School and Community Theater Management

School and Community Theater Management

A HANDBOOK FOR SURVIVAL

Lawrence Stern

ALLYN AND BACON, INC.

Boston   London   Sydney

Library of Congress Cataloging in Publication Data

Stern, Lawrence, 1935–
    School and community theater management.

    Bibliography: p.
    Includes index.
    1. College and school drama—Handbooks, manuals,
etc. 2. Community plays, etc.—Handbooks, manuals,
etc. 3. Theater management—Handbooks, manuals,
etc. I. Title.
PN3178.T68S75   792'.02   79–1079
ISBN 0-205-06174-5

Production Editor: Robine Storm van Leeuwen
Manufacturing Buyer: Linda Card
Design Editor: Paula Carroll

Printed in the United States of America

In memory of Lou Rifkin

Contents

Preface

A few months after my first book was published, I served as a judge at the thirty-second Annual Drama Festival sponsored by the Drama Teachers Association of Southern California. One festival official, a teacher at a Los Angeles high school, stared at my nametag and said, "Are you *the* Lawrence Stern who wrote *Stage Management*?"

"Yes," I said, a bit surprised that anyone would remember my name even after reading my book.

"I require all of my student directors and stage managers to read your book, and I want you to know how much work it's saved me."

Those were very rewarding words, and I'm pleased to say that I've heard them many times since.

I decided to see if I could apply the same nuts-and-bolts approach used in *Stage Management* to other theater problems.

The result you hold in your hand. In this book I identify several school and community theater problems and provide practical solutions.

I've had a lot of help. My first book was written mainly from personal experience, but *School and Community Theater Management* required the shared experience of many talented people. I would like to thank them all, my colleagues who work in theater, the students who assisted me, and the teachers and community theater people who took time to answer my questionnaires.

My special thanks to Sheldon Altfeld, S.I.A. Productions, Inc.; John W. Andrus, President, The Palos Verdes Players; Billy C. Creamer, Dapplegray Intermediate School; Rowena Dores, Allyn and Bacon, Inc.; Mary Jane Evans, Southern California Educational Theatre Association; S. Ezra Goldstein, Editor, *Dramatics;* Katherine Melke, Columbus Junior High; Jacqueline Melvin, President, Southern California Educational Theatre Association; Norman Mennes, Los Angeles City College; Jean Mullin, Paul Revere Junior High; Leon S. Paule, The Morgan Theater; Robert M. Roen, Allyn and Bacon, Inc.; Irv Rosen, President, Kentwood Players; Sheri Smith, President, Drama Teachers Association of Southern California; Jacqueline Tays, Verdugo Hills High School; Maris Ubans, California State University—Los Angeles; Anne Vardanian, Mission Viejo High School; and Pam Woody, California State University—Los Angeles.

A very special thanks to Mrs. Carol Berger Kato for reading my manuscript and insuring that I did not write theaterese.

Lawrence Stern
Los Angeles

PART ONE

School Theater

CHAPTER ONE

Objectives and Curriculum

It is easy to overlook the importance of theater education, because people tend to judge it solely by its productions. Its main purpose, however, is student development. Through a carefully planned theater curriculum, students can achieve six important objectives: (1) individual development, (2) self-expression, (3) problem-solving techniques, (4) improved social attitudes, (5) evaluation skills, and (6) an awakening to theater. Production work is merely a part of the teaching process.

OBJECTIVES

Before outlining the curriculum, let's see how drama contributes to the achievement of each objective.

Individual Development

Drama exercises allow students to use their own ideas, attitudes, feelings, fantasies, and memories. They thus gain a fuller understanding of themselves—where they're at and what their inner workings are. And as they perform before their peers and see and feel their reactions, they gain even greater insight into themselves.

Being on the drama team—engaging in classroom exercises and production work—will give them a sense of belonging and the esteem of their peers. Drama can offer this sense of belonging to students who haven't found it in scholarship, athletics, or student government.

Self-expression

The ability to communicate thought and emotion is the core of the theater. This skill is equally vital to the well-functioning individual. Classroom exercises in drama emphasize the improvement of voice quality and enunciation and the communication of emotion through voice, facial expression, and posture. Thus, students develop poise and generally improve their ease of manner. The teaching of acting techniques also emphasizes an individual's ability to listen to others, feeling their thoughts and emotions and reacting sensitively to them.

Problem-solving Techniques

In drama, more than in any other subject, students find the opportunity to develop and apply problem-solving techniques.

There are two major problems related to every play. The first is the conflict faced by the central characters. The second is the problem of mounting the production successfully.

Studying the problems faced by the characters, the students learn to define them. They become aware of causes and solutions, seeing the interaction of the character traits and the problem.

As members of a production unit, from a classroom exercise to a major mainstage production, students learn to work cooperatively with others in problem solving. They join a team effort to cope with the many problems that arise in getting the material on its feet.

Social Attitudes

When studying a play, students are able to work with ideas in exceptionally personal and meaningful ways. The thoughts and emotions of thousands of playwrights—of imaginary and historical characters—are the students' to relate to, to understand, and to evaluate.

When students enact a role, they must evaluate the ideas of the character. Concepts of values—honor, love, honesty, loyalty, etc.—may be explored critically in a drama class.

Students also have an immediate laboratory for application of social values—acceptance of responsibility, cooperation, initiative, etc. Producing a play thrusts them into a social framework, each dependent on another. There is an explicit order, and all participants quickly realize that they are responsible to others and that others are responsible to them. They learn to use, control, and inhibit their own creativity so that they can contribute to the whole production, a process that is basic to democratic society.

Evaluation Skills

Drama classes demand that students develop evaluation skills. The students are constantly called upon to judge the work of playwrights, acting companies, fellow students and themselves. They learn to be discerning and critical. They learn to deliver criticism in such a way that it will effect change and not build resentment. Of even greater importance, they learn to accept and benefit from criticism.

Awakening to Theater

As participants in making theater, or as audience members, the students will be introduced to an art form that has great potential for their lifelong recreation and entertainment. Their interest in dramatic criticism will be stimulated. They will see how the principles of theater apply to movies and television. Since music, dance, and painting are necessary to theater, the students will also be introduced to those art forms.

THE CURRICULUM

Having reviewed these significant objectives of theater education, we now examine the means to achieve them. What follows is an outline of a possible theater curriculum for a high school. It is not intended as a standard, but as a guide. It is up to teachers and students to determine what will and will not be taught in each classroom. The curriculum will depend on the needs of the class and the time available.

A DRAMA CURRICULUM

I. Evaluating Student Needs

(What is the experience level of the class? How much do they know about theater? Have they been to a performance or have they seen only movies and television? What do the students see as their needs? The class will be more valuable to them if they take part in planning the semester's goals and activities.)

A. Overview: Introduction to What Theater Is
1. Communication of thought and emotion
2. Live art form
B. The Various Forms of Dramatic Arts
1. Reading play scripts
2. Readers' theater
3. Live theater
(a) Drama
(b) Comedy
(c) Musicals
(d) Revues
(e) Opera

Classroom Exercises and Projects

1. Discuss and define theater, its forms, and its elements.
2. Have students see live theater as a planned field trip or as an individual assignment.
3. Have students see and report on other forms of dramatic arts.
4. Have students tour a live theater plant and meet production personnel.
5. Have advanced students and guest artists demonstrate forms of live theater to the class.
6. Have students present to the class reactions (criticism) of dramatic forms seen.
7. Discuss current opportunities to see live theater and other dramatic forms.

4. Movies and television
5. Dance
C. Elements common to most forms of dramatic arts
    1. actors
    2. audience
    3. stage
    4. scenery
    5. properties
    6. lighting
D. Overview of Possible Contents of This Specific Class
E. Determination by Students and Teacher of Class Content

II. Making Theater Happen

(An Overview of the People Who Make Theater)

A. Playwright
B. Actor
C. Director
D. Producer
E. Scene Designer
F. Costume Designer
G. Stage Manager
H. Wardrobe Mistress
I. Business Manager
J. Publicity Director
K. House Manager
L. Musical Director
M. Musician
N. Choreographer

8. Discuss newspaper reviews of dramatic arts.

Useful References

Motter, Charlotte Kay. *Theatre in High School: Planning, Teaching, Directing.* Englewood Cliffs, N.J.: Prentice-Hall, 1970.

Ommanney, Katherine Anne, and Schanker, Harry H. *The Stage and the School.* 4th ed. New York: McGraw-Hill Book Co., 1971.

Tanner, Fran Averett. *Basic Drama Projects.* 3rd ed. Pocatello, Idaho: Clark Publishing Co., 1977.

Classroom Exercises and Projects

1. Discuss the duties of each member of the theater staff.
2. Discuss the qualifications and training necessary and desirable for each position.
3. Prepare an organizational chart showing who is responsible to whom in the school's theater. Compare this to a chart prepared for a professional theater.
4. Have students interview staff members of an educational theater, a community theater, or a professional theater and

O. Dancer
P. Scene Technician

III. The Play

A. Elements
1. Plot
    (a) Exposition
    (b) Initial
         dramatic
         incident
    (c) Rising action
    (d) Climax
    (e) Falling action
    (f) Denouement
2. Characters
    (a) Protagonist
    (b) Antagonist
    (c) Growth,
         change in
         course of play
3. Setting
    (a) Place
    (b) Time
    (c) Mood
4. Dialogue
5. Conflict
6. Theme (author's
    purpose)
7. Other elements
    (a) Antecedent
         action
    (b) Obstacles,
         crises, and
         complications

report on their duties and
background.
5. Have students read
    biographies of famous
    actors, directors, managers,
    etc., and report to the class.

*Classroom Exercises
and Projects*

1. Define terms and give
    examples.
2. Have students read a play
    and report on its elements,
    type, and style.
3. Have students identify the
    elements, type, and style of
    an assigned TV program or
    movie.
4. Have the class discuss how
    a well-known story (fairy tale
    or Aesop's fable) would be
    treated in various styles and
    types.
5. Present cuttings from
    various types of plays.
    Compare elements and
    style. Use recordings or
    films to illustrate types and
    styles. Ask advanced
    students to present scenes
    from a variety of types and
    styles.

Useful References

Hatlen, Theodore W. *Orientation to
the Theater.* 2nd ed. Englewood
Cliffs, N.J.: Prentice-Hall, 1972.

(c) Obligatory
scene
B. Types of Plays
1. Drama
2. Tragedy
3. Comedy
4. Melodrama
5. Fantasy
6. Farce
7. Satire
8. Black Comedy
C. Styles
1. Realism
2. Naturalism
3. Romanticism
4. Classicism
5. Expressionism
6. Theater of the
Absurd

Wright, Edward A., and Downs, Len-
thiel H. *A Primer for Playgoers.* 2nd
ed. Englewood Cliffs, N.J.: Prentice-Hall, 1969.

IV. Individual Stage Movement
and Pantomime

A. Difference between
Onstage and Offstage
Movement
1. Concentration
2. Posture
3. Economy of
movement
4. Grace of movement
5. Rhythm
B. Pantomime Methods
1. Selection,
simplification, and
exaggeration
2. Use of hands alone
3. Use of whole body

*Classroom Exercises
and Projects*

1. Show films of good
pantomime, or bring in
advanced students or guest
artists to demonstrate
pantomime skills.
2. Discuss elements and
desirable principles of stage
movement and pantomime.
3. Assign to students
individual movements and
pantomimes for presentation
to the class.
4. Assign pantomimes to
groups of students.

4. Expression of
   emotion and
   attitudes
5. Relaxation,
   flexibility, control

C. Reflection of Specific
   Characters with
   Pantomime

V. Group Movement and
   Pantomime, Pantomime
   Interaction

   (Sometimes it is desirable
   to introduce group
   activities first to get
   students working in a less
   self-conscious atmosphere.)

5. Ask students to watch
   people in silent situations
   (waiting for a bus, riding an
   elevator, etc.) and then
   present their observations to
   the class.
6. Pantomime easily
   recognizable scenes from
   literature, history, and other
   sources.

Useful References

Fleming, Gladys A. *Creative Rhyth-
mic Movement: Boys and Girls
Dancing.* Englewood Cliffs, N.J.:
Prentice-Hall, 1976.

Heinig, Ruth B., and Stillwell, Lyda.
*Creative Dramatics for the Class-
room Teacher.* Englewood Cliffs,
N.J.: Prentice-Hall, 1974.

McCaslin, Nellie. *Creative Dramatics
in the Classroom.* 2nd ed. New
York: Longman, Inc., 1974.

VI. Voice

   A. Characteristics
      1. Volume
      2. Pitch
      3. Rhythm
      4. Variety
      5. Pronunciation
      6. Enunciation

*Classroom Exercises
and Projects*

1. Play records of popular
   songs, poetry, and drama
   that exemplify good speech;
   discuss how the artists
   demonstrate principles of
   good speech.

7. Intonation
8. Accent
B. Breath Control
C. Tone Quality
D. Stage Speech
E. Vocal Characterization

2. Have students read selected paragraphs; evaluate their speech.
3. Prescribe individual voice improvement drills.
4. Conduct group drills.

Useful References

Fisher, Hilda B. *Improving Voice and Articulation.* 2nd ed. Boston: Houghton Mifflin Co., 1975.

Houston, Neal B., and Quinn, John J. *Phonetikon: A Visual Aid to Phonetic Study.* Glenview, Ill.: Scott, Foresman and Co., 1970.

Lessac, Arthur. *The Use and Training of the Human Voice: A Practical Approach to Speech and Voice Dynamics.* 2nd ed. New York: Drama Book Specialists, 1967.

Machlin, Evangeline. *Speech for the Stage.* New York: Theatre Arts Books, 1966.

McLean, Margaret Prendgast. *Good American Speech.* rev. ed. New York: E. P. Dutton and Co., 1968.

VII. Improvisation

A. Importance to the Actor
B. Spontaneity
1. Thinking on feet
2. Responding

Classroom Exercises and Projects

1. Discuss the meaning and application of improvisation.
2. Give two students a prop. Ask them to improvise a scene related to the prop.

        (a) Material objects
        (b) Actions
        (c) Setting
        (d) Emotions
  C. Use of Conflict

3. Give students a setting. Ask them to improvise a scene within the setting.
4. Give two students an emotion each. Have them improvise dialogue, retaining their assigned emotions through part of the scene. Then have them switch emotions.
5. Show students a picture and have them improvise a scene based on the picture.
6. Read a short story, poem, fable, or popular song lyric. Have students improvise scenes based on it.

Useful References

Spolin, Viola. *Improvisation for the Theater: A Handbook of Teaching and Directing Techniques.* Evanston, Ill.: Northwestern University Press, 1963.

VIII. Stage Basics

  A. Stage Terminology
     1. Stage directions
     2. Blocking notation
     3. Actors' jargon
        (a) Stepping on lines
        (b) Blocking another character
        (c) Focus
        (d) Other

Classroom Exercises and Projects

1. Define and give examples of acting vocabulary.
2. Demonstrate stage directions and blocking notation.
3. Have students practice basic movements to see if they can demonstrate desirable principles.
4. Have students take blocking

B. Basic Movement
1. Crossing/turning
2. Entering/exiting
3. Sitting/standing
4. Handling props
5. Falling/fainting
6. Eating/drinking
7. Embracing/kissing
8. Laughing/crying
C. Concentration
D. Use of Observations
E. Use of Remembered Emotions
F. Responsibilities of the Actor
1. Self-discipline
   (a) Rehearsal routines
   (b) Line memorization
2. Cooperation
3. Implementing intent of playwright and director
4. Accepting and learning from criticism

notation in pages of a script reproduced for that purpose. Have students repeat the scene to see if they can move accurately from their own notation.

Useful References

Benedetti, Robert. *The Actor at Work.* rev. ed. Englewood Cliffs, N.J.: Prentice-Hall, 1976.

Blunt, Jerry. *The Composite Art of Acting.* New York: Macmillan Publishing Co., 1966.

Kahan, Stanley. *Introduction to Acting.* New York: Harcourt, Brace and World, 1962.

Selden, Samuel, and Heffner, Hubert. *First Steps in Acting.* 2nd ed. New York: Irvington, 1964.

IX. Memorization

A. Value to the Actor
B. Techniques of Greek Orators
C. Association
D. Linking

Classroom Exercises and Projects

1. Discuss principles of memorization.
2. Play memory games in the classroom. (For example,

present a tray of various small items to the class briefly. Ask students to write down as many as they can remember. Review principles of memorization and present another tray with a different variety of items. Allow the students to see for themselves that they can increase their ability to remember by applying principles.)

3. Assign paragraphs to be memorized (and later presented to the class), emphasizing methods of memorization. Ask students to time themselves so that they can see how long it takes to commit a body of material to memory.

Useful References

Lorayne, Harry, and Lucas, Jerry. *The Memory Book.* New York: Ballantine Books, 1975.

X. Oral Interpretation

    A. Reading
       1. Pre-reading and analysis
       2. Setting mood with voice
       3. Characterization
    B. Readers' Theater

Classroom Exercises and Projects

1. Discuss differences between reading aloud and oral interpretation.
2. Play records of poems and essays to demonstrate effective oral interpretation.

C. Reciting from Memory
D. Scene Work

3. Invite advanced students and guest artists to perform.
4. Ask students to interpret poems and essays, both by reading and from memory.
5. Stage a reading of a one-act play.

Useful References

Coger, Leslie I., and White, Melvin R. *Readers Theatre Handbook: A Dramatic Approach to Literature.* rev. ed. Glenview, Ill.: Scott, Foresman and Co., 1973.

Sessions, Virgil, and Holland, Jack. *Your Role in Oral Interpretation.* 2nd ed. Boston: Holbrook Press, 1975.

XI. Creating a Role

A. Study of Character
   1. Physical characteristics
   2. Psychological traits
   3. Socioeconomic status
   4. Speech traits
B. Understanding Character's Relationship to Others

Classroom Exercises and Projects

1. Review acting performances in plays, movies, and TV, emphasizing actors' methods of creating roles. Compare types of actors and their approaches to their work.
2. Have students read biographies of actors that emphasize their craft and how they create roles.
3. Ask students to write a few paragraphs of analysis on a character in a play. They are to find out as much as they can from the playwright's words (what the character

does, what he says, what others do to him, what others say about him) and then extend the biography by induction.

4. Have students act, act, act, act! (improvisational scenes, sketches, dialogues, scenes, full parts in fully staged plays)

Useful References

Albright, Harry D. *Working Up a Part.* 2nd ed. Boston: Houghton Mifflin, 1959.

Boleslavsky, Richard. *Acting: The First Six Lessons.* New York: Theatre Arts Books, 1956.

Checkhov, Michael. *To the Actor.* New York: Harper and Brothers, 1953.

Funke, Lewis, and Booth, John E., eds. *Actors Talk about Acting.* New York: Avòn Books, 1973.

McGaw, Charles J. *Acting Is Believing.* 3rd. ed. New York: Holt, Rinehart and Winston, 1975.

Stanislavski, Constantin. *An Actor Prepares.* New York: Theatre Arts Books, 1936.

Stanislavski, Constantin. *Building a Character.* New York: Theatre Arts Books, 1949.

XII. Directing

    A. Principles

        1. Interpreting thoughts and emotions of playwright through media of actors and designers

           a. Establishing overall style, tone, and purpose

           b. Helping actors interpret lines

           c. Guiding actors in developing characters

        2. Casting

        3. Blocking

           a. Destination

           b. Motivation

        4. Pacing

           a. Tempo versus speed

           b. Variety

        5. Polishing interactions

        6. Harmonizing all phases of production

    B. Mechanics

        1. Before rehearsals

           a. Play analysis

           b. Director's notebook

           c. Cutting

           d. Pre-blocking

        2. During rehearsals

        3. During performance

Classroom Exercises and Projects

1. Invite guest directors to discuss how they mount a play.
2. Discuss qualifications of a director.
3. Have students read biographies of famous directors and commentaries by them. Have students report on specific rehearsal procedures and methods of directors.
4. Give students the opportunity to direct scenes.

Useful References

Albright, Hardie. *Stage Direction in Transition.* Encino, Cal.: Dickenson Publishing Co., 1972.

Cole, Toby, and Chinoy, Helen K., eds. *Directors on Directing.* rev. ed. Indianapolis: Bobbs-Merrill Co., 1963.

Dean, Alexander, and Carra, L. *Fundamentals of Play Directing.* 3rd. ed. New York: Holt, Rinehart and Winston, 1974.

Hodge, Francis. *Play Directing: Analysis, Communication and Style.* Englewood Cliffs, N.J.: Prentice-Hall, 1971.

Kozelka, Paul. *The Theatre Student: Directing.* New York: Richards Rosen Press, 1968.

C.   Stage Management (as
     support to the director)

Stern, Lawrence. *Stage Management:
A Guidebook of Practical Techniques.* Boston: Allyn and Bacon,
1974.

XIII.   Playwriting

A. Springboards
B. Characterization
C. Theme
D. Plotting
E. Mechanics

(Review III, emphasizing creating
rather than analyzing.)

*Classroom Exercises
and Projects*

1.   Select poems, fables, short
     stories, and newspaper
     articles that students can
     dramatize.
2.   Ask students to outline an
     especially good
     improvisation, writing out
     the highlights of dialogue, to
     see if they can capture the
     essentials.
3.   Ask students to rewrite a
     scene from a well-known
     play in their own idiom.
4.   Guide students in writing
     one-act plays.

Useful References

Cole, Toby, ed. *Playwrights on Playwriting: The Meaning and Making
of Modern Drama.* New York: Hill
and Wang, 1961.

Grebanier, Bernard. *Playwriting: How
to Write for the Theater.* New York:
Thomas Y. Crowell Co., 1961.

XIV.   Technical Theater

A.   Scenery Design and
     Construction
     1.   Interpretation of
          playwright's
          intent

*Classroom Exercises
and Projects*

1.   Introduce class to shop
     areas, tools, and equipment.
2.   Demonstrate use of tools
     and equipment.

4. Safety orientation
5. Construction process
   (a) Flats
   (b) Units
   (c) Set pieces
6. Painting
7. Shifting

2. Practical considerations
   (a) Budget
   (b) Space
   (c) Time
   (d) Labor
   (e) Materials
   (f) Shift requirements
   (g) Shift equipment
3. Design process
   (a) Floor plan
   (b) Sketches/ models
   (c) Perspective drawings
   (d) Line drawings

3. Give students practical exercises in construction to demonstrate their use of tools and equipment.
4. Talk through a design problem.

Useful References

Burris-Meyer, Harold, and Cole, Edward C. *Scenery for the Theatre.* 2nd rev. ed. Boston: Little, Brown and Co., 1972.

Gassner, John, and Barber, P. *Producing the Play and the New Scene Technician's Handbook.* rev. ed. New York: Holt, Rinehart and Winston, 1953.

Parker, W. Oren, and Smith, Harvey K. *Scene Design and Stage Lighting.* 3rd ed. New York: Holt, Rinehart and Winston, 1974.

Philippi, Herbert. *Stagecraft and Scene Design.* Boston: Houghton Mifflin Co., 1953.

Welker, David. *Theatrical Set Design.* 2nd ed. Boston: Allyn and Bacon, 1979.

B. Lighting
   1. Purpose of light
   2. Control of light
      (a) Intensity
      (b) Color
      (c) Direction
   3. Types of lighting instruments
      (a) Plano-convex

Classroom Exercises and Projects

1. Demonstrate how various lighting instruments are used.
2. Demonstrate effect of gels and their impact on sets, costumes, and makeup.

  (b) Elipsoidal
    reflectors
  (c) Fresnels
  (d) Floods/strips
  (e) Special
    effects
 4. General principles
  (a) Mood lighting
    for comedy
    and tragedy
  (b) Relationship
    of color of
    lights to set,
    costume,
    makeup
    colors
  (c) Most
    commonly
    used gels
    and their
    application
  (d) Crosslighting
 5. Processes
  (a) Diagramming
  (b) Safety
    procedures
  (c) Hanging
  (d) Focusing
  (e) Plots/cue
    sheets

C. Costuming
 1. Interpretation of
   playwright's
   intent
  (a) Period
  (b) Nationality
  (c) Season
  (d) Mood

3. Talk through the lighting
process with respect to
mounting a play with which
the students are familiar.

4. Ask students to hang, focus,
and gel an instrument.

Useful References

Bellman, Willard F. *Lighting the Stage: Art and Practice.* 2nd ed. New York: Chandler Publishing Co., 1974.

McCandless, Stanley. *A Syllabus of Stage Lighting.* 11th ed. New York: Drama Book Specialists, 1964.

Selden, Samuel, and Sellman, Hunton D. *Stage Scenery and Lighting.* 3rd ed. Englewood Cliffs, N.J.: Prentice-Hall, 1959.

Classroom Exercises and Projects

1. Have students write descriptions of costumes for one historical and one modern dress play.

2. Have students draw costume designs.

(e) Social status

(f) Economic status

(g) Character traits

2. Elements

(a) Materials

(b) Color

(c) Line

3. Execution

(a) Safety procedures

(b) Measurements

(c) Patterns

(d) Sewing

(e) Dyeing

(f) Cleaning

(g) Upkeep

D. Makeup

1. Needs for makeup

(a) Reflect playwright's intent

(b) Counter effect of stage lighting

(c) Counter effect of distance

(d) Characterization

(e) Changes in character

(f) Corrective

2. Principles of makeup

(a) Human anatomy

3. Have students evaluate costumes in a production they have seen.

Useful References

Barton, Lucy. *Historic Costume for the Stage.* rev. ed. Boston: Walter H. Baker Co., 1961.

Russell, Douglas A. *Stage Costume Design: Theory, Technique and Style.* Englewood Cliffs, N.J.: Prentice-Hall, 1973.

Classroom Exercises and Projects

1. Demonstrate materials, principles, and techniques.
2. Have students make up for both youth and age.
3. Have each student depict a character by makeup alone.

Useful References

Buchman, Herman. *Stage Makeup.* New York: Watson-Guptill Publications, 1971.

Corson, Richard. *Stage Makeup.* 5th ed. Englewood Cliffs, N.J.: Prentice-Hall, 1974.

        (b)   Light and shadow
        (c)   Color
        (d)   Safety precautions
   3. Materials
        (a)   Bases (stick, tube, pan)
        (b)   Liners
        (c)   Rouges
        (d)   Powders
        (e)   Crepe hair
        (f)   Spirit gum
        (g)   Other
   4. General types
        (a)   Straight
        (b)   Youth
        (c)   Age
        (d)   Character
   5. Special effects
        (a)   Moustaches
        (b)   Beards
        (c)   Noses
        (d)   Scars
        (e)   Black eyes
        (f)   Blood
        (g)   Other
   6. Makeup charts
E. Sound Effects
   1. Function
        (a)   Reflect playwright's intent
        (b)   Create mood
        (c)   Focus attention
   2. Sources of sound
        (a)   Devices
        (b)   Tape

Classroom Exercises and Projects

1. Have students demonstrate in classroom various sound effect devices, such as sheet of tin for thunder.
2. Play a sound effect record to demonstrate sources.

(c) Records
3. Commonly used effects
   (a) Phone bell
   (b) Door buzzer, chimes
   (c) Automobile sounds
   (d) Rain, thunder
   (e) Birds, crickets, cats, dogs
   (f) Other
4. Sound plots

F. Properties
   1. Importance
      (a) Reflecting playwright's intent
      (b) Enhancing mood
      (c) Aiding characterization
      (d) Affecting actors' timing
   2. Construction
   3. Finding and keeping sources
   4. Care and storage
      (a) Backstage
      (b) During shifts
      (c) After play
      (d) After run
   5. Prop plots

Useful References

Kenton, Warren. *Stage Properties and How to Make Them.* Reprint. New Rochelle, N.Y.: Sportshelf and Soccer Associates, 1974.

XV. Theater History

A. Origins
1. Storytelling
2. Pantomime
3. Dance
4. Chanting
5. Religion
B. Oriental
1. Noh plays
2. Kabuki
C. Greek Theater
D. Roman Theater
E. Medieval Theater
1. Guilds
2. Mystery Plays
3. Morality Plays
F. Renaissance Theater
G. Elizabethan Theater
H. Restoration Theater
I. French Neoclassic
Theater
J. Eighteenth-Century
Theater
K. Nineteenth-Century
Theater
L. Modern Theater
M. Evolution of the
Physical Stage

*Classroom Exercises
and Projects*

1. Play excerpts from records
of classic plays pointing out
characteristics of the period.
2. Read scenes from selected
plays.
3. Stage scenes from selected
plays.
4. Compare similar scenes
from plays of different
periods, showing how the
playwrights handled the
same theme in different
ways.
5. Analyze theme, characters,
plot, and dialogue of a
classic play and then show
what changes you would
make in writing the same
play today for a modern
audience.
6. Plan a field trip to see a
modern presentation of a
classic or to see a movie
adaptation.
7. Have students report on a
play and its author, showing
how the author's life
influenced what he or she
wrote. Also have them show
how the political and
religious atmosphere at the
time of writing influenced
what was written.

Useful References

Brockett, Oscar G. *History of the
Theatre.* 3rd. ed. Boston: Allyn and
Bacon, 1977.

Freedley, George, and Reeves, John A. *A History of the Theatre.* rev. ed. New York: Crown Publishers, 1968.

Gassner, John. *Masters of the Drama.* 3rd ed. New York: Dover Publications, 1953.

XVI. Black Theater

A. Plays
B. Playwrights
C. Actors and Actresses
D. Social History of Blacks in United States as Reflected in Theater

Classroom Exercises and Projects

1. Ask individual students to report on the aspect of black theater in which they are most interested.
2. Stage scenes from black theater.
3. Stage a pageant with scenes from black theater that reflect the history of blacks in the United States.

Useful References

Abramson, Doris E. *Negro Playwrights in the American Theatre.* New York: Columbia University Press, 1969.

Hatch, James V., and Shine, Ted, eds. *Black Theatre, U.S.A.: Forty-Five Plays by Black Americans, 1847–1974.* New York: The Free Press, 1974.

King, Woodie, and Milner, Ron, eds. *Black Drama Anthology.* New York: Columbia University Press, 1972.

Oliver, Clinton F., and Sills, Stephanie S., eds. *Contemporary Black Drama.* New York: Charles Scribner's Sons, 1971.

Turner, Darwin T. *Afro-American Writers.* Arlington Heights, Ill.: AHM Publishing Corp., 1970.

Keep abreast of new and better books that will assist you by adding your name to the mailing lists of the publishers that specialize in books on theater arts.

Allyn and Bacon, Inc.
Longwood Division
470 Atlantic Avenue
Boston, Massachusetts 02210

AMS Press, Inc.
56 East 13th Street
New York, New York 10003

Cornell University Press
124 Roberts Place
Ithaca, New York 14850

Crown Publishers, Inc.
1 Park Avenue
New York, New York 10016

Da Capo Press, Inc.
227 West 17th Street
New York, New York 10011

The Fireside Theater
Garden City, New York 11530

Burt Franklin & Co., Inc.
235 East 44th Street
New York, New York 10017

Indiana University Press
10th and Morton Streets
Bloomington, Indiana 47401

National Textbook Co.
8259 Niles Center Road
Skokie, Illinois 60076

University of Miami Press
Drawer 9088
Coral Gables, Florida 33124

University of Texas Press
P.O. Box 7819
Austin, Texas 78712

University of Washington Press
Seattle, Washington 98105

Annotated Bibliography of New Publications in the Performing Arts is a list of the latest books in drama that are available through The Drama Book Shop, 150 West 52nd Street, New York, New York 10019.

CHAPTER TWO

Lesson Plans

A lesson plan is an organizational tool that suggests ways to carry out a lesson. I use the word suggest because a lesson plan won't tell you exactly what to do and how to do it. You will have to adjust each plan to meet your needs, using your own judgment.

The important things to consider are your needs and the needs of your students. What specific objectives do you want to achieve? What are the best ways to achieve them? Sometimes there are many ways to attain a single drama objective. Decide which approach will work best considering the time available, the number of students, and the mood of the students.

HOW LESSON PLANS HELP YOU

If you are a beginning teacher and feel that you need lesson plans, you certainly do. They will give you the basic guidance you need to carry out your daily work. They will give you a detailed approach to implementing the curriculum.

Some experienced teachers say they never use them, or that all of their lesson plans are in their heads and they feel no need to have them in written form.

Yet even experienced teachers agree that written lesson plans are a very convenient way to exchange ideas with other teachers, to pick up new ideas, to pass instructions to substitute teachers, and to direct student assistants.

My experience when facing my first drama class was that I needed, but did not have, adequate lesson plans. I had already taught English and felt comfortable in an English classroom. I had a master's degree in theater arts. However, I felt ill prepared to teach drama. I believe that many people, like myself, study theater without intending to teach. They learn the subject matter, but all too quickly forget the methods their instructors used to teach. Lesson plans can be a useful reminder of those methods.

In addition, lesson plans can refresh your memory on what techniques work for you in your classroom and why other plans fail. They can help you to reach objectives by making the best use of your classroom time. They can help you to evaluate and to improve your techniques. And finally, they help you to use constructively short periods of time that suddenly become available.

FIVE SOURCES

1. Some teachers teach what they were taught in the way that they were taught. They use the lesson plans that their teachers used, or what they remember of them.

2. Some teachers create their own lesson plans. Fired up by necessity, perhaps by a problem that they encounter in the classroom or while staging plays, they devise a solution on the spot. Starting with an objective, they find a new procedure to help their students reach that objective. This can be very rewarding. Are you using your creative abilities to the fullest in devising lesson plans?

3. Some teachers read and adapt. That's what you're doing here. There are many good books on acting, directing, and teaching theater that contain classroom exercises. There are also a few highly recommended books of basic lesson plans. (See the list at the end of this chapter.)

4. Live theater, television, and movies can trigger lesson plans. Example: in a sketch on TV, a man waiting for a subway train is confronted by a machine played by another actor. It's a "compliment machine." The man pays the machine a quarter and it says something nice about the man. It starts to say something else but stops in mid-compliment and holds out its hand for another quarter. The sketch is clever. The teacher thinks, why not try other machine-human confrontation scenes with one student playing a human and the other a machine? This might be a useful lesson plan to help students improvise.

5. Exchanges of plans with other teachers can be productive. Unfortunately, it's hard to schedule visits to other drama classrooms. Usually there's only one drama teacher in a school. It would help if more teaching time could be freed for exchange visits.

Setting up a lesson plan exchange through the mail is possible, but expensive and time-consuming. Most of the plans in this chapter were obtained in a mail exchange among members of the Drama Teachers Association of Southern California.

When you attend festivals and theater conventions, don't hesitate to ask your fellow drama teachers for help. (E.g., "I'm having a terrible time getting my students to enunciate. What do you do in the classroom to promote clear and distinct pronunciation on stage?")

FORMAT

The lesson plan format used in this chapter includes the title, the area of curriculum in which the plan can be applied, the objective, the materials needed, and the procedure.

The statement of objective is listed not only for the teacher, but also for the students. A vital part of any lesson is motivating the students. If they know the purpose of an activity, they will be much more responsive. Don't assume that the students understand, as you do, the desirability of doing a specific exercise. Explain it to them. Take the time to let them know what's in it for them. Show them how this specific objective fits into the overall plan of work for the week or the semester.

Materials needed are listed separately so that you don't launch into a lesson and find you need some materials that you didn't prepare in advance. These lesson plans assume a classroom setting with blackboard and chalk. All of them may be carried out on a stage with the help of a portable blackboard.

It is extremely important that you personalize—add your own comments to each plan as you try it. If you find that a plan doesn't work for you, make a note. Include the date that you tried the plan, the time you took, and an analysis of what went wrong or what could be improved. Perhaps next semester you will want to try the same plan again with a different class. Then your notes will help you to alter the plan so that it will be more effective for you.

The following brief collection of lesson plans is not a total approach to teaching every objective in the curriculum. It is not a complete semester's work for any hypothetical class. Nor is it aimed at any specific level of work. My intent is simply to demonstrate a variety of plans in hopes that you will want to start your own personal collection.

There are no time limits suggested. You will want to note the time you devoted to a plan and the number of participating students, such as "two periods for a class of 25." When you want to use the plan again, you will have a good idea of how much time you should budget.

Peruse, enjoy, adapt, and apply.

DRAMA LESSON PLAN 1

Lesson Title: Interviews and Introductions
Area: I—Evaluating Student Needs
Objective: Students will feel comfortable in talking to one another and in talking to the class as a whole. (One of many break-the-ice exercises to get the class feeling relaxed, loose, and comfortable.)
Materials: Pencils and paper
Procedure:

   A.   Write on board, "Interviews and Introductions."
   B.   Explain that the objective of today's exercise is simply to get to know one another.
   C.   "Pretend that you are to appear on the 'Johnny Carson Show' as a guest. Write three questions that you would like Johnny Carson to ask you about yourself."
   D.   Give the class time to write the questions.
   E.   Break the class into pairs. Ask the students to exchange papers and inter-

view their partners. Explain that following the interviews each student will introduce his partner to the class.

F.   After ample time for interviews, ask students to rise one at a time to introduce their partners. (Emphasis on the other student and what the other student wants known about himself should help to make students lose their self-consciousness.)

G.   Thank each student for his introduction. Use names as much as possible: "Thanks, Arthur, for introducing Anna. It was interesting to hear about Anna's travels."

H.   Summarize: "Today we learned something about our classmates, and incidentally, we also learned how easy it is to get up and talk in this class."

Lesson Plan 1 submitted by Billy C. Creamer, Dapplegray Intermediate School. Reprinted by permission.

DRAMA LESSON PLAN 2

Lesson Title: Passing Exercise
Area: IV B—Individual Stage Movement and Pantomime
Objective: Every student will learn to apply all the senses—smell, taste, sight, hearing, and touch—to pantomime. Students will learn to take time and care in the handling of imaginary objects. Students will learn to react to the pantomime of others.
Materials: Deck of three-by-five-inch cards with a single item written on one side of each: an ice cube, sand, mud, one long hair, a pin, a bottle of soda with the cap on, a teaspoon of hot chocolate, a feather, a small cactus, a peeled onion, pepper, a worm, bubble gum, a conch shell, a baby rattle, etc.
                   Film on pantomime

Procedure:

A.   Write on the board the title "Pantomime—Passing Exercise," the definition of pantomime, and a list of the five senses.

B.   Review the meaning of pantomime and the importance of pantomime in the theater.

C.   Show a film (*Pantomimes, In the Park,* or another short film exemplifying good pantomime).

D.   Explain the objective (above) of the passing exercise. Ask students to see where they can apply each of the five senses.

E.   Select four to six students to sit in a row facing the remainder of the class.

Tell the class that you will show the participating students the card telling them what they are to pass. "The objective is to see how well these students can apply their senses of smell, taste, sight, hearing, and touch. The objective is not to guess what they are passing. It's fun to guess, but if shouted, guesses interfere with concentration. Then I will have to tell the whole class in advance what is being passed. You'll have a chance to tell what you think was passed after all the students on stage have passed the object."

F.   Do not criticize any of the work but praise good application of pantomime skills that you observe: "I like the way Harry made that bigger than life. It's good to exaggerate in pantomime as long as we keep some essential truths about the item." "I like the way Joyce wiped her hands after she passed the object. Joyce was still reacting to the object after it left her hands."

G.   Summarize: "Today we learned to apply all of our senses to simple pantomime tasks. We also thought about exaggeration, completion, using the whole body, and not rushing an action. We will apply all of these ideas to our future work in pantomime."

Lesson Plan 2 submitted by Lawrence Stern, Manual Arts High School.

DRAMA LESSON PLAN 3

Lesson Title: Characterization in Pantomime
Area: IV C—Individual Stage Movement and Pantomime
Objective: Students will introduce characterization into their pantomime work.
Materials: None
Procedure:

A.   Write on board, "Characterization in Pantomime."

B.   Explain importance of characterization in pantomime. Cite examples from plays where roles demand characterization in pantomime.

C.   Ask individual students to volunteer to perform the same basic pantomime as three different characters:

1.   You go into a restaurant to order a meal as

a.   a teen-age boy who is very hungry

b.   a middle-aged woman who has very little appetite and sees nothing on the menu that she wants

c.   a very old man who is hungry but must limit his choice to what he can afford.

2. You are trying on dresses in a shop as
   a. a very fat woman who has trouble being fitted
   b. a young girl looking for a pretty dress to wear to a dance
   c. a secretary who is trying to find the most appropriate dress to wear on her first day of work in a new job.
3. You are visiting an art museum. You look at the exhibition as
   a. an artist who knows the painter whose work is on display
   b. a woman who thinks she should go to museums but does not appreciate the pictures
   c. an elderly woman who has been ill and is enjoying visiting her favorite museum for the first time in many months.
4. You are exercising in a gymnasium as
   a. a young man who loves all athletics
   b. a fat man whose doctor advised him to exercise to lose weight
   c. a child who has never seen gymnasium equipment before.
D. Summarize principles of characterization in pantomime and praise particular efforts of students that exemplify those principles.

Lesson Plan 3 from *Creative Dramatics in the Classroom,* Second Edition, by Nellie McCaslin. Copyright © 1974 by Longman Inc. Previously published by David McKay Company, Inc. Reprinted by permission of Longman Inc.

DRAMA LESSON PLAN 4

Lesson Title:	Machines,* Part I
Area:	V—Group Movement and Pantomime
Objective:	Students will learn to coordinate their movements. They will experience a sense of cooperation, sharing, and ensemble spirit.
Materials:	None

Procedure:
   A. Write "Machines, Part I" on the board.
   B. Divide the class into groups of five to ten. Have each group select a machine or assembly line that makes something or does something. Ask each group to make a list of its moving parts.
   C. Review the machines and parts selected by each group with the whole class.

*In her book *Improvisation for the Theater* (Evanston, Ill.: Northwestern University Press, 1963), Viola Spolin included an exercise called "Part of a Whole." This is the original source of the many variations called "Machine" in use throughout the country today.

D. Choose one group to lead off by sending one of its parts to the stage. Direct other parts to join the part moving on stage, taking on the rhythm of the moving part, until the machine is complete. Some students may be spare parts, replacing parts that wear out.

E. Have groups perform one at a time.

F. Summarize: "Today we learned the importance of working with others, as well as sharing our imaginative ideas."

Sample Imaginary Machine

Part 1:   Use one hand as an anvil and the other as a hammer. Pound with a slow steady rhythm.

Part 2:   After Part 1 is running well, Part 2 joins and puts an imaginary piece of metal on the anvil.

Part 3:   Removes the metal.

Part 4:   Receives the metal and puts it in a box.

Part 5:   Hands raw material to Part 2.

Part 6:   Works as a motor to drive Part 1.

Part 7:   Closes the box and hands it to Part 8.

Part 8:   Places a label on the box and passes it to Part 9.

Part 9:   Stacks boxes.

Part 10:   Carries away the stacked boxes.

Lesson Plan 4 submitted by Josephine Zarro, S. M. White Junior High. Reprinted by permission.

DRAMA LESSON PLAN 5

Lesson Title: Machines,* Part II

Area: V—Group Movement and Pantomime

Objective: Students will learn to move freely on stage and to adjust their movements to the movement of other students.

Materials: None.

Procedure:

A. Write "Machines, Part II" on the board.

B. Discuss need to improve pantomime techniques even more.

C. Ask the students to sit on stage, spread apart from one another. Ask them to think of a machine with moveable parts and visualize it clearly in their mind's eye (eyes closed).

*See footnote for Drama Lesson Plan 5.

D.   Ask them to take on the character of that machine and slowly become it.

E.   Encourage them to begin shaping their bodies to fit their machines and move as their machines would.

F.   Slowly have them stand, open their eyes, and continue to concentrate on their machines using their whole body.

G.   Once everyone is comfortable with his machine, ask him to begin moving with a rhythm suited to the machine. (Some will protest that their machines are stationary; ask them to imagine that their machines have grown legs and are part of a cartoon.)

H.   Ask them to freeze as you explain the next step.

I.   Ask them to begin to move again and to confront another machine, standing in front of it but continuing to move in rhythm.

J.   If either of the confronting machines would like, he may abandon his own movement and become a part of the other's machine. Each member of the two-party machine may adjust its movement to accommodate the added part.

K.   If neither wishes to change, they each move on to confront another machine.

L.   The exercise is over when everyone is part of one machine. (Once I witnessed a typewriter confront a train for a long time; finally, one by one, the typewriter parts gave way to the train to become tracks.)

M.   Often the last few objects become too unwieldy to move about on stage or the students become frustrated when neither side will give in. But it's better, I think, not to stop until they join together. If they know this and are tired of the exercise they will yield.

N.   Summarize: "Today we learned a little more about movement on stage and about adjusting our movement to the movement of others."

Lesson Plan 5 submitted by Donna Kristiansen, Costa Mesa High School. Reprinted by permission.

DRAMA LESSON PLAN 6

Lesson Title: Getting to Know You

Area: V—Group Movement and Pantomime

Objective: Students will become aware of the importance of nonverbal communication.

Materials: None.

Procedure:

A.   Write on the board: "Getting to Know You."

B. Explain why nonverbal communication is important in acting.

C. Ask students to take the stage and move about freely greeting one another without any words, using only smiles, nods, and handshakes. "Make sure that you have greeted everyone."

D. Stop the greeting and demonstrate another greeting by clasping wrists. Ask all the students to greet one another this way.

E. When this round is complete, demonstrate greeting by clasping elbows. Ask the students to greet one another in this manner.

F. Next try a hands-on-shoulders greeting. Go on to a hug if the students wish.

G. Resume seats to discuss the emotions aroused as each greeting became more friendly and intimate.

H. Summarize: "People can, and often do, communicate good wishes and greetings nonverbally. Often the nonverbal action of the actor is more communicative than his dialogue."

Lesson Plan 6 submitted by Cathy Binns, Chino High School. Reprinted by permission.

DRAMA LESSON PLAN 7

Lesson Title: Frozen Titles (Frozen Pictures)
Area: V—Group Movement and Pantomime
Objective: Students will learn to transfer mental pictures to visual presentation using their bodies creatively. Students will develop ways of working together under pressure.
Materials: None.
Procedure:

A. Write "Frozen Titles" on the board.

B. Explain the importance of being able to communicate silently and the desirability of being able to work under pressure.

C. Divide the class into small groups.

D. Ask each group to choose three titles from any of the following categories: plays, books, movies, fairy tales, nursery rhymes, proverbs, or great moments in history.

E. Give the groups 10 minutes to prepare "frozen pictures" that illustrate their choices. They may not use any props or costumes, but may illustrate the picture using bodies as props, etc. (such as one student being a tree, rock, or chair that another student is climbing or sitting on). Part of the preparation time should be used to rehearse transitions between the titles, getting from one picture to another quickly, smoothly, and entertainingly.

F. Call upon each group to present its three titles holding each frozen picture until "change" is called. Give a little more class observation time for the difficult ones, a little less time for the less complicated. When all three titles have been completed, the class guesses the titles. Difficult ones may be restaged using suggestions made by the audience.

G. Summarize: "Today we learned to use our bodies to form pictures, to communicate silently with an audience."

Lesson Plan 7 submitted by H. K. Baird, Charter Oak High School. Reprinted with permission.

DRAMA LESSON PLAN 8

Lesson Title: Circus
Area: V—Group Movement and Pantomime
Objective: Students will learn to use pantomime in representing animals, people, objects, and situations.
Materials: None
Procedure:

A. Write on the board, "Circus."

B. Explain that the following exercises will challenge the student's ability to channel previously used pantomime skills.

C. Tell the students to create a circus. Brainstorm the types of acts they would like to see and list them on the board: lion tamer, tightrope walker, clowns, fire-eater, etc.

D. Ask the students to select an act they would like to perform; have them pick assistants as needed. Pick one master of ceremonies. Use some students for sound effects.

E. Give the students 10 minutes to prepare their act. The master of ceremonies prepares a running order.

F. Circus should be presented very spontaneously. While one group is performing, the remainder of the class should react as a circus audience.

G. Summarize: "Today we improvised acts using pantomime, movement, creativity, and past experiences to create an imaginary environment."

Lesson Plan 8 submitted by Diane DeMarco, Luther Burbank High. Reprinted by permission.

DRAMA LESSON PLAN 9

Lesson Title: Symphony of Emotion
Area: VI E—Voice, Vocal Characterization

Objective: Students will learn to express emotions freely and vary the degree.

Materials: None

Procedure:

   A. Write on board: "Symphony of Emotion."

   B. Explain the importance of expressing the emotions freely.

   C. Select five or six students to face the remainder of the class, standing close to one another.

   D. Assign an emotion, attitude or feeling to each student, such as love, hate, happiness, sadness, anger, jealousy, disgust, silliness, stupidity.

   E. Use your hands to "conduct" the students, pointing to them to turn them on, raising hands to increase intensity, lowering hands to decrease intensity, and using a horizontal cutting motion to stop them immediately.

   F. Whenever a student is on, he is to express the emotion or attitude assigned to him. He is to use sounds or nonsense syllables of his choice, but not words. He is to use facial expressions and his whole body when possible.

   G. Turn on the students one at a time to introduce their emotions to the audience. Then mix and match, love with hate or happy and sad with disgust. Get them all going at once and then cut down to two.

   H. Students may guest conduct if you like.

   I. Summarize: "Today we learned to be very free in the expression of our emotions. We also learned that we could easily control the intensity."

Lesson Plan 9 submitted by Teri Argula, Holmes Junior High. Reprinted by permission.

DRAMA LESSON PLAN 10

Lesson Title: Situation Dialogues

Area: VII B 1—Improvisation, Spontaneity

Objective: Students will gain experience improvising scenes.

Materials: List of situations below

Procedure:

   A. Write "Situation Dialogues" on the board.

   B. Explain the objective. Emphasis may be placed on voice, pantomime, remaining in character, or another aspect.

   C. Ask two students to take the stage and give them one situation from the list below. Ask them to immediately start ad-libbing the situation.

   D. Summarize: "Today we learned to improvise by doing just that."

Situations

1. You meet with a teacher to explain why your report card grade was too low.

2. You teach someone how to drive a car.

3. You try to sell a product to a person who doesn't want to be bothered.

4. You try to tactfully advise a dear friend that he has bad breath.

5. You hurriedly try to return a Christmas present to an irritable clerk.

6. You fire one of your firm's oldest employees.

7. You are very shy but must ask a young lady for a date.

8. You argue with a stranger at a library over a book on a table.

9. You tell your child that there is no money to pay for his graduation expenses.

10. You tell an overbearing waiter that you cannot pay for the meal you just ate.

11. You refuse your daughter permission to attend a dance.

12. You apologize to a classmate for spilling water on him.

13. You reluctantly accept a speeding ticket from a policeman.

14. You plead for permission from your parent to attend an R-rated movie.

15. You quarrel with a neighbor about whose car is better.

16. You argue with your brother over which TV program to watch.

17. You try to convince a hard-to-manage child to go to bed.

18. You retrieve your baseball from a neighbor whose front window you just broke.

19. You catch one of your students cheating on a test.

20. You try to protect your treehouse from workmen who want to cut down the tree.

Lesson Plan 10 submitted by Ann-Marie Barry, Wilmington Junior High. Reprinted by permission.

DRAMA LESSON PLAN 11

Lesson Title: Wandering Speech

Area: VII B 1—Improvisation, Spontaneity

Objective: To give students practice in improvising and communicating ideas within a selected situation.

Materials: Three-by-five-inch cards with one situation on each.

Procedure:

    A.   Write on board "Wandering Speech."*

    B.   Explain the objective.

    C.   Explain the basic situation: One student is to delay the other from getting information or completing a task by means of chattiness, changing the subject or digressing. "Hostility is not a part of this exercise. The chatty person is not to deliberately set up an obstacle. The digression is to be a purely innocent, friendly one."†

    D.   Select/assign situations from the list below. Add others or have students devise. (A variety of situations may be written on three-by-five-inch cards; pairs of students would then pick a card.)

    E.   Have pairs of students present their situation.

    F.   Summarize: Point out that students were inventive during an ongoing scene within bounds of a chosen situation.

Situations

1. Chatty customer and salesman in department store. The customer has come to buy his wife's (her husband's) Christmas present.

2. Chatty nurse and hospital visitor at the hospital's information stand. The visitor needs an admission card to get on the elevator.

3. Chatty security guard and airline passenger. Passenger is anxious to board plane about to depart.

4. Chatty telephone operator and person anxious to report an emergency.

5. Chatty desk sergeant and person needing to report a crime in progress.

*This lesson plan was taken from *Improvisation for the Theater,* by Viola Spolin (Evanston, Ill.: Northwestern University Press, 1963). Reprinted by permission.
†Ibid.

DRAMA LESSON PLAN 12

Lesson Title: Emotional Transitions
Area: VII B 2 d—Improvisation, Spontaneity
Objectives: Students will learn to make emotional transitions believably.
Materials: Two index cards with ten to twelve emotions written on each (love, fear, anger, hate, despair, etc.)

Procedure:

A. Write on the board: "Emotional Transitions."

B. Explain the necessity of being able to make emotional transitions.

C. Select two students to be "directors" and give them the index cards.

D. Select two students to be "actors" and assign each to a director.

E. Give the two actors a simple situation to improvise, such as a judge questioning a ticket offender. Tell them that they are to play the scene according to the emotions called out by their directors. They are not to break character when the emotions are called out. They are to make transitions as smoothly as possible without destroying the continuity of the scene.

F. Encourage the directors to call out another emotion when a scene is dragging. They should call out emotions that will make the scene more interesting. For instance, if the judge is playing boredom and the offender is playing anger, the judge's director might call out "love." (The judge need not love the offender; he might love giving fines, or having power, as long as the emotion is justifiable.)

G. Several situations should be tried with different directors. Students are usually very free in this type of exercise as they are never stuck for what to play with a variety of emotions being fed to them.

H. Summarize: "Today we learned to apply a variety of emotions to a scene and to make smooth transitions."

Lesson Plan 12 submitted by Sydell Weiner, Northview High School. Reprinted by permission.

DRAMA LESSON PLAN 13

Lesson Title: Trust!
Area: VIII F 2—Stage Basics, Responsibilities of the Actor
Objective: Students will learn to trust each other and to accept responsibility

for the physical well-being of another student. They will also begin to overcome shyness in touching one another.

Materials: Blindfolds for half the class.

Procedure:

A. Write on the board: "Trust!"

B. Explain why trust is important in dealing with classmates and fellow actors.

C. Have the students discuss the meaning of the word "trust."

D. Using their definitions, explain that the objective of today's lesson is to become trustful of one another.

E. Have students rearrange the room or stage so that a maze of obstacles is formed from tables, chairs, and rehearsal furniture.

F. Break students into pairs, asking close friends not to work with one another.

G. One of each pair is to be blindfolded by the other. The "sighted" is then to lead the "blind" through the maze. Point out that the sighted have a responsibility to the blind.

H. When all have passed through the maze, have the blind and sighted exchange blindfolds and go through the maze again.

I. At the completion of the exercise, ask students to express the trust they felt or didn't feel, and the responsibility they felt when they were the sighted member of the pair.

J. Summarize: Point out that although we are not blindfolded when acting, we must be able to trust one another for lines, cues, actions—and therefore, we must be responsible.

Lesson Plan 13 submitted by Barbara Gerber, Nimitz Junior High. Reprinted by permission.

DRAMA LESSON PLAN 14

Lesson Title: Character Exploration

Area: XI A—Creating a Role, Study of Character

Objective: Students will learn to develop characterization through creative writing and performance.

Materials: Pencils, paper, and props (if desired, provided by actors)

Procedure:

A. Write "Character Exploration" on board.

B. Explain the importance of being able to explore a character.

C. Every student is to pretend that he is portraying a character in a play. (Example: Amanda in *The Glass Menagerie*.)

D. Build an imaginary character you've encountered in the play—one who is talked about but not seen. (Example: Laura's business teacher.)

E. Write a biography of the character, creating a full picture of that person's life.

1. See the character in your mind's eye.

2. Let us know how you feel about that character and why. Be specific.

3. Describe an incident that occurred when you were together. Make it relevant to the play. (Example: Business teacher tells Amanda that Laura has dropped out of school.)

F. Read the biography to us. Choose who your audience represents. Explain why you are telling your audience. (Example: Laura's classmates at the business school.)

G. Summarize: "Today we learned to explore characterization, a process that can be helpful to us when we prepare to play roles."

Lesson Plan 14 submitted by Joy Diskin, Harvard High School. Reprinted by permission.

DRAMA LESSON PLAN 15

Lesson Title: Cold Readings with Subtexts

Area: XI B—Creating a Role, Understanding Character's Relationship to Others

Objective: Students will become aware of auditioning procedures. Students will attempt to grasp and display the intent of the author while adding the emotional subtext given by director.

Materials: TV scripts, if available; play scripts, if not
A list of various emotional subtexts

Procedure:

A. Write on the board: "Preparation for Auditions."

B. Explain that you are primarily concerned in this exercise with the directability of the student actors as they reveal it in the audition process.

C. Pair off the students giving them unfamiliar scripts. Specify the scene and pages they are to read.

D. Give each pair about five minutes to look over the script.

E. Take each student aside, after the prep time, and whisper or show him his emotional subtext. (E.g., to Actor A, "Your partner has just killed your dog, which you loved very much.'' To Actor B, ''You see your partner is a spider, and you are deathly afraid of spiders.'')

F.   Allow each actor to ponder his subtext a few moments. Remind them that the author's words are just a vehicle through which emotions are to be delivered to the audience.

G.   Ask students to read.

H.   Following the reading, ask each to reveal what he was getting in the way of emotion from his partner.

I.   Ask the class for their opinions as to what emotions were coming across.

J.   Following this discussion, reveal the subtexts to the class and critique the work of the actors, being as positive as possible.

K.   Summarize: ''Professional actors must frequently audition with cold readings and must learn to easily and quickly apply any emotional subtext that a director might throw them.''

Lesson Plan 15 submitted by Bill Seymour, Van Nuys Junior High School. Reprinted by permission.

DRAMA LESSON PLAN 16

Lesson Title: Skits from the Newspaper

Area: XIII A—Playwriting, Springboards

Objective: Students will learn to use a newspaper article or ad as a springboard for a skit.

Materials: Selected newspaper articles and ads, possibly Thermofaxed or reproduced for distribution to students

Procedure:

A.   Write on the board: ''Skits from the Newspaper.''

B.   Explain that the assignment is to use an article or an ad as a source for a skit. Explain that many professionally written sketches evolve from newspaper items.

C.   Pass out articles and ads.

D.   Read an article aloud.

E.   If an overhead projector is available, write on a transparency using Sharpie pens. Otherwise use the blackboard. Discuss and then write:

1.   Setting—Draw a simple stage plan

2.   Characters—and select students to play them

3.   Props

4.   Basic action

5.   Some significant lines of dialogue

F. Ask students to take the stage and improvise the scene.

G. Possibly assign a student director to polish the scene.

H. Summarize: "Today we learned to use a newspaper article as a springboard for a skit. Tomorrow bring in a newspaper article or ad that your group can use as a skit. Tomorrow you will be allowed time to plan, improvise, and then rehearse your skit. The following day you will present your skit to the class."

Lesson Plan 16 submitted by Janis Parker, Andrew Carnegie Junior High. Reprinted by permission.

DRAMA LESSON PLAN 17

Lesson Title: Halloween Costumes
Area: XIV C—Technical Theater, Costuming
Objective: Students will gain the practical experience of designing and making a mask and/or costume for their own use.
Materials: A ghost story, flashlight, drawing paper, colored pencils, costume- and mask-making materials.

Procedure:

A. Write on board, "Halloween Costumes."

B. Explain that with the coming of Halloween it is a good time to use mask/costume-making skills to prepare for trick or treatin' and costume parties. Discuss costumes and masks used by students during previous Halloweens.

C. "Darken the room as you would for showing a film. Arrange desks in a semicircle with the teacher in the center. Using a flashlight, read a ghost or mystery story." (Poe's "Tales of Terror" is excellent.)*

D. Review elements of costuming—line, color, materials.

E. Ask each student to design a mask or costume suitable for his personal use during Halloween. It may be a sketch or it may be made from appropriate materials. Or, the sketch may be done in class and the costume made at home with results to be paraded in class.

F. Summarize by pointing out how individual masks and costumes reflect good techniques in design and construction.

*This lesson plan was adapted from the "calendar section" of STAGE: A Handbook for teachers of Creative Dramatics, by Natalie Bovee Hutson (Stevensville, Mich.: Educational Service, Inc.). The chapter suggests how teachers may use holidays and anniversaries of historical events to motivate lessons in dramatics.

DRAMA LESSON PLAN 19

Lesson Title: Makeup for Thin Old Age
Area: XIV D—Technical Theater, Makeup
Objective: Give each student the opportunity to apply his own makeup with a common class goal.
Materials: General makeup materials or individual makeup kits, if available.
Procedure:

A. Write on board, "Makeup for Thin Old Age."

B. Explain that in school, community, and even professional theater it is often necessary for younger actors to play older characters. Also explain that it is often necessary for actors to do their own makeup.

C. Review principles of makeup with emphasis on character and old-age makeup. (If possible, use visual aid such as filmstrip "Elementary Stage Makeup," from Olesen, 1535 Ivar Avenue, Hollywood, California 90028.)

D. Distribute handout showing general placement of shadows and wrinkles (see Figure 2–1).

E. Write on board the following procedure or hand out duplicated procedure to students:

1. Apply a pale grease base.

2. Using maroon or brown liner, with brush or fingertips shade the:
    a. eye sockets (These should have the heaviest shadows.)
    b. indention below cheek bones
    c. temple hollows
    d. side of nose
    e. mouth corners
    f. under jaw and chin
    g. depressions on both sides of throat cartilage

3. Using maroon or brown liner (do *not* use pencil) draw wrinkles where they naturally form in the:
    a. forehead
    b. between the eyes
    c. outer eye corners (called crow's feet lines)
    d. curved smile line from nose to mouth corners
    e. vertical lines below and above the lips

4. With white liner, highlight above all the wrinkles

5. Using white liner, above each shadow, highlight the bones:

    a.   over the eyebrows
    b.   cheekbones
    c.   chin point
    d.   line of lower jaw
    e.   throat cartilage

6. With your fingertips carefully blend together the edges of highlight, shadow, and base. The effect should be subtle. Avoid the stark wrinkle lines that plague many amateur jobs.

7. Thin the lips by applying foundation over them. Allow only a small portion of the natural lip coloring to show.

8. Whiten hair and eyebrows. Make the latter bushy by brushing the wrong way.

9. Powder the makeup.

10. Apply a beard and mustache, if needed.

11. Make up the hands by shading the depressions with gray and brown and highlighting the bones with yellow or white.

12. Properly arrange the character's hair.

F. Summarize principles of makeup by pointing out how each individual student's work makes good use of appropriate ideas and techniques.

Lesson Plan 19. This material taken from *Basic Drama Projects,* third edition, by Fran Averett Tanner. Caldwell, Idaho: Clark Publishing Company, 1977. Reprinted by permission.

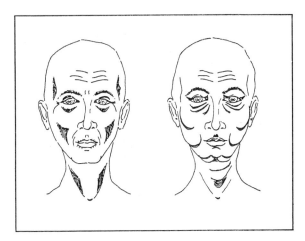

Figure 2–1. Old Age. Shadows and wrinkles shown must be highlighted and blended well.

| Gibberish Selling | A86 |

PREPARATION
Lead-in: Gibberish Introduction (A85).
Audience players.

FOCUS
On communicating to an audience.

DESCRIPTION
Single player, speaking Gibberish, sells or demonstrates something to the audience. Allow one or two minutes clock time per player.

SIDE-COACHING
Sell directly to us!   See us!   Sell to us!   Share your Gibberish!   Now pitch it!   Pitch it to us!

EVALUATION
What was being sold or demonstrated? Was there variety in the Gibberish? Did player see us in the audience or stare at us? Was there a difference between selling it and pitching it?

NOTES
1. Insist on direct contact. If players stare or look over the heads of the audience, ask them to "pitch" their sale, until the audience is actually seen. "Pitching," as practised in carnivals or department stores, requires direct contact with others.

2. Both audience and player will experience the difference when staring becomes seeing. An added depth, a certain quiet, will come into the work when this happens.

3. Allow a student-player to be the timekeeper who calls time at the halfway point —"half-minute to go!"—and at the end.

EXPERIENCE AREAS
Theater: What (Activity)
Showing, Not Telling
Space Object Game/Exercise: Making the invisible visible
Gibberish Series
Communication: Without Real Words
Non-Verbal Communication Game/Exercise

© 1975, Viola Spolin

Figure 2–2. A Card from the Theater Game File, by Viola Spolin. The file contains 204 sequenced theater games or exercises on five-by-eight-inch cards. A handbook gives directions for their use. The file is recommended for use from elementary through college classes.   (St. Louis, Mo.: CEMREL, Inc., 1975. Reprinted by permission.)

Look into the following sources for other excellent ideas:

Hutson, Natalie Bovee. *Stage: A Handbook for Teachers of Creative Dramatics.* Educational Service, Inc., P.O. Box 219, Stevensville, Michigan 49127. (Recommended for teachers of elementary school.)

McCaslin, Nellie. *Creative Dramatics in the Classroom.* 2nd ed. Longman, Inc., 19 West 44th St., New York, New York 10036. (Recommended for teachers of younger students.)

Spolin, Viola. *Improvisation for the Theater.* Northwestern University Press, 1735 Benson Avenue, Evanston, Illinois.

Spolin, Viola. *Theater Game File.* CEMREL, Inc., 3120 59th Street, St. Louis, Missouri 63139.

Tanner, Fran Averett. *Basic Drama Projects.* 3rd ed. Clark Publishing Co., c/o Caxton Printers, P.O. Box 700, Caldwell, Idaho 83605.

YOUR ADDENDUM

Now that you have reviewed the plans, do you have any that you would like to add? I would like to include more plans in the next edition of this book. If you know of a good one that you would like to share with other drama teachers, please take the time to send it to *The Stage Manager,* Box 1901, Los Angeles, California, 90053. Thank you!

CHAPTER THREE

Box Office
and Reservations

A pleasant, well-programmed box office worker is a great asset to a theater's public relations. In many cases, the box office attendant's greeting will be the only personal contact theatergoers will have with the theater. They are more apt to return to a theater if they feel at home there.

Consider the following exchange:

Box Office Attendant (BOA):	[*Smiling*] (A) Good Evening. May I help you? (B)
Ticket Purchaser:	Yes, I have these tickets for last night, but then our babysitter got sick, and I was wondering if I could exchange them for two tickets for tonight.
BOA:	Babysitters can really be a problem. (C) I wish I could help you by exchanging those tickets. (D) Unfortunately, our box office rules state that exchanges must be made three hours before the performance, or we can't honor the tickets. [*Points to posted rule.*] (E) [*Pause*] Perhaps Mr. Wilson, our house manager,

can help you. Why don't you speak to him? He's in the lobby wearing a blue cardigan. (F)

(A)   Everyone responds favorably to a warm smile, and anyone can learn to smile. Box office workers may need to be reminded of the importance of their demeanor in dealing with the public. You can't legislate a smile on an attendant's face, but you can call attention to its desirability. When you write your box office procedures, you might start with a gentle reminder and an earnest plea. (See Figure 3-1.)

(B)   The smile should be accompanied by a personal greeting and the offer of assistance.

BOX OFFICE PROCEDURES

1.   Remember to smile and be friendly with customers. If you make them feel at home, they will want to return here. Your smile can be a great asset to our theater.

2.   Strive for accuracy in all of your written work and in every transaction.

3.   Start the day by initiating the Daily Report. Enter the amount of cash on hand as you fill the change drawer.

4.   In pulling tickets, remember to dress the house.

5.   Cross off sold tickets on the seating chart for the performance.

6.   Confirm and finalize each transaction with window customers: "Here are your two tickets for 'Name of Production,' for Friday evening, November 21. Curtain is at 8:30. Parking information is on the envelope. Thank you!"

7.   Answer phone: "State Playhouse. May I help you?"

8.   If time permits, ask customers if you may add their names to the mailing list.

9.   Copy driver's license numbers on checks. Do not accept checks for more than cost of tickets.

Figure 3-1. Instructions to Box Office Personnel (incomplete). Revise this list to make it applicable to your theater. Then add any other rules and procedures that will be helpful to you, and post the list in the box office.

BOX OFFICE RULES

1. Reservations may be made by phone—555-7043

2. Tickets may be exchanged 24 hours prior to a performance, but no later.

3. Reserved tickets must be picked up 30 minutes prior to curtain or the reservations will be cancelled and the tickets sold.

4. Checks are acceptable with driver's license or student I.D. Checks in excess of the amount of purchase will not be accepted.

5. Absolutely no refunds will be made on any ticket sales.

6. Absolutely no unauthorized persons are allowed to enter the box office.

Figure 3-2. Box Office Rules (incomplete). These rules should be posted for the public.

(C) Purchasers should be given some feedback. It may be the only understanding they have received all day. Even if the box office attendant only repeats their orders, the purchasers see that they are communicating and that the attendant understands what they want or what their problems are.

(D) The attendant should grant in fantasy what he or she cannot really deliver. "I wish I could do that, but . . . ." This kind of statement shows the attendant's desire to accommodate the theatergoers. It puts the attendant on their side against the cruel world of rules and regulations. But if the statement is not sincere, it should be left out.

(E) The attendant should point out the applicable box office rule, if necessary. These rules should be posted in or near the box office in plain view of prospective ticket buyers. (See Figure 3-2.) Ticket envelopes and backs of tickets are also good places to write rules.

(F) If a customer is not satisfied, the attendant should refer him or her to higher authority. Of course there are exceptions to the rules, but the box office attendant should be instructed not to make any. The theater manager or a faculty member should smooth out any problems that may occur, deciding whether the good will of the customer is worth more than strict adherence to box office rules.

Having noted the importance of the box office attendant's attitude, we can now discuss box office procedures in general, starting at the beginning.

PREPARING THE BOX OFFICE FOR BUSINESS

Before the box office is opened for business, change must be prepared, tickets racked, and house seats pulled.

Preparing Cash

The amount of cash on hand should be kept to a minimum. Selling tickets for whole dollar amounts, or even half dollar amounts, can reduce the need for a lot of change. A cash drawer and safe should be provided for convenient storage and handling. A regular procedure should be followed in counting the starting monies and reporting them. (See Figure 3-20 for opening monies form.)

Checking Tickets

Another regular procedure should be the checking in of tickets from the printer. Tickets are as valuable as money; therefore, they should be carefully controlled. They should be inspected on arrival for accuracy of printing and correct information—particularly, correct seat numbers.

If reserved seats are being sold, the tickets must be racked; that is, they must be placed in specially designed ticket racks so that their distribution corresponds roughly to the seating plan of the theater. This allows the ticket seller to grasp the correct tickets quickly without having to sort through all of the tickets for that performance. (The racks are discussed below under Equipment.)

Count the tickets as you place them in the rack, making sure that the number of tickets for each row corresponds to the number of seats for that row on the seating chart. This check will help you to find printing errors.

Pulling House Seats

As soon as the tickets have been racked, pull the house seats—four to ten seats withheld from sale for use by the management. They are good seats that may be used for press, as complimentary tickets, or to take care of last minute emergencies. The number of tickets that must be set aside as house seats will vary from theater to theater. Experience will determine what number to set aside. Once determined, the same number is pulled for every performance and not sold by the box office until the box office is directed to do so by the theater manager or faculty supervisor—or until a prearranged time, say two minutes before announced curtain.

House seats should be scattered throughout the house, comprising a few seats from alternate rows rather than a whole row or block. That way, if the house seats are not used and cannot be sold at the last minute, there won't be a completely empty row or block in the audience.

House seats are the best cushion against mistakes, or alleged mistakes, made in the reservation of tickets. If patrons arrive on a sold-out night claiming they have reservations, and the box office attendant finds their tickets set aside for the following night's performance, the house manager might decide to give them house seats as a public relations gesture.

SERVING THE CUSTOMER

The walk-up sale (window sale) of tickets hours or days before the performance is the basic box office transaction. After the smile and warm greeting, the box office attendant should give the customers any information they may need to purchase tickets. A flyer for the current production should be in easy view, giving the dates and times of performance and the cost of tickets. In theaters with large capacities and reserved seating systems there should also be a seating chart (see Figure 3–3) showing which seats are still available.

Sometimes it is convenient to cover a seating chart with plastic so that sold seats may be crossed out in crayon. This type of chart can be placed on the counter of the box office in easy view of both seller and buyer.

After giving buyers all the information they require, the attendant should recommend seats to meet their needs and dress the house (discussed below) at the same time.

For each customer, the seller pulls the tickets, places them standing up in an envelope, holds them in hand, waits for direct eye contact with the buyer, and repeats the specifications: "Four tickets for Friday night,

November 21." The seller then takes the customer's money, hands over the tickets, allowing the customer to check the tickets and place them all the way into the envelope, and returns change.

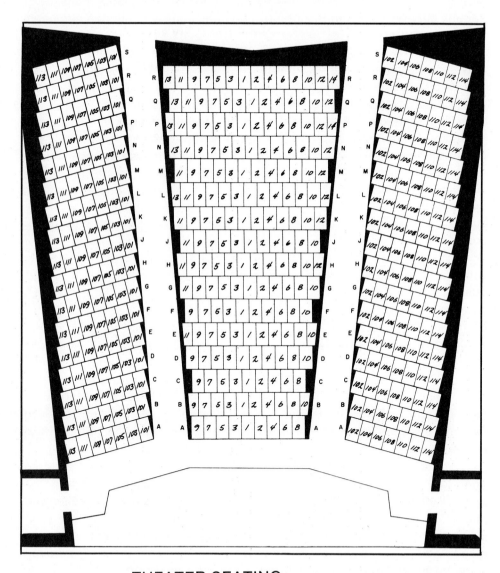

THEATER SEATING

Figure 3-3. Seating Chart of State Playhouse, California State University, Los Angeles. There are 422 seats.

The box office attendant can then finalize the transaction with a hearty "Thank you," a warm smile, and a parting, "I know you'll enjoy it."

The attendant might ask customers if they are on the mailing list, giving them forms if they are not. Time allowing, the attendant can even fill out the forms for the customers.

Box office attendants must maintain a cheery and optimistic attitude about productions for which they are selling tickets, regardless of cast gossip, reviews, or their own personal evaluations based on rehearsals or parts of the production seen.

If they feel bad about selling tickets to a turkey, they can remind themselves of their need for professionalism—that they have a job to do and do well. If necessary, they should give a better performance with their cheerful sales techniques than the leading actor gives on stage!

Sometimes it is helpful if the box office attendant reminds the buyer about the content of the production. "We don't feel that the play is suitable for children." Presumably this warning is on the flyer and other publicity, but the box office attendant should be well informed about the content of the play so that he or she can advise customers.

Check-cashing policy should also be posted. If checks are acceptable with presentation of a driver's license, student I.D., or credit cards, the posted rules should make clear that checks in excess of the amount of purchase will not be accepted. The box office attendant should copy identifying numbers on the check.

DRESSING THE HOUSE

The box office in a reserved seat house and the ushers in a nonreserved situation are responsible for dressing the house—that is, seating the audience so as to elicit the maximum response, whether it be applause, laughter, or tears. If you have ever attended a play in a nearly empty auditorium, you know what a chilling experience it can be. You feel much more comfortable when you are surrounded by people, and you are more apt to respond to the production when others about you are responding.

Generally, seats in the front center of the center section should be filled first. Then the seats around those should be filled, moving left and right of center, across aisles, and nearer and farther from the stage.

People who are experienced in theater management tend to take the dressing of the house for granted. But inexperienced box office personnel (and ushers in nonreserved houses) may not understand it. Take time to instruct them, emphasizing that they have a role to play in molding individuals into a responding audience by determining that they sit close to others and are not isolated.

Since the exact dressing pattern may vary with the configuration of your theater, you should place a chart in the box office, showing how you expect the attendant to dress the house when selling tickets (see Figure 3-4).

If your house gets sold out, the dressing process will have been unnecessary. But if the house is half filled or less, the audience distribution may make a significant contribution to how much people enjoy the production. It definitely contributes to cast morale.

It is standard practice in many English theaters to request that patrons in the less expensive seats move forward to fill the empty seats prior to curtain.

RESERVATIONS

Reservations may be taken by telephone, by mail, or in person. It is necessary to get the name, address, telephone number, date of performance (and time if there are two performances that day), number of tickets, price, and amount due or paid. Paid reservations are considered sold tickets; they may not be resold by the theater. Establish a deadline for paying for reservations. Usually it is thirty minutes before curtain. For a very popular attraction, however, you might want to change it to twenty-four or even forty-eight hours.

Telephone Reservations

Most theaters accept telephone reservations. The practice is highly recommended, because it offers customers such a convenience. (The procedure has but one major drawback—the customer who makes a reservation and then fails to pick up the tickets. But that situation can be dealt with, and such customers are in the minority.)

Attendants should be taught to answer the phone: "Playhouse box of-

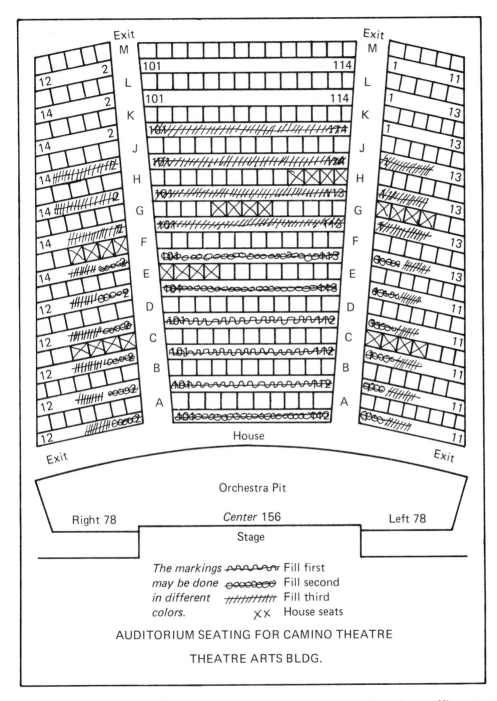

Figure 3-4. Dressing Chart. Colors may be used to show box office personnel which seats are to be filled first.

fice. May I help you?'' They can't smile over the phone, but if they can put a smile in their voices, they should. Depending on proximity to performance time and number of seats already sold, attendants might also add, ''Good seats for tonight's performance are available,'' thus anticipating the caller's probable first question. (Of course, many calls will simply be for information, and the attendants will be able to refer to flyers for coming performances.)

If time allows and the ticket racks are at hand, the attendant should pull the tickets while the customer is on the phone and place them in a reservations envelope. The attendant then repeats the specifications for the tickets, ''Four tickets for Friday night, November 21,'' and fills out a printed or hand-stamped ticket envelope (see Figure 3–5). Pulling the tickets while the customer is on the phone avoids errors in filling orders.

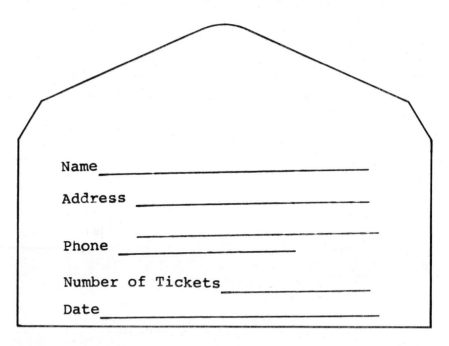

Name _____

Address _____

_____

Phone _____

Number of Tickets _____

Date _____

Figure 3–5. Ticket Envelope. An envelope may be printed or hand stamped with an outline of the information needed to make a reservation. Other items that might be included on the envelope are the box office phone number, parking information, a map of the theater's location, or box office rules such as ''No mistakes rectified after leaving window'' or ''Tickets may not be exchanged.'' Some theaters sell space on the envelopes to advertisers.

Sometimes it will be impossible to pull tickets immediately, as in cases when the customer requests reservations for a production whose tickets have not yet been racked.

Either way, attendants must take the time to complete information, and they must work accurately. Asking a man named Smith how he spells his last name is *not* going too far! And getting his complete first name is mandatory. It will not be uncommon to have two people with the same last name making reservations for the same performance. Time and accuracy used in taking the reservation might well pay off when there is a long line at the box office just a few minutes before curtain.

Getting the address and phone number can serve a couple of purposes. Both items serve as a check if there are two people with identical names. The phone number may be used to confirm reservations (discussed later in this chapter), and the address may be added to a mailing list.

If more than one person works in the box office, the need for accuracy and careful printing is increased.

The attendant should try to be brief when making reservations, assuring customers that they will be given the best seats still available and trying not to get into lengthy discussions of seat locations.

The attendant should end the conversation with: "Curtain time is 8:30. Reservations not picked up by 8 P.M. will be *cancelled."* This statement allows the box office to sell unclaimed tickets during that half hour prior to curtain. In practice, the tickets may be held later, depending on the demand, but the theater should make it clear to the customer exactly when it has the right to sell them. The word *cancelled* seems to be the most effective for this purpose.

If attendants can't pull tickets when talking on the phone, they should pull them as soon as they hang up. They should file the tickets, in their envelopes, in a reservations file. If the tickets are for the very next performance, they go directly into a reservations rack in alphabetical order (see Figure 3–24).

The length of time in advance of curtain when tickets must be paid for or cancelled, varying from fifteen minutes to forty-eight hours, must be decided by the theater manager. Saving the envelopes of cancelled reservations can help in two ways. First, irate customers who arrive after their tickets have been sold can be shown that the tickets had been reserved for them. Second, the manager can see the number of cancellations and decide whether the time period should be adjusted, or if greater emphasis should be placed on confirming reservations.

THEATER 20

INSTRUCTIONS TO ANSWERING SERVICE

1. Answer: "Theater 20 Box Office"

2. Take reservations:
    Ninety per evening (Do not accept more than four in a party!)
    Write on three-by-five-inch note cards: name
                                              number in party
                                              phone
                                              night of performance
                                              Be sure to total!

3. Give alternate dates of performance if requested performance is sold out. (See flyer for dates.)

4. Advise all parties:
    Curtain time is 8 P.M.
    Reservations will be held until 7:45 P.M.
    Subscribers must bring their cards.
    A subscriber card is good for one guest.
    Tickets are $3 for nonsubscribers and subscribers without cards.

5. Address: 5060 Fountain Ave.

6. Parking: More than ample parking is available adjacent to the theater; it is free and clearly marked.

7. Standbys are admitted at 7:50, first come, first served.

8. For other matters, call:
    subscriptions: Mrs. J. Duro Pampinelli   555–7273
    theater parties: Mrs. Paula Ritter   555–3421
    auditions: Mr. Ralph Twiller   555–2436
    backstage: 555–8387

9. Turn reservations over to house manager, Teddy Spearing, only.

Figure 3–6. Briefing Sheet for an Answering Service.

The walk-up customer should take precedence over the phone reservation. This might simply mean answering the phone, asking the caller to hold the line ("Playhouse box office. One moment please."), and completing the transaction with the window customer. Of course, the box office attendant would resume the conversation with "Thank you for waiting. May I help you?" The attendant might even ask phone customers to call back in five minutes, or take their numbers and call them back.

        The Answering Service   Some theaters find it desirable to use an answering service. Would it be economically sound for you? In rough figures the service might cost you between $50 and $100 per month. (Fees vary from service to service and with the type of service.) A typical fee might be $25 per month plus 10¢ per message over 100 messages. If your answering service took 541 messages in one month, your bill might be $79.10 for that month.

If those 541 messages resulted in 850 reservations at $3 per ticket, you would be spending 3 percent of your box office receipts on the service. How would that compare to hiring an attendant to work part time, say 40 hours per month?

It works well for a small (100-seat) theater in Beverly Hills, but would it work for you?

There are two basic answering service systems. In the first, the answering service number is used, and the person answering the ring says, "Thank you for calling 555–3212." In the second, the answering service picks up the theater phone line and says, "Thank you for calling Theater 20." The second plan is slightly more expensive, but it gives theater personnel the option of answering on the theater premises. In either case, the answering service number is used on all flyers and publicity releases.

The theater gives the answering service a briefing sheet (Figure 3–6), a supply of three-by-five-inch reservation forms (Figure 3–7), and a flyer for the production. The service uses a very simple chart (Figure 3–8) to keep track of reservations.

Each time a customer makes a reservation, the service fills out a reservation form and subtracts the number in the party from the total number of seats it is authorized to reserve. (In the case of the 100-seat theater described here, the house manager withholds ten house seats to accommodate VIPs and patrons who contribute heavily to the theater.)

When all seats for a performance have been reserved, the service is able to recommend other performances. It tries to discourage standbys, but tells callers that if they insist, they may go to the theater to await last minute cancellations. They will be admitted on a first come, first served basis after signing in at the theater. Note that the waiting list (standby list) is made up by the theater and not by the service.

THEATER TWENTY RESERVATION FORM	
Name	MRS. ARTHUR NEWMAN
Number in Party	3
Phone	555-7617
Which Performance? (Date)	SATURDAY. JANUARY 24
Totalled?	✓

Figure 3-7. Reservation Card Used by Answering Service. Different colored cards may be used if the service takes reservations for two plays in the same month by the same theater.

The house manager picks up the reservation forms from the answering service the night before opening and once each evening during the run. Of course, no reservations are taken at the theater.

The answering service never handles tickets or money.

Occasionally, the service takes a reservation and forgets to subtract the number in the party from the number of seats available on the chart. The "totalled?" section of the reservation card is a guard against that. A rushed answering service worker can stack four or five reservations and then go back and tally them.

An advantage of the answering service is that a customer can call around the clock. Your box office is thus open twenty-four hours a day. This decreases the hours that an attendant must be working in the box office. A simple sign in the box office window can advise buyers that "Reservations may be made at any time by calling 555-5643. Tickets must be picked up half an hour before curtain. The box office is open 7-9 P.M. daily."

THEATER 20 RESERVATIONS

First Week   Prisoner of Second Avenue

Jan. 20	Jan. 21	Jan. 22	Jan. 23	Jan. 24
Tuesday	Wednesday	Thursday	Friday	Saturday
90 22	90 25	90	90 28	90 13
88 20	86 24	88	89 27	88 11
87 18	84 20	86	87 25	84 10
84 17	83 18	85	85 23	82 7
81 16	81 16	81	83 20	80 5
79 13	79 13	77	82 17	79 3
75 11	78 10	75	81 15	77 2
73 9	77 8	73	79 13	74
71 8	75 7	70	75 9	71 SOLD
70	73 5	68	73 7	68 OUT
66	71 2	66	71 3	66
63	67	64	69 1	62
62	64 SOLD	63	67 SOLD	60
58	62 OUT	62	65 OUT	58
56	60	58	63	55
55	58	56	62	49
53	57	54	60	45
51	53	48	58	41
49	50	45	57	40
47	48	44	56	39
45	47	40	54	37
41	45	38	52	35
40	43	36	50	33
39	41	34	48	31
36	39	31	46	29
35	37	29	43	27
34	34	27	41	24
29	32	25	40	22
27	30	23	38	20
25	27	19	35	18
		17	32	16
			30	14
			29	

Figure 3-8. Tally Sheet Used by Answering Service.

65

The Answering Device   At California State University, Los Angeles, the music department uses a recording device leased from the phone company (about $12 per month, year-round) to help handle reservations. It has been in use for over five years. The department finds it very effective.

Calls for tickets to *Orpheus in Hell* are answered with a few bars of Offenbach's cancan music before a pleasant voice states that good seats are available for the evening's performance. Callers are asked to state name, phone number, date of performance, and number of tickets wanted—after the beep. They are assured that if they are not called back, their tickets will be waiting at the box office.

The management feels that the music helps to take the curse off of being answered by a mechanical device.

Like the answering service, the answering device, leased or purchased (roughly $90 to $150) might be a way for you to extend your box office hours or cut down on employee hours.

Mail Reservations

Flyers that solicit mail orders, whether for single performances or the season, should require customers to send in stamped, self-addressed envelopes with their requests for tickets. Besides saving you the expense of the stationery and stamps, this procedure avoids loss or delay in the mails due to addressing errors.

The advantage of mail orders is that they may be handled when the box office is not busy. The disadvantage is that the customers may not select their seats and sometimes may be requesting tickets for a performance that is already sold out.

The mailed request should be given priority over the telephone or window sale, because the writers actually ordered their tickets before the others. They deserve the best seats still available. So the box office attendant should fill mail orders before opening the box office to the other sales. In practice, however, this is not always done.

Instead of filling out a ticket envelope, the box office attendant should fill out a three-by-five-inch card for each customer, noting the name, address, phone, number of tickets, dates of performance, seat numbers, and date the tickets were mailed from the box office. The cards should be filed in alphabetical order so that they can be found easily. If the tickets get lost in the mail, they can be duplicated.

In the flyer soliciting mail orders, it's wise to ask customers for their phone numbers and an alternate date that they can attend in case the performance they request is sold out. If a customer does not specify an alternate date, you may want to call and discuss alternatives.

If the mail order arrives too close to the performance date to insure delivery on time, the tickets should be held at the window, just like a telephone reservation. This policy should be made clear on the flyers soliciting mail orders. If possible, call the customer to explain.

Checks and money orders must be scrutinized to insure that you have received the correct amount. If the payment is not correct, you can phone or write the customer to ask for the difference. A form note can be used. (See Figure 3–9.) In both cases, you do not pull the tickets until the correct amount has been received. Keep incorrect orders and accompanying checks in a separate file.

Usually, mail order receipts are tallied separately from other box office sales.

Despite the inconveniences and labor involved in processing mail orders, it is desirable to continue the practice. Purchase by mail is convenient for the theatergoer. Mail orders also give the earliest indication of the popularity of a production. They allow the theater manager to increase or decrease publicity in other areas as required.

Confirming Reservations

Too often, people who reserve the best seats in the house don't bother to use their tickets! Therefore, some theaters find it practical to call the reserved ticket holders the evening before the performance or the afternoon of the performance. This procedure can reduce the number of reservations that are held up to the last minute and then cancelled.

"This is State Playhouse calling. Do you expect to use the tickets that you have reserved for tonight's performance? . . . Good. This is just a reminder that they must be picked up before 8 P.M. or we will have to cancel the reservation. . . . Thank you!"

It is unfortunate that a small percentage of those called will respond by saying that they will not be able to attend or will only be able to use two of the tickets they have reserved.

It may take too much time and energy for your attendant to confirm reservations. If it is desirable to confirm, perhaps you can find someone outside the box office to do this chore. (This would also keep the box of-

APRIL 13, 1979
_____
date

WE WOULD LIKE TO HELP YOU . . . . BUT

_____ We are sold out (of price) (of date) specified.

_____ Price desired available, but not locations requested.

___✓___ Because of limited mailing time, tickets are
being held at the box office. Please pick up
before _8 PM_ .

___✓___ Payment not correct (~~or included~~). Please
remit $4.00 .

_____ Please give alternate dates from your choice of
_____.

_____ Failed to state date and performance.
_____ matinee?   _____ evening?

_____ Check returned for signature.

_____ Number of tickets and price not indicated.

Please mail to: State Playhouse Box Office
ATTN: CARMEN COOPER
5151 State University Drive
Los Angeles, CA 90032

Figure 3-9. Form Note Used When There Is a Mail Order Problem.

fice's telephone open.) In the long run, confirming reservations can cut down on empty seats and the number of last-minute exchanges at the window.

WAITING LISTS

In the happy event that you can't accommodate all who are waiting to see your show, prepare a waiting list so that you can distribute cancelled reservations on a first come, first served basis. Besides the name, get the number in the party. Obviously you cannot accommodate a party of four with a single cancelled reservation, so you would want to be able to go down the list until you found a party of one.

MAILING LISTS

Keeping a mailing list is a publicity function that is often turned over to the box office.

An effective mailing list includes the names of those who have an avid interest in theater and live within a comfortable distance of your theater. Where are you more likely to find such people than in your theater? Therefore, start your list by putting a guest book in your lobby, with a sign above it asking those interested in being on the mailing list to write their names and addresses in the book. (You might prefer to use a printed form card and a deposit box.)

To add to this basic list, you can consider several sources. Add the faculty of your college or university. Borrow membership lists from nearby community theaters and related art groups—music, dance, and fine arts. Choose selectively from lists compiled by other campus groups for concerts or guest lectures.

You will also want to consider rosters of other groups that may have theater-prone members: the museum, country clubs, city officials. You might even add from the Yellow Pages the names and addresses of all the doctors, lawyers, and certified public accountants. (In a large city you would select only those whose phone numbers had prefixes that were in your area.)

A copy of the complete mailing list should be kept in the box office so that the attendant can update it by adding the names of those persons who phone in or mail in orders. Deletions and changes must also be made when people move and send you a change of address or when a flyer is returned.

On all your mailings you should write near the address, "ADDRESS CORRECTION REQUESTED." The post office charges a small fee to return the mail to you with the new address, but it will save you the cost of future undeliverable flyers. When the new address is out of your area, you delete the entry.

There are many mechanical means of addressing your flyers. Check your Yellow Pages under Addressing Machines and Supplies. The simplest type uses a card master that can be prepared on a typewriter and then stenciled directly onto the flyer. The addresses can be maintained in a card file rather than in list form. They are easy to use and change that way. The cards may also be punched so that you can quickly pull categories of addressees (faculty members, incoming freshmen, etc.). This gives your mailing list added versatility, since you can select certain types of potential audience for a specific production.

Of course, if your school is large enough to have a computer services department, you may find that you can easily obtain a printout list and computer-prepared address labels that merely have to be applied to your flyers.

TICKET EXCHANGES AND REFUNDS

A sign prominently posted in the box office and notes on the tickets or envelopes should make it unmistakably clear just what your theater's exchange and refund policy is: "Tickets may be exchanged 24 hours prior to a performance, but no later. Absolutely no refunds on ticket sales." Policy in this matter can only be determined by experience, and it should be reviewed periodically by the theater's management.

There are two main problems in the exchange of tickets. The first, and lesser of the two, is the added work for the box office during its busiest time.

The second problem occurs when you have a complex ticket system like the double-stubbed or coupon. Then the box office attendant must be sure to resell the returned tickets for the price at which they were originally purchased so as not to throw off box office records. If for any reason this can't be done, the box office attendant has to go through all the stubs and patch together the returned tickets. It's time-consuming and devoutly not to be wished for!

If a customer wants to return tickets on the last night of a run, the theater manager may want to issue an exchange ticket good for any future production.

LOST TICKETS

Tickets lost or left at home are an all-too-frequent hassle. If there's a record of the sale in the box office, such as a list of reserved seats that were ordered by mail, the attendant can merely verify that the individual did purchase the tickets, and issue a house pass. In most cases the customer will be referred to the house manager, who must decide whether or not to accept the story of the lost tickets. The house manager may then issue house seats. But the manager has every right to deny entry.

STANDING ROOM

In the event of a sellout performance, and if fire regulations allow, you may want to issue standing room tickets. The simplest way is to use a "standing room" hand stamp on a house pass.

Standing room is an accepted custom in London and on Broadway. Usually, standees are admitted at reduced prices. They inspect the audience for empty seats during the first act and seat themselves at the first intermission when possible. When community theaters have a sellout, they tend to extend the audience into the dressing rooms, pulling out every folding chair available and setting them up in the aisles. Again, fire regulations *must* be observed!

TICKETS

In my haste to get to the more important things like the smile on the face of the box office attendant, I neglected to discuss the commodity in which the box office deals—tickets. A ticket is a little piece of paper that says you have paid for space to see a production. Sometimes you haven't even paid—in which case it's a little piece of paper saying that you are invited.

There are all kinds! In its simplest form a ticket could be a blank piece of paper, distinguishable only by its shape or color, or perhaps by some distinctive punch mark in it. At the other extreme is the computerized, logo-embossed ticket that is suitable for framing, and may cost your theater upwards of $350 for a six-performance run. In between are a variety of general-admission and reserved tickets.

General-Admission Tickets

A general-admission ticket entitles the bearer to a seat in the theater, but it does not specify which seat. There are two types of general-admission ticket: roll-type and card-type.

Roll-Type   The type of ticket that is issued to you at a movie theater is the roll-type general-admission. (See Figure 3–10.) It comes printed with wording such as, "Admit one—No refund." On the reverse side there might be a statement that the theater reserves the right to refuse admission. The tickets are numbered consecutively. If necessary, you can hand stamp such a ticket with the date.

The ticket serves as a pass from the box office past the door attendant. The door attendant can rip the ticket apart, giving the customer a piece and retaining the other piece to count the number of paid admissions.

If you use a stubbed roll ticket (Figure 3–11), the box office or door attendant can retain the stub to count sales.

Using rolls of tickets of two different colors would allow you to keep an accurate account of two different prices of admission (general/student-faculty or children/adult).

Figure 3–10. Roll-Type Tickets. Note the consecutive numbering.

(Courtesy of Dillingham Ticket Co., Los Angeles, California.)

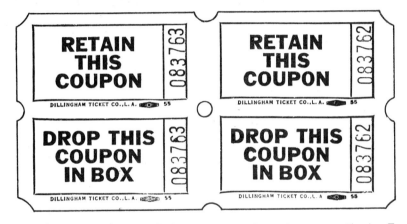

Figure 3–11. Stubbed Roll Tickets. Tickets are numbered consecutively. Each ticket has two parts, perforated. (Courtesy of Dillingham Ticket Co., Los Angeles, California.)

Card-type   The card-type, often used by high schools and community theaters, is the next step up in nonreserved tickets. It can usually be made in the high school print shop, ordered from a local printer, or run off on a mimeograph machine or spirit duplicator.

If publicizing the show is a function of the tickets, the card-type is obviously more useful than the roll-type. Card tickets usually have the names of the production and the producing company, the name and address of the theater, the date or dates of performance, and the time of curtain. (See Figure 3–12.) The reverse side may be printed with box office rules: "No refunds." "Tickets may not be exchanged for any other performance."

"This play is not recommended for children." "Curtain time strictly observed. Those arriving after the curtain will not be seated until the first intermission."

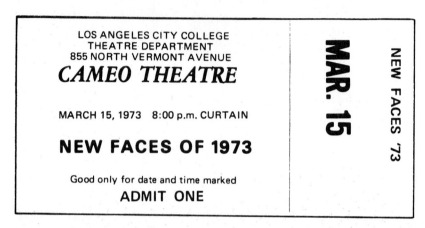

Figure 3–12. Card-Type General-Admission Ticket.

(Courtesy of Theatre Department and Academy, Los Angeles City College.)

You can keep track of card-type tickets by numbering them consecutively. The tickets can also be stubbed so that they can be made into booklets for convenient handling. Using two colors allows you to account for a dual pricing structure or two categories of seats, such as orchestra and balcony.

Programs as Tickets   In small houses, you can save the cost of tickets entirely by using the program as a ticket. Simply stamp the program with the date and have your box office attendant issue it. If stubs are necessary for accounting purposes, perforate one corner of the program to be removed by the door attendant. (The removed corner would prevent the program from being reused as a ticket.)

Advantages and Disadvantages   If you can do without reserved seating, the roll-type and card-type tickets offer a few advantages. They are inexpensive and are easy to obtain and use. Just like reserved tickets, they can help you not to oversell a production if you don't issue more tickets than you have seats. They can also help you in accounting.

A few of the disadvantages of nonreserved seating are that persons with sight or hearing problems or other physical disabilities cannot preselect an appropriate seat, and the best seats in the house can't be reserved for VIPs. But even with general admission tickets, arrangements can be made to accommodate such people. Audience members usually observe reserved signs placed on seats and won't move them without the permission of the ushers. Ushers should have no difficulty asking customers to move to accommodate the disabled, even without such signs.

Reserved Tickets

Size of the theater and cost of admission seem to be factors in leading theatergoers to expect reserved seats. Generally when they pay three dollars or more per ticket or go to a theater that seats at least 250, they expect to be presented with a reserved ticket rather than a general admission ticket. Notice that the quality of the production they expect to see is not a factor in their expectation of reserved seating arrangements!

The advantage of reserved seating is certainty. Upon arrival the customers will be taken directly to their seats. They won't have to get there early and forage for good seats. (But if all the seats in a 300-seat house are good, why should reserved seating matter? And do you really need reserved seating in a house seating 400 if your audiences average only 250?)

The reserved ticket designates a specific seat, usually by section, row, and seat number. Sections may be alphabetically labeled, with Section A at the viewers' left as they face the stage. Or in a three-section auditorium divided by two aisles, the sections might be labeled Left, Center, and Right. Or they might not be labeled at all. Instead, the ticket would be printed with an aisle designation (A or B). Seat numbers of one or two digits would be in the side sections, and three-digit seats would be in the center section. (See Figure 3-3.)

Sometimes it is helpful in very large auditoriums to print the tickets for each section in a different color, matching the color of the seats.

Methods of numbering seats in a row also vary from theater to theater. (Compare seating charts in Figures 3-3 and 3-13.)

There is no foolproof way to designate sections or to number seats in a large auditorium; invariably there will be misunderstandings: "My wife has seat number 3, and I have seat number 1. Are you sure we're sitting

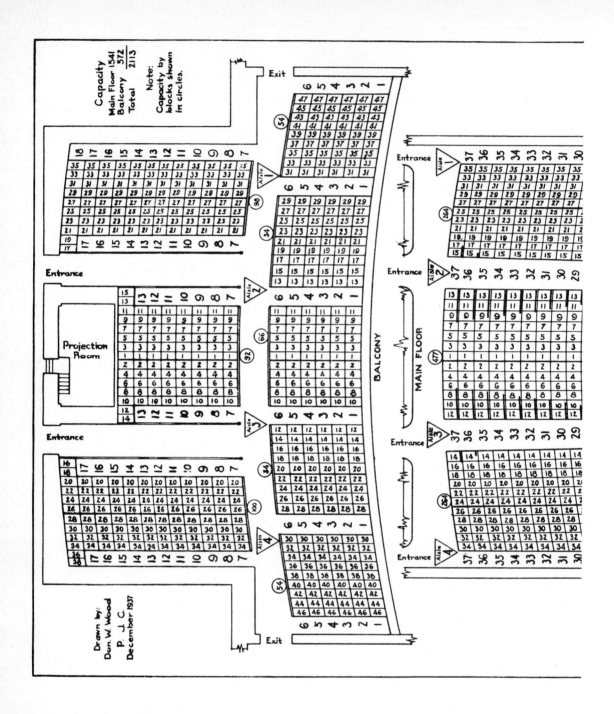

Figure 3-13. Seating Chart for a Large House.

76

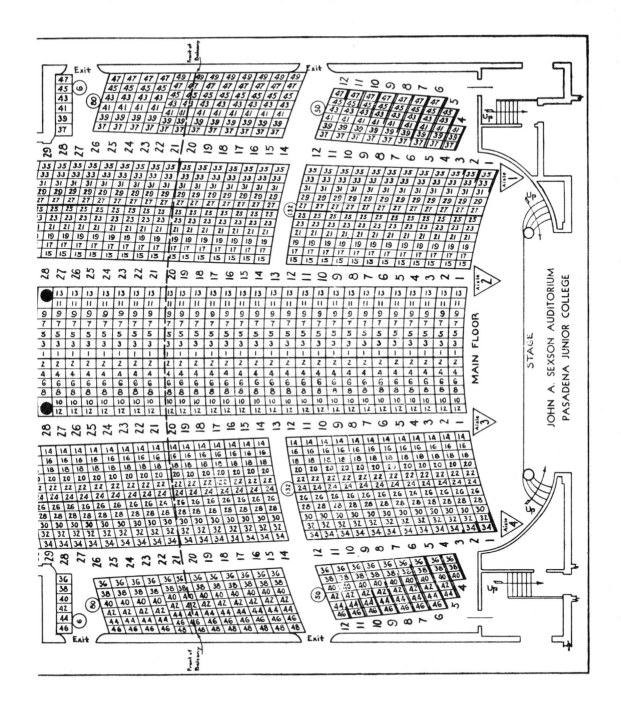

JOHN A. SEXSON AUDITORIUM
PASADENA JUNIOR COLLEGE

together?" "I wanted to be near the stage and you gave me Section B. Isn't that in back of Section A?" Of course, the ushers, box office attendant, and house manager are there to assist in these matters.

Assuming that your seats and sections have already been numbered and designated, your problem is to get the correct markings on each ticket. Whether you prepare your tickets yourself with the help of your staff or order them from a printer, you must be extremely careful to identify the seats correctly.

The card ticket may be used as a reserved seat ticket by adding the words "Section _____ Row _____ Seat _____" and leaving enough room for your most careful writers to fill in the letters and numbers by hand.

Or you may use professionally printed tickets, done by a firm that specializes in theatrical tickets or by a local printer. (Look under "Tickets" in *Simon's Directory of Theatrical Materials, Services and Information,* 5th ed. [New York: Package Publicity Service, 1975].) Once you have submitted your seating chart, the printer can send you sets of tickets for each of your productions—for a price.

Information sent to the printer must include the following:

1. The number of tickets—one for every seat in your house (a "set").

2. The number of sets required for a run.

3. Section designations, row designations, seats in the row (or other designations for the identification of seats). Include your seating chart if at all possible.

4. Stock selection—the quality of stock you want the ticket printed on, assuming that the printer offers a choice.

5. Color of stock, stripings, or other ornamentation. You may want various colors for different sections, various colors for different dates of performance, or combinations of stripes and colors for different dates. Some printers will include the logo of the play, the picture of the star, or the emblem of the producing company. (How fancy can you get?)

6. The name of the theater (and the location).

7. Title of production.

8. Performance dates. If two per day, specify matinee and evening.

9. Curtain time(s).

10. Ticket price.

11. Box office rules, ranging from "No refunds" to "Exchanges of tickets must be made 24 hours before curtain time."

Single-Stubbed   The single-stubbed ticket (Figure 3-14) has a small stub that can be detached from the body of the ticket. If the seat location is printed on the stub, the stub is handed to the theatergoer and the body of the ticket is retained by the door attendant for an audit of box office sales. Sometimes the main body of the ticket has the seat location printed on it, and the stub has only the serial number of the ticket. Then the door attendant retains the stub. There are many variations, but the essential feature of each is that the door attendant keeps an easily detachable part of every ticket to check on box office sales.

Figure 3-14. Single-Stubbed Ticket.

(Courtesy of Theatre Department and Academy, Los Angeles City College.)

When there is only one category of admission—one price for the ticket—the single-stubbed ticket should suffice.

Double-Stubbed   The double-stubbed ticket is advantageous when there are two categories, or prices, of admission, such as student admission and general admission (see Figure 3-15). As each ticket is sold at the box office, the attendant removes the stub that designates what price it was sold at. Since every seat in the house can be sold at either price, this is the easiest way of accounting. The door attendant can then remove another perforated section of the ticket that has the performance date on it. Or the attendant can retain the main portion of the ticket and give the theatergoer a stub with the seat location. Again, the part retained by the door attendant serves as a check on box office sales.

Figure 3–15. Double-Stubbed Tickets.   (Courtesy of Dillingham Ticket Co., Los Angeles, California.)

Computer Tickets   Some firms specializing in tickets have gone to the computer-printed ticket. (See Figure 3–16.) House specifications are put on a tape, so seat numbering specifications or seating chart need not be referred to with subsequent orders. One advantage is speed. Cost per ticket is about the same. (See *Simon's Directory of Theatrical Materials, Services and Information* for more information.)

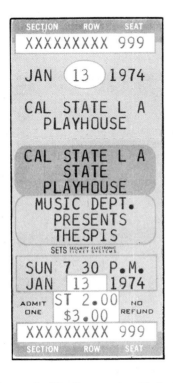

Figure 3–16. Computer Tickets. Different colors can be used for different days.

(Courtesy of SETS Tickets, Sierra Madre, California.)

If your university has a computer services section, it might be desirable to investigate the cost of preparing tickets through that office.

Designing for Special Needs

Do not allow tradition to inhibit the design of your tickets. The ticket in Figure 3–17 was designed to meet a very special need. It was felt

```
LOS ANGELES CITY COLLEGE
THEATRE ARTS DEPARTMENT
855 North Vermont Avenue

CAMINITO THEATRE
8:30 p.m. Curtain

"THE INVESTIGATION"

Admit One $1.00
```

82   Nº   Nº 82

Nº 82   CAMINITO THEATRE GOOD THIS DATE ONLY

TEAR ON DOTTED LINE

Please note

THE INVESTIGATION is a devastating accounting of the destruction of ten million people at the Auschwitz Concentration Camp.

Peter Weiss, whose "Marat/Sade" stunned audiences throughout the world, involves his audience totally in "The Investigation" by raising inescapable questions, vitally pertinent to today's problems, about a citizen's relationship to the society in which he lives. To what extent are we accountable for our own actions? Does conformity with a prevailing social or political code of behavior absolve us of individual responsibility? If our government, perporting to act for the good of our whole society, enforces a code that conflicts with our own convictions, should we resist — and when — and how?

The dialogue of "The Investigation" was not invented. Rather, the actual testimony of the accused and their accusers has been distilled to bring out what is essential to the author's concept. From the testimony of the survivors comes a literal, sickening account of the procedures at Auschwitz: The gas chambers, the mass cremations, the starvations, the brutality, the medical experimentation — all parts of a routine whose goal was impersonal efficiency in exterminating large numbers of human beings.

"The Investigation" is not a pretty play. It may shock, disgust, and revolt you. But if you are willing to be involved in humanity, you must see "The Investigation."

Figure 3-17. Ticket with Warning.   (Courtesy of Theatre Department and Academy, Los Angeles City College.)

that audience members must be strongly warned about the play's content. Therefore, a personal warning was a part of each ticket, and not on the reverse side of the ticket. Theatergoers had to separate the warning from the ticket themselves. The college management therefore felt it had done its best to ward off future complaints about content. It worked well.

Group Rate Tickets

Both universities and community theaters use group rate plans under various names—contract, group benefit, organizational discount, or theater party. The purpose is to guarantee the sale of a large block of the whole house, especially on a slow night. Groups may use this type of plan to raise funds or simply to enhance their recreational programs. The sales aspects are described in Chapter 13, but three box office aspects should be considered here.

1. As the name implies, group sales should be handled as a group, that is, all at once. The box office should not be burdened with a lot of small transactions pertaining to a single group sale. Ideally, the box office should only have to pull the tickets set aside for the sale and receive the funds. This should be made abundantly clear to the group in the contract or letter agreement.

2. The contract must specify exactly when all monies must be turned over to the box office—usually one hour or more before curtain. The problem is that some groups will take out more tickets than they can sell and wait until the very last minute to return them, making it highly improbable that the box office can move the tickets. A no refund, no exchange policy on group sales should be enforced. But if you are going to allow a return, it should be on terms favorable to the box office. Explain that tickets must be returned one week before the performance, the box office will sell the group's returned tickets only after all remaining seats in the house have been sold, and the group will be held financially responsible for unsold group seats.

3. The box office should keep track of the number of groups and the total number of group tickets scheduled for each performance. With discounts ranging from 10 to 40 percent, it would be possible to sell out the house and still lose money. The group sales person must prevent this kind of problem.

You may want to stamp tickets used in group sales with a unique hand stamp for accounting purposes. If you use a single-stubbed ticket you can pull the stubs when the tickets go out and attach them to the contract. With the double-stubbed ticket you can pull one stub and then stamp both the ticket and the remaining stub.

Season Tickets

To the theatergoer, the season ticket offers the possibility of saving from 10 to 33 percent on the price of admission. To the box office, the season ticket means long hours of filling orders, exchanging tickets, and ironing out problems. (The advantages and disadvantages of planning a season are discussed in Chapter 12.)

Coupon Book

One approach to season ticket sales is the coupon book. Usually the number of coupons in the book is equal to the number of productions in the season, or a multiple thereof. Use of the coupons may be at the discretion of the customer, or the theater may state exactly how they are to be used.

Examples:

Each coupon could be good for admission to only one production. ("This coupon good for one admission to *Hamlet,* any performance.") Or each coupon could be good for one admission to any performance of any production during the season. The customer would decide how many coupons he wanted to use to see which performances of what productions. Many variations are possible (e.g., "Coupons may be used only for the Tuesday, Wednesday, and Thursday night performances.")

Rules concerning the use and exchange of the coupons should be spelled out for the customer on the cover of the coupon book. They may include the following:

1. Refund policy: No refund will be made for this coupon book, either in whole or in part.
2. Coupons are transferrable. They may be used by you or your guests.
3. The coupon guarantees you a reserved seat at one of the productions listed on the coupon.

4. Mail exchanges will be accepted only after the mail exchange date on the coupon and must be accompanied by a stamped, self-addressed envelope.

5. Telephone reservations will be accepted only after the telephone order date on the individual coupons and must be picked up 30 minutes prior to the curtain or be cancelled.

The last two rules are intended to help space the work of the box office. Careful system design will prevent your box office from being overwhelmed.

Coupons for succeeding seasons should be of distinct color and design to avoid any possible confusion.

The Patron Book   The patron book, a variation of the coupon book, is used to raise funds for community and professional theaters. Rather than offering a lower price per ticket, it offers the theater patron a higher price per ticket and some fringe benefits, such as an earlier date to make reservations, a listing in the program as a patron, and a tax deduction receipt.

The Strip Ticket   The strip ticket (see Figure 3–18) contains the same information as the coupon ticket but is laid out on a single piece

Figure 3–18. Strip Tickets. An additional area separated by a perforation may be printed alongside the tickets (not shown here but see Figure 3–17). This area may contain information on exchange of tickets or parking, an order blank for the coming season, procedures for changing seats, a map of the area with emphasis on freeways and offramps that lead to the theater, etc. The strip ticket should be designed so that it will fold or fit into standard envelopes. (Courtesy of Dillingham Ticket Co., Los Angeles, California.)

of paper or stock, usually with perforated lines separating the individual tickets. The advantage of the strip ticket over the coupon book is that it is cheaper to print and does not require assembling. On the other hand, the coupons can be processed faster by the box office.

Without coupon books or strip tickets you would have to order and rack (or at least file) all tickets for the entire season, and then pull the customer's order. In a large house with a great number of performances during a season, that would be impossible!

Complimentary Tickets

Guests of the house must be issued a ticket to admit them without paying. This unfortunate custom can be accommodated most easily by issuing a list of those deserving *comps,* to the box office. When the individual picks up the tickets, the box office attendant can stamp them with a hand stamp (being sure to stamp the stub and ticket of a single- or double-stubbed ticket). This will keep your accounting straight.

If there are too many comps to be handled in this manner, complimentary ticket vouchers or exchange tickets (see Figure 3–19) may be issued.

Comps are issued for many reasons. Besides those sent to the press in the hope of reviews, some are issued to VIPs whose presence would benefit the theater (members of the city council, administrators of city and state governments, executives of the university, etc.). Often comps are

```
┌──────────────────────────────────────────────────────┬────────┐
│                  EXCHANGE TICKET                       │        │
│               DRAMA PRODUCTION TRUST                   │        │
│            California State University, Los Angeles    │        │
│   5151 State University Drive • Los Angeles, California 90032   │
├──────────────────────────────────────────────────────┤        │
│                                                        │        │
│                  THE PATRIOTS                          │        │
│                                                        │        │
├──────────────────────────────────────────────────────┤        │
│  Call  224-3344  for  reservations  and  then present this │    │
│  exchange  ticket at  Box Office. Good for one compli- │        │
│  mentary ticket to event indicated above.              │        │
│     STATE PLAYHOUSE   •   ARENA THEATRE                │ (1406) │
└──────────────────────────────────────────────────────┴────────┘
```

Figure 3–19. Exchange Ticket. This can also be used as a complimentary ticket.

(Courtesy of California State University, Los Angeles.)

issued for services rendered to the theater—the loan of a prop, the repair of equipment, etc. And finally, comps are frequently issued to cast members for their guests.

No matter how hard you try to keep down the comp list, it seems to grow. So establish your comp policy and post it for all to see. Then assign one person, the meanest person on the staff (or the one who has to pay the theater's bills), to handle the comps. Give him or her a lengthy rehearsal on how to say no without feeling guilty. You might practice with the line, "I wish I could give you a complimentary ticket, but we have a strict comp policy and we must be fair to all."

Often it is hard to say no, but cast, crew, and staff will respect your consistency if you post the comp policy and then stick to it.

One way to handle the comp situation is to have an invited audience for a dress rehearsal or an invitational preview, issuing all comps for that specific rehearsal. This serves those who demand comps and also provides the theater with a service, as it gives the director and cast the response of a live audience before opening night.

Papering the House

Comps are sometimes called "paper," and filling the house with unpaid guests to surround a critic with a responsive audience or keep up the cast morale is called "papering the house." Sometimes the producer will resort to papering on an opening night. The idea is that a less critical, nonpaying full audience will be more responsive. A handful of paying customers might withhold applause pending receipt of their money's worth. At its most productive, papering can result in good word-of-mouth publicity. The decision to paper must be weighed carefully. If done to excess, it lessens the value of the paid ticket. On the other hand, you might find it difficult to scare up a free audience when necessary, even when you send a bus over to the nurses' residence.

Deadwood is the term used for unsold tickets. Sometimes the term is also used for unpaid tickets, or comps.

Refund Voucher

A refund/exchange voucher may be helpful when an exchange cannot be avoided and other tickets the customer wants are not available.

The voucher may be applied to an unspecified production in the future. For customers who cannot use their tickets for the last performance of a run, or the last play of a season, the voucher might be the last step short of handing back cash.

BOX OFFICE RECORDS

On every day that the box office is open, even when there is no performance, a daily report should be prepared showing the cash flow—how much money was on hand when the box office opened (for purposes of making change) and how much was on hand when the box office closed (see Figure 3–20)—and the number of tickets sold. This report may also include the hours the box office was open and a description of any unusual incidents.

A ticket report (Figure 3–21), used to tally tickets sold for a specific performance, lists all categories of tickets sold, tickets not used (deadwood), and the house manager's count. The report allows the house manager to see a discrepancy between the number of tickets sold and the number being used.

A weekly report on ticket sales may be desired, especially if a production runs longer than one week. This would allow the management to compare income/sales with publicity and other factors to see if any last-minute changes should be made.

The run report (Figure 3–22) gives the tallies for the whole run. It includes the number of performances, the performance capacity, the run capacity, and the total income. This report allows the theater management to evaluate the financial success of the run.

Check carefully with the Internal Revenue Service to interpret regulations applicable to your situation concerning taxable income. The government will tell you what records must be kept.

Generally, you must keep all unsold tickets and all stubs for a period of one year, or until they have been processed by your theater's accountant. With or without ticket stubs, you must keep a log of all sales. All box office records must then be kept for three years and are always subject to government audit.

Laws pertaining to tax exemptions for nonprofit theaters and educational theaters may be found in Section 501(c)(3) of the Internal Revenue Code. Community theater groups and school theaters both file Form 1023,

CALIFORNIA STATE UNIVERSITY, LOS ANGELES---THEATRE TICKET SALES REPORT

EVENT_____ DATE_____

CASH FUND START	CASH FUND END	___COMPLIMENTARY TICKETS___ n/c_____
# DENOM $	# DENOM $	GENERAL ADMISSION @_____ $_____
CHECKS	CHECKS	STUDENT ADMISSIONS @_____ $_____
20.00	20.00	SPECIAL ADMISSIONS @_____ $_____
10.00	10.00	LESS:
5.00	5.00	REFUNDS GEN. ADM. @_____ $_____
2.00	2.00	" STU.ADM. @_____ $_____
1.00	1.00	" SPEC." @_____ $_____
.50	.50	NET SALES
.25	.25	CASH OVER $_____
.10	.10	CASH SHORT $_____
.05	.05	I CERTIFY THAT THE ABOVE REPORTS ARE
.01	.01	TRUE AND CORRECT.

TOTAL CHANGE_____   TOTAL CASH_____

LESS CHGE _____

CASH RECEIPTS_____

BOX OFFICE MANAGER   CASHIER

REMARKS

$_____TAKEN OUT OF BOX OFFICE FOR DEPOSIT_____

DATE   SIGNATURE   THUMBPRINT!

Figure 3-20. Box Office Daily Cash Report. The thumbprint is a joke. Don't take it seriously.

(Courtesy of California State University, Los Angeles.)

```
DRAMA PRODUCTION TRUST

BOX OFFICE REPORT                          Theatre: _____

                                           Play_____
                                                _____

                                           Date: _____
```

	Number	Price	Total
Student Admission tickets sold			
General Admission tickets sold			
Special Admission tickets sold			
Total tickets sold			
Total income			
Season ticket exchanges issued			
Complimentary tickets issued			
Total tickets used			
Box office Cash Total			
Cash Over			
Cash Short			
Tickets not used			
Attendance (House Manager's Count)			

```
_____
Box Office Manager

COMMENTS:
```

Figure 3–21. Ticket Sales Report.   (Courtesy of California State University, Los Angeles.)

```
                              Number of performances:

                              Performance capacity:

                              Total capacity:




Theatre:   _____

Play:      _____

Dates:     _____


Season tickets sold:

Season tickets used:

Student Admission tickets sold:      @ $         — Income:  $

General Admission tickets sold:      @ $         — Income:  $

Special Admission tickets sold:      @ $         — Income:  $

                                     @ $         — Income:  $

                                     @ $         — Income:  $

                                     @ $         — Income:  $

                            Total Income:        $_____


Total tickets sold:

Complimentary tickets issued:

Total tickets used:

Attendance (House Manager's count):



DRAMA PRODUCTION TRUST

PRODUCTION FINANCIAL STATEMENT
```

Figure 3-22. Financial Report for Run of Play.   (Courtesy of California State University, Los Angeles.)

"Application for Recognition of Exemption." Community theaters use code 088, and educational theaters may use 030, 037, or 045, depending on how their theater's income is used.

If satellite box offices are used, each should submit a daily report that can be appended to the daily report of the central box office.

In cases where petty cash for use of department heads is handled through the box office, receipts signed by authorized personnel must be obtained and added to daily reports.

Periodically it is desirable to hold a spot audit in which the house manager or a faculty supervisor reviews a report by checking it against the theater manager's count and the deadwood. This insures that no mistakes by box office personnel are being made repeatedly, unintentionally or otherwise.

Regular audits of the box office should be carried out at the end of the season or every three months if your theater is operated throughout the year.

THE PHYSICAL BOX OFFICE

The box office should be decorated to catch the attention of passersby. In some cases this will mean adding display windows, bulletin boards, or kiosks. Publicity photos, blurbs, and flyers should be posted. Find other displays that will create interest in the current production: scene sketches, costume designs, dolls in costume for a period show, flags, pictures of the first page of the script in the playwright's handwriting, whatever. Similar displays of coming productions in the season, if space allows, are also effective. And if you have still more space, stills from past productions help to establish your history for the prospective customer.

Music can be an excellent lure to your box office. Obviously, with a musical, you could play the score or other music by the same composer. For a straight play, any music of a suitable mood might help to draw the customer's ear and then his eye.

Because the box office usually offers a room with limited access and maximum security, it is often selected as a storage place for non-box office records such as reference copies of past flyers, handbills, posters, and pictures of past productions. It is amazing how fast this material consumes space. If you are in a planning or rebuilding phase, you will want to allow for ample shelving and storage cabinets. In design, ease of function and safety are paramount considerations. Ample light, heat, and ventilation are required.

HOURS

To determine the hours your box office will be open, start with the bare minimum—one hour before curtain and one half hour after curtain for each performance. Add the number of hours necessary, beyond this, to accomplish related paperwork and process mail orders. Then add the hours you feel the box office should be open for walk-up business. All of these hours need not be consecutive. There is usually a lull from 5 to 7 P.M. when the box office can be closed. It may be practical to keep it open in the morning from 11:30 to 12:30 to accommodate lunch-hour ticket buyers. Whatever hours you find most practical, be sure to post them clearly at your box office and on all flyers. Hours may be modified by use of an answering service or answering device (described earlier), in which case the number should be posted outside your box office.

There are several options for setting up remote, or satellite, box offices. On a large college campus, where the theater building is not centrally located, you may want to place a booth on the main walkway to grab the attention of more of your potential customers, and also as a convenience to regular ticket buyers. In a college town you may want to do as many community theaters do—use space in a store on the main street. This means convincing the merchant to donate space. There is obviously a publicity value for the merchant. On all your flyers and in all radio and TV spots, the store's name would appear. ("Tickets may be purchased at Nate's Drugstore.") In addition, the merchant would be cited in the program. Finally, and most important, the merchant might save a few dollars on income taxes by deducting the value of the space donated to the theater.

Often one store, frequently a music store, will serve as a central box office for many events. If you know of such a store, you should explore the possibility of selling your tickets there.

Finally, consider the possibility of setting up a satellite box office in the shopping center nearest your theater.

STAFF

The position of box office attendant requires reliability, honesty, courtesy, a pleasant personality, and the ability to deal with figures as well as with people. Hiring and retaining such a person presents a problem for any theater.

Try to limit the number of box office workers to *one.* As soon as you have more than one, you have the problem of fixing responsibility for any chaos that might ensue.

In most colleges the box office is under the control of one member of the theater faculty. But in some large universities, one box office is set up to handle all ticket events on campus, including sports events. In such cases the control of the box office goes to the university's financial manager.

EQUIPMENT

Ticket racks are a necessity if you have a large theater. A rack allows you to store tickets and organize them for easy access. Build your own rack if you can. You will be able to pattern the rack to correspond with the sections of your theater or your ticket prices. Plan enough rack space to hold the tickets for a few performances.

An important feature of a rack is a cover that can be locked.

You may find it convenient to use metal rack cabinets from theatrical supply houses. (See *Simon's Directory of Theatrical Materials, Services and Information.*) These racks are convenient to use. They may not conform to the layout of your theater, but they are small, lockable, and portable. A typical metal rack comes with four rows of twenty-six compartments. (See Figure 3–23.)

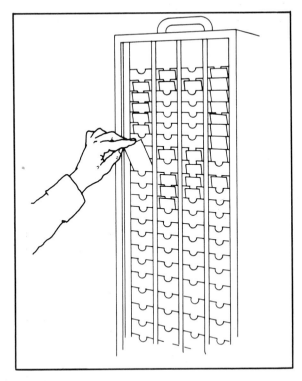

Figure 3-23. Metal Cabinet Ticket Racks. Portable, lockable cabinets are convenient to work with.

Reservation racks (usually only one is needed) are simple to build and may also be purchased (see Figure 3-24). They have enough compart-ments to place reserved tickets for a specific performance in alphabetical order. You also need file space for keeping reserved tickets for future per-formances and other box office records.

The cash drawer should be lockable and contain compartments for bills and change. A floor safe is desirable if you can afford one.

Other equipment will vary with the needs of your operation: telephone, preferably a direct line; adding machine with tape output; typewriter; seating charts; theater stationery; calendar; clock; ticket envelopes; bank deposit slips; pencil sharpener; waste basket; and a moistener so that your box office attendant doesn't have to lick the envelopes and stamps on outgoing mail.

You should have the address and phone number of a fast and conve-

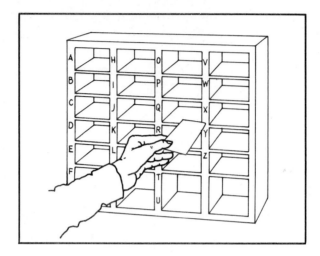

Figure 3-24. Reservations Rack. Reserved tickets are filed in alphabetical order.

nient maker of rubber, stamps. Depending on your operations, you may want the following stamps: Matinee, Group, Complimentary, Season. You also may want a ticket envelope stamp (see Figure 3-5) and a stamp with the name of each play that you produce.

REVIEW AND SIMPLIFY

The above information is not going to solve all of your box office problems. It won't balance your money with your tickets sold, it won't prevent you from giving your customers the wrong end of the ticket, and it won't cut down the number of requests for refunds or complaints about seat locations. But it will increase your *awareness* of your box office operations. There are no perfect rules for the management of all box offices. What works well for the community, college, high school, or professional theater next door, might not work for you at all. So it's important that you adjust to meet your needs.

Don't get into a rut. Review your operations periodically. Set up a committee to review problems with your box office attendant on a regular basis, with either a debriefing following every run or a session every three months.

Simplicity is the last word. The fanciest tickets and the most glorious box office don't make great theater. Strive for simplicity in your operations.

CHAPTER FOUR

Festivals

Festivals and *tournaments* are two terms used to describe drama events in which more than one group presents work to an audience or judges, or both. Sometimes *tournament* is used to describe a competitive event and *festival* a noncompetitive event, but generally this distinction is not observed. *Festival* is used below for both.

Festivals promote the improvement of theater. They give theater people the opportunity to meet to present their dramatic skills and to see what their fellow theater workers are doing (and how well). They offer opportunities for exchange of ideas, competition, and social contact. Participants get a chance to "go on the road," to play in an unfamiliar environment. They have an opportunity to evaluate themselves by the reactions of judges and a new audience. Participants may also measure themselves by comparison to the other groups entered.

The festival may be used as a marketplace, bringing together groups and individuals who can hire the groups for appearances at other locations.

A festival should have all the values of a traditional play. In addition, it should give the festival audience a chance to experience a wide variety of theater within a single day. Audiences become more discerning as a result of attending festivals.

Festivals often result in joyful, stimulating, exciting, and rewarding experiences.

FESTIVAL FORMAT

Here are four basic ways to organize a festival. There are a great many variations on these formats.

Plan A

All of the participants prepare a production with a time limit of about forty-five minutes. Usually each company chooses its own material, but sometimes the festival rules specify the work to be performed. It may be a scene from a play or musical, a one-act play, or an original script written for the festival, depending on the festival rules. One at a time, each group presents its work to a panel of judges and an audience composed of other festival participants and invited guests. A single auditorium and a single panel of judges are used.

This system is the simplest and works well if there are a limited number of entrants. With a dozen entrants, using a schedule that grants forty-five minutes to each group, fifteen minutes between groups to change sets and to allow the audience to stretch, and forty-five minutes to an hour for lunch and dinner, such a festival might start at 9 A.M. and end—by the time the judges had conferred, tabulated their evaluations, and awarded trophies—at midnight. It's a long day for the judges and the festival managers. It is also a long day for any audience members who want to see the entire festival.

In its favor, however, it must be said that this plan is very fair to entrants; they all get to present their work under exactly the same conditions. (But do impatient judges give the last performers the same consideration they give the early ones?)

Plan B

Entrants invite festival judges to see their work at their home theater. From all the entrants, a few are selected to present their works at the finals held in a central location. With just a few plays to be evaluated in the finals, cuttings from each play may be performed during one evening. Or the complete plays may be presented on three successive days, with afternoon and evening performances at a centrally located theater. Or the top three groups may present their complete plays on three successive evenings in competition and the next five groups may present cuttings during the mornings and afternoons, not in competition but as showcase. The judges in the preliminary rounds need not be the same ones who judge the finals. Although initially some entrants may have material advantages (lighting, sets) by performing in their own theaters, judges can compensate for this in their evaluations. In the final rounds, all entrants are on an equal footing.

Award categories may have to be limited or adjusted. For example, if there is usually an award for best lead actress, judges may agree that the finest performer in this category was not invited to the finals. Either they give an individual award on the basis of points during the initial home ground evaluation or they leave out this category and make only group awards. Such a festival might also elect to give no trophies or awards, but rather offer the entrants an evaluation and possibly souvenir pins for participation.

Plan C

The festival is composed of many different five- to ten-minute events—individual pantomime, group pantomime, individual humorous, individual serious, group humorous, group serious, group special event, etc. Each school may enter as many events as it chooses. Teams of judges watch the events in rounds and submit ratings. At the end of the first two rounds, after each group in each category has been seen in competition with other entrants by two sets of judges, the ratings are tabulated and the winners proceed to the semifinals.

In the semifinal round another panel of judges rates each entrant, and those with the highest ratings go on to the finals. In this round, entrants are evaluated by still another panel of judges, and winners are selected. The winners then perform for the entire festival audience composed of guests, entrants, and judges.

As complex as this plan is, it can work smoothly and effectively and allow some seventy schools in a metropolitan area to take part during a single day with a schedule that may run from 8 A.M. to 5 P.M. Winning entrants have to repeat their scenes five times during the day, but since the scenes are short and there is much time between performances, this is not too much of a hardship. Those eliminated during the early rounds have a chance to watch the work of those still in competition.

Plan D

Plan D must be held at a large facility such as a university or multi-theater art complex. Ten to twenty-five participating groups perform one-acts, children's theater, or cuttings in a carnival atmosphere. Each entering group presents its selection two to five times during a period of one to three days. There may be ten to fifteen different "theaters" operating simultaneously, with starting times overlapping. Audience groups may be scheduled to see specific performances, or they may arrive at the festival at any time during the day, examine the schedule, and then go to see the entrant that is performing next or wait and see another group that is scheduled to perform fifteen minutes later. In this type of festival, the entire audience is not expected to see every entering group, but it is hoped that there will be something for everyone. Entering groups do not usually compete for trophies, but judges may submit written evaluations or critique orally.

PLANNING

Regardless of the format you choose, organization and long-range planning are absolutely essential to its success. Festival planning should start with a meeting of the festival staff, at least six months to a year before the festival. It is important to allow enough time to organize the festival and to do all the supporting work.

The number of participants and the size of the audience should be carefully estimated at the initial meeting. The number of invitations, programs, judges, etc., will depend on this estimate, and very little advance work can be done without it. The date(s) of the festival, the host campus or theater, and the overall festival theme, if any, should also be determined at that meeting, because all publicity from then on should emphasize the date(s), place, and theme.

Here are some of the individuals and committees usually needed to make a festival run smoothly:

1. Producer (Executive Director, Chairperson)
2. Rules
3. Registration
4. Judges/Evaluators
5. Tabulations/Evaluations
6. Programs
7. Publicity
8. Guests/Hospitality
9. Facilities (Technical Director, Room Chairperson)
10. Stage Crew (Stage Manager)
11. Associate Producer or Reviewers
12. Food/Refreshments
13. Business Manager/Trophies

Some of the committees may be combined (such as rules and registration, business manager and trophies, and judges and evaluation). But it is desirable to break up duties as much as possible so that individual chairpersons can do a small job very well rather than accepting a lot of responsibility and carrying it out marginally.

It is also usually preferable to have one individual responsible for the work of each committee rather than appointing cochairpersons. Each chairperson may recruit a deputy chairperson and should recruit as many committee members as are needed to carry out the work of the committee.

Following are brief descriptions of the work of individuals and committees, with some discussion of the problems that must be faced. Since the specific work of individuals and committees varies with the type of festival, letters A–D are used following each entry to denote the types of plan to which it applies.

Festival Producer (A, B, C, D)

The top executive officer, regardless of title, coordinates all committees, troubleshooting any problem that they cannot resolve. He or she presides over festival planning and critiques and serves as figurehead for the festival.

The producer's most difficult problem is delegating authority to individuals and committee chairpersons. An effective producer motivates capable individuals to accept responsibility.

The producer does not get bogged down in the actual work of the committees. If a committee chairperson becomes ill during a critical period before the festival, the producer finds a new chairperson; the producer does not take over the sick person's work.

A producer's effectiveness is not measured by how much he or she does, but by how much he or she has done. (Before you accept a job as a festival producer, embroider that last sentence on a sampler.)

The initial planning meeting is very important for the producer. He or she should review the production calendar or schedule with all the chairpersons and ask them to determine deadlines for the completion of their work.

Three important principles should be applied in setting up the production calendar:

1. Plan delays! Play the "What if . . . ?" game. Example: What if it takes the registration chairperson two more days than planned to get in all the names of the entrants? How will this delay affect the work of the program chairperson? After answering such questions, space deadlines so that there is room between interdependent deadlines. You now plan a three-day period between the registration deadline and the deadline for the program chairperson to get the names to the printer.

2. Set up minor checkpoints with each chairperson. Instead of establishing one deadline for each chairperson's completed work, set up deadlines or checkpoints for small parts of that work. Ex-

ample: Instead of establishing a single deadline for the program chairperson, establish deadlines for artwork completed, copy edited, material to the printer, etc.

3. Plan deadlines as far in advance of the festival as is comfortable. Example: At the initial planning meeting, decide on the type of trophies. What deadline should be established for obtaining the trophies? Two weeks before the festival? Three? Four? When possible, schedule deadlines so that they do not coincide with other deadlines. This will allow you to deal with one item at a time.

Applying these three principles allows the producer the comfort of checking on minor problems throughout the organization stage rather than facing total panic the day before the festival.

Committee chairpersons should be encouraged to submit an information copy of all work to the producer as it is completed. The producer should also call and meet with chairpersons periodically to insure that they have not run into snags or delays.

The producer also works with the chairpersons, especially the publicity chairperson, when a figurehead is needed. If a newspaper runs a picture headed, for example, "Mayor Presents Festival Proclamation," the smiling, relaxed individual accepting the proclamation is likely to be the producer.

After the festival, the producer should hold a critiquing session with all committee chairpersons. Each chairperson should discuss the major problems he or she encountered. Emphasis must be placed on what the chairperson had not been adequately prepared to do. The chairpersons should then write brief notes to their hypothetical successors (even if they plan to be around next year). They can attach samples of their work, such as the illustrations in this chapter. With the materials gathered into a festival procedures file or book, the next year's chairperson can start planning with the benefit of past years' experience.

The person who is appointed festival producer should be someone who has had experience as chairperson of one or more committees during prior festivals. It should be clear to all committee chairpersons that their work will be considered when staff appointments are made for future festivals.

The work of a festival producer is unquestionably time-consuming. Principals and department chairmen must recognize this fact. If possible, they should reduce the teaching hours or other responsibilities of producers to allow them adequate time to devote to their festivals. In some cases student teachers, teaching assistants, or students can be recruited to assist producers. Above all, however, producers must delegate authority and not overcommit their own time.

Rules (A, B, C, D)

The rules chairperson is responsible for writing, updating, and distributing the rules of the festival. At some Plan C festivals, the rules committee holds session during the entire festival to make judgments on reported infractions.

Some rules that have worked for various festivals in Southern California are included here as examples: Figure 4-1 gives the rules used by the Adult Drama Association of Los Angeles in a Plan A festival; Figure 4-2, the Southern California Educational Theatre Association, Plan B; Figure 4-3, The Drama Teachers Association of Southern California, Plan C; Figure 4-4, the Southern California Educational Theatre Association, Plan D.

Rules should be reviewed prior to the initial planning meeting for the festival. Any proposed revisions should be brought to the attention of the entire committee—and sometimes to the attention of the entire membership of the sponsoring organization—before they are made.

ADULT DRAMA FESTIVAL

WHERE: Bing Theatre
          Los Angeles County Museum of Art
          5905 Wilshire Boulevard
          Los Angeles, California
WHEN: Saturday, March 19, 1977
          10:00 am to 11:00 pm
          NOTE: If more than fifteen (15) groups apply, we shall extend the Festival to Friday, March 18,
                1977, 7:00 pm to 10:00 pm.
WHO: All community theatre groups are eligible to participate.
WHAT: Community theatre getting together to present their best.
WHY: To promote and promulgate proper community theatre.

RULES AND REGULATIONS

PARTICIPATION

1. Theatre groups must be members of the Adult Drama Association in order to compete in the Festival.
2. Participation is limited to theatre groups in Los Angeles County.
3. Audience: admission is free, but no one will be allowed entry while a production is underway.

PRODUCTION MATERIAL

1. Scripts can be one-act plays, one act from a larger play, or adaptations. Rights and royalties for copyrighted materials are the responsibilities of the individual theatre groups.
2. Maximum time limit for a production is 30 minutes, curtain-to-curtain. A total of 15 minutes is allowed for set-up and strike; the 15 minutes can be divided between set-up and strike at the discretion of the theatre group. The 30 and 15 minute time limit are separate units.
   PENALTIES for time overruns are as follows:
   A production is "downed" one level (e.g., from first place to second place) for a one minute overrun, two levels for two minutes overrun, etc. and disqualified for anything over five minutes.
   Penalties apply to production and direction categories, but not acting categories.
3. In fairness to all participants, it is recommended that participating groups try to stay relatively close to a 30-minute production time. We can thus stay "on schedule" for the total time of the Festival.
4. Material should be selected on its potential for demonstrating acting and directing capabilities of the participants, for these are the sole criteria upon which the productions will be judged.

   Friday evening, March 18, has been reserved so that groups may make a visual inspection of the Bing Theatre. It is hoped that the technical crew will be at their stations to demonstrate the capabilities of the theatre, e.g., how a sound system might be patched in, a curtain pulled, or a light dimmed. No rehearsals will be allowed at this time. Each participating group will be sent a floorplan of the Bing Theatre stage when their entry is received, so that they may rehearse accordingly. However, Friday, March 18, may be used as part of the competing Festival if more than 15 groups participate. If so, another evening will be designated for inspecting the theatre.
5. Simple risers, chairs, tables, couch and cubes will be provided. Should a group wish to rely on specific furniture units that hold a play together, the transport and storage of these materials must be their responsibility.
6. The theatre is beautifully equipped to brightly light the stage (or moodily dim it). Special lighting plots cannot be accommodated.

ENTRY PROCESS

1. Send in the NOTIFICATION OF ENTRY as soon as possible to get the time slot of your choice. The non-refundable entry fee of $10.00 must accompany this Notification. Details such as cast members are not required when you send in this Notification.
2. When your Notification of Entry is received, you will be mailed an entry packet which includes (1) The Bing Theatre floor plan, (2) A form to fill in with program information, i.e., name of play, cast members, director, publisher, and selection of scene, (3) A complete list of flats, risers, furniture that you will need. The form must be returned by February 15, 1977, to get your information in the program.
3. THE DEADLINE FOR RECEIPT OF THE NOTIFICATION OF ENTRY IS FEBRUARY 1, 1977. It is important that your prompt attention be paid to this deadline, because Los Angeles County insists that you adhere to these rules.
4. The Notification of Entry must be accompanied by an application form for membership in the Adult Drama Association if you are not already a member group. The membership fee is $10.00 per year. Enclose the check with application.

MISCELLANEOUS

1. Three to five judges from the field of professional theatre will critique performances; these will be written and presented to participating groups at an A.D.A. meeting.
2. Awards of Best Production, Second Place and Third Place, Honorable Mention, Best Director, Best Actor, Best Actress, Best Supporting Actress, and Best Supporting Actor will be made at the conclusion of the festival.
3. The first fifteen (15) entrants will perform on Saturday, March 19, 1977. Should more than 15 groups enter, latecomers will perform on Friday, March 18, 1977, and awards will be made after the Saturday performance.
4. As many of you know, the best way of getting to know other members of the A.D.A. is by working with them. How about volunteers for house management, backstage coordination, etc.? We need you.

Figure 4-1. Rules for a Plan A Festival—Adult Drama Association.

(Courtesy of Los Angeles County Department of Parks and Recreation.)

RULES FOR HIGH SCHOOL THEATRE FESTIVAL 1975

I. Eligibility:
1. Any secondary school in Southern California is eligible to enter. (See Section VI)
2. Members of the company must be duly enrolled in the entered high school. (Exceptions: A production requiring children's roles incapable of being played by high school actors, i.e., the boys of Medea and Jason in Medea, may be included.)
3. Only one play may be submitted by each high school.
4. Productions must be directed by an accredited faculty member within the entered school.
5. Each production must adhere to the rules and regulations as herein stated or be disqualified. Evaluators may report possible violations which the Committee will investigate and determine whether disqualification is necessary. Entry fees will not be refunded.

II. Type of Play:
Any type of full length play of educational value that is generally intended for adult audiences, i.e. not child audiences, is acceptable. Musicals and original material are not acceptable. Music may be included if it is incidental to the production, leaving a production that is clearly recognizable as a drama rather than a musical comedy or musical play.

III. The Company:
The company must be limited to thirty students including cast and crew. The company screened by the evaluators must be that which is used at C.S.U.N.

IV. Production Requirements:
To avoid difficulties in executions at C.S.U.N., plays must be produced for or adaptable to the proscenium stage. Weight and size of scenery should correspond to the limitations specified by the American College Theatre Festival. Simplicity in setting and technical effects is recommended. (1,000 cubic feet)

V. Evaluations:
The Festival Committee will provide qualified evaluators to screen the production during the play's scheduled run at its campus site.

VI. Costs:
1. Entry fee is $35.00 and membership in SCETA. Each school provides its own production costs.
2. The Festival Committee will provide, through entry fees, ticket sales, the following to the shows selected for reproduction:
   a. Costs for the play's reproduction, i.e. additional royalty, additional rental of costumes and props(not to exceed Festival revenue).
   b. Transportation costs for the companies and their theatrical baggage.

VII. The Festival Committee reserves the right to refine, expand, or adjust the rules of the Festival if circumstances demand such action.

VIII. Directors must participate in Festival Activities.

IX. Deadlines:
1. The deadline for Festival entries is October 20th.
2. Productions must be presented by December 13th. No evaluations will be made after that date.

X. Each Director & School is responsible for 10 tickets to each of the three performances at C.S.U.N.

Figure 4-2. Rules for a High School Festival (Plan B). C.S.U.N. stands for California State University, Northridge. SCETA is the Southern California Educational Theatre Association.

(Used by permission of the Southern California Educational Theatre Association.)

```
                      FALL DRAMA FESTIVAL--1975

            EVENTS                  TIME LIMITS        POSSIBLE ENTRIES
   I    Individual Pantomime     5 min.                        1
  II    Group Pantomime          5 min.                     2 to 8
 III    Individual Humorous      5 min.                        1
  IV    Individual Serious       5 min.                        1
   V    Group Special Event      9 min.                     2 to 8
  VI    Group Humorous           9 min.                     2 to 8
 VII    Group Serious            9 min.                     2 to 8

       SCHEDULE
       8:00-8:30                  Registration
       8:30-8:45                  Assembly
       9:00-10:20                 Round I
       10:25-11:45                Round II
       11:45-12:15                Luncheon
       12:15                      Assembly:  Semi-finalists
                                                 announced
       12:30-1:40                 Semi-Final Round
       1:45                       Assembly:  Finals announced
       2:00-3:15                  Final Round
       3:15-4:15                  Awards Assembly
```

ENTRY FEE

Entry fees are $2.50 per participant up to $50.00 maximum fee per
school. This entry fee includes programs for each participant up
to 20. To order more programs, 25¢ per additional program must
be sent. (A limited number of programs may be sold at the festival for 25¢ each.) DTASC MEMBERSHIP DUES ($6.00) must also
be sent with entries unless paid earlier this school year.

ENTRY DEADLINE

  SENIOR HIGH: Entries and fees must be postmarked or delivered
                not later than MIDNIGHT, WEDNESDAY-OCTOBER 15.
  JUNIOR HIGH: Entries and fees must be postmarked or delivered
                not later than MIDNIGHT, WEDNESDAY-OCTOBER 8.
  LATE ENTRIES WILL NOT BE ACCEPTED. ANY HARASSMENT REGARDING THE
  ENTRY DEADLINE SHALL BE REFERRED TO RULES COMMITTEE WHICH CAN
  DISQUALIFY ENTRIES FOR THE NEXT FESTIVAL.

TIME LIMITS

  TIME LIMITS WILL BE STRICTLY OBSERVED. PARTICIPANTS WILL BE
  STOPPED WHEN TIME HAS EXPIRED, BUT WILL NOT BE DISQUALIFIED.

GENERAL STANDARDS FOR JUDGING OF ACTING EVENTS

  1. Manner of approach to the audience.
  2. Use of appropriate speech and acting techniques.
  3. Characterization.
  4. Theatrical effectiveness and general excellence of performance.

SPECIFIC RULES

1. A memorized introduction is recommended though not required. If
    it is given it must be included in the time limit.

Figure 4-3. Rules for a High School Festival (Plan C).

(Used by permission of the Drama Teachers Association of Southern California.)

2. Where an introduction is used, the student making the introduction is considered a participant. In individual events the participant must make his own introduction if he chooses to have one.

3. Selection is to be memorized.

4. No participant may perform in more than one event. However, a participant may portray more than one character and may enact a character of the opposite sex.

5. Sound effects are permissible but only through the use of a participant's hand, feet, or mouth. No manufactured devices may be employed.

6. No director, parent, or student may attempt to influence the decision of any judge or discuss in the hearing of a judge the merits of any participant.

7. No director or parent may act as a judge in a section in which he has a participant.

8. The opinion of the judges as to the excellence of the performance and the judges' decision as to the ranking of the contestants should not be challenged. Any protest regarding rules violations should be made to the Rules Committee.

9. Only published or professionally produced material is to be performed in any event, except pantomime.

10. No Shakespearean material may be used. Verse drama is acceptable.

11. The terms "serious" and "humorous" refer to the mood of the selection performed, not necessarily to the form of the work from which the cut is taken. (That is--a humorous scene or monologue might be cut from a tragedy, for example.)

12. No properties may be used except available classroom furniture, such as a table and chairs. They may be used in any manner, except in pantomime.

13. Participants shall wear acceptable school clothing, including shoes, but no costumes may be worn. It is permissible to color coordinate and to dress in the mood of the scene. Special footwear (i.e., tennis shoes, ballet slippers, etc.) is acceptable for all events.

14. Clothing may be used (example: hands in pockets) but not removed or put on.

15. Each participating director must serve either as a judge or on a committee. The Rules Committee is given the authority in extreme circumstances to disqualify all entries of an entire school for unsportsmanlike conduct and/or discourteous behavior by the director, students, or parents.

Figure 4-3. (*continued*)

16. Students are not to be notified of placement in any rounds. Semi-finalists and finalists will be announced at the scheduled assemblies.

17. A school with only boys or only girls enrolled in its student body may join with one other school which has only the opposite sex enrolled to enter as a "team" in competition. Rules and fees will apply to such a team as to a single school.

18. Specific events, such as pantomime and the Special Event, have specific rules which are given herein following the standard rules.

19. All entries must be directed and/or supervised by members of DTASC.

20. In a four-year school, 9th grade is considered part of the junior division, while 10th, 11th, and 12th grades are part of the senior division.

RULES FOR PANTOMIME

1. Pantomime is defined as a dramatic (either humorous or serious) performance by actors using only dumb show.

2. No music is to be used in pantomime.

3. The pantomime is to be prepared and to have an introduction consisting of a title which is not more than ten words.

4. The pantomime is not to exceed five minutes.

5. Words may be mouthed in pantomime, as long as there is no vocal utterance.

6. Chairs are allowed in pantomime. No other furniture or property is to be used. No chairs may be moved during the pantomime.

7. Each performer may pantomime any number of characters and may pantomime characters of the opposite sex.

SPECIAL EVENT RULES

1. To honor the Bicentennial, DTASC chose Carl Sandburg's poem, The People, Yes. A composite or straight cutting may be taken from any part or parts of the poem.

2. Participants may number 2 to 8 and the time limit imposed is nine minutes.

3. Humming or chanting of any music may be used as background, but no lyrics may be used from any other source.

Figure 4-3. (*continued*)

DRAMA TEACHERS ASSOCIATION OF SOUTHERN CALIFORNIA

IMPROVISATION

RULES -- STANDARDS -- PROCEDURES -- EXAMPLES

1. Four participants must be entered, no more, no less.
    May be four boys, or four girls, or three and one or
    two and two. The sex does not matter, nor does the
    combination.
2. Spectators will be allowed to watch all rounds of
    improvisations, including semifinal and final. They
    must, however, remain in the room until the round is
    over.
3. In rounds one and two, and in the semifinal round, the
    participants will be in the room and may watch because in
    the first three rounds the situations will be different.
    In other words, the same situations will not be given
    to each group in a room in Rounds one, two, and semifinal.
4. Situations will be in a sealed envelope for each room.
    Participants will select their own envelope.
5. Improvisation introductions will consist of a title of
    not more than ten words.
6. In the final round, the participants will not be
    allowed to watch. They will be placed in another room,
    well out of hearing distance, and will perform one
    group at a time. After performing, the group may watch
    the others perform. The order of the final performance
    will be determined by drawing numbers.
7. Up to two minutes of preparation time will be allowed
    within the five-minute time limit. Less time in
    preparation may be taken and the entire five minutes
    does not have to be used up in Rounds one, two, and
    semifinal.
8. A visual warning will be given to all performers at
    the end of three minutes and at the end of four minutes.
9. At five minutes, if the improvisation is not completed,
    the group will be told to stop.
10. In the final round, the improvisation must be (including
    the preparation time) over three minutes.
11. In the final round the situation, as in the first three
    rounds, will be in a sealed envelope. However, in
    the final round there will be two sealed envelopes
    for each group. The four finalists in each group must
    choose a member who will not be involved in the
    situation until the final two minutes. This member
    will have the second sealed envelope, which may be
    opened once the other three begin. The fourth member
    who has the second envelope will act as the <u>deus ex
    machina</u>, the surprise element. He or she will enter
    the situation during the final two minutes (at the time
    the three-minute mark is reached).

Figure 4-3. (*continued*)

CHILDREN'S THEATRE FESTIVAL
PHILOSOPHY, RULES AND EXPLANATIONS
(ABBREVIATED FORM)

I. Statement of Philosophy

Recognizing a continuing need to raise the standard of
theatre for the child audience, the Southern California
Educational Theatre Association has established the
following goals for their annual Children's Theatre
Festival:

A. To encourage educational, commercial, community
   and recreational theatre for the child audience,
   to enrich the lives of children and to contribute
   to the development of discerning audience members
   of the future.

B. To bring selected professionals in contact with
   one another and their productions in order to
   promote sharing of talents, techniques, and goals.

C. To provide a showcase for productions and focus
   the attention of the media and the public on the
   productions created by professionals from the
   educational, commercial, community and recreational
   theatres.

D. To strive to obtain sufficient profits and subsidies
   in order to underwrite the expenses of all festival
   participants, thus eliminating artist exploitation.

E. To provide a weekend of family entertainment at a
   reasonable cost to the public.

Since the festival strives to create an atmosphere of mutual
support, no awards or ratings will be given to the participants.
A board of reviewers will evaluate each performance in order to
encourage each member of each production company to improve his
theatrical skills. Critics from the commercial media will be
invited to review each production.

II. Eligibility

A. Any Children's Theatre Producer in Southern California
   who is invited by the Festival Committee and whose
   producer or director is a member of SCETA.

B. Members of the acting company must be of college age
   or older. Exception: an occasional child's role,
   i.e., Tiny Tim in "A Christmas Carol."

Figure 4-4. Children's Festival Rules (Plan D).

(Used by permission of the Southern California Educational Theatre Association.)

III. Size of Company

The company must be limited to a maximum of 20 persons.

IV. Type of Play

Any type of full length production, scripted or improvisational, including scripted puppet theatre.

V. Production Facilities

The Executive Producer of the 1976 Festival will supply technical details to invited companies.

VI. The Executive Festival Producer will forward application forms to producers selected by the Festival Advisory Committee. All companies will be reviewed. The Festival Advisory Committee reserves the right to refuse participation to companies whose shows do not meet the expected criteria.

January 18.......Deadline for receiving application forms, plot synopsis, background information on Company, 8 x 10 action shots of group (rehearsal pictures or shots from previous productions) and $35.00 deposit. $25.00 is refunded if Festival commitments and deadlines are met.

March 15........Deadline for sample program (printed by individual producer) 8 x 10 glossy black and white photographs from production, for newspaper publication and media. 35mm color slide for TV. Glossy pictures are not acceptable for television.

VII. Expenses

A. The Festival Committee will provide theatre facilities for the individual and collective companies participating in the 1976 Festival.

B. The host campus will provide minimum technical assistance without cost to the producer.

C. Participating producers will pay their own production costs and author's royalties and provide transportation for their company and their theatrical baggage, including scenery.

D. When Festival revenues permit, companies may be assisted in defraying expenses.

Figure 4-4. (*continued*)

E. Each participating producer will provide a sufficient number of programs for each performance -- delivered to the house staff upon arrival.

F. Companies seeking financial assistance must submit detailed estimates 30 days in advance of the festival dates.

G. The $35.00 entry fee will be considered a deposit guaranteeing appearance at the festival. If the company exhibits its production and meets scheduled deadlines for sample programs, pictures, etc., $25.00 will be refunded. If the $5.00 process fee was included with indication of interest form, the entry fee is $30.00.

VIII. Liability

The Festival liability waiver must be signed by the chief administrative officer of the production organization or his designee. If the policy of the individual company requires release or field trip permission forms for its members, all arrangements relating to those forms are the sole responsibility of the producer.

IX. Board of Reviewers

A. The appointed Director of the Reviewing Board will select a panel of reviewers from the educational and professional theatre community to review each show presented. Although no prizes or awards will be given, a written critique will be presented to each producer by a minimum of three reviewers. Specific procedures and evaluation forms will be provided by the Director of the Board of Reviewers.

B. Each producer is expected to serve as a reviewer for at least one production other than his own.

X. Registration

A. The producer must submit the final registration form along with the thirty-five dollar($35.00) check by January 18, 1976.

B. Make checks payable to: Children's Theatre Festival.

Mail to: Children's Theatre, Executive Producer
Dr. Pam Woody
Department of Speech, Communication and Drama
California State University, Los Angeles
5151 State University Drive
Los Angeles, California 90032

Figure 4-4. (*continued*)

CRITERIA FOR PLAYS FOR CHILDREN
PARTICIPATING IN THE SOUTHERN CALIFORNIA
CHILDREN''S THEATRE FESTIVAL

All children's theatre productions entered in the Southern California Children's Theatre Festival will be previewed by members of the Festival Advisory Committee or an approved evaluator. Shows may not be changed between preview performance and the Festival, except for changes approved by the Festival Advisory Committee. The Festival reserves the right to refuse participation to companies whose shows do not fulfill the criteria stated below.

A. Shows should be designed to appeal to children rather than adults and should be intended for a <u>stated</u> age range.

B. Shows should demonstrate an integrity of style, whether it be audience participation, formal theatre, improvisational theatre, or story theatre.

C. If a show is audience participation oriented there must be built in audience controls and the actors must work with and listen to the children.

D. The direction should demonstrate an understanding of pace, reasonably creative movement, the necessity for variety, appropriate casting, and respect for children.

E. The acting should be consistent and the actors should appear to enjoy performing for and working with children. The illusion of the first time is vital, particularly with shows that tour and do many performances.

F. The literature should not show characters rewarded for evil or include unnecessary violence. The play should treat all characters fairly and not poke fun at any race, religion, nationality, sex, color or way of speaking with the exception of regional accents.

G. The costumes, sets and makeup should be executed with some style and unity and should be appropriate for the production. They must be in good condition.

H. The length of the show should be appropriate to the style of the show.

Audience participation plays for K-3   30 - 50 minutes
Formal play for 2-6 grade   60 - 75 minutes

I. No intermissions are allowed.

Figure 4-4. (*continued*)

NOTE: The Festival Advisory Committee reserves the right
to refine, expand or adjust the rules of the
festival, if circumstances demand such action.

The participating producers agree that all interpre-
tations of regulations and decisions of the Festival
Committee are final, including the selection of participating companies, and that no recourse will be
initiated against the Executive Festival Producer,
the Festival Advisory or Working Committees or SCETA.

I have read these rules and criteria and agree to abide by them
and return one copy with my entrance fee to the Executive Producer,
by the stated deadline:

Signed _____

Date _____

Figure 4-4. (*continued*)

Complete rules should be mailed out with the invitations to participate. You might want to send out two copies with instructions that the second copy be signed and returned with the registration forms. This might promote study of the rules and compliance. It is also helpful to underline or use asterisks to call attention to rules that have been changed since the last festival.

One possible system for handling infractions at a Plan C festival is as follows: Anyone (participant, judge, or observer) may report an infraction to a room chairperson. The room chairperson then fills out an infraction form (Figure 4-5) and sends it to the rules committee. The event is allowed to continue, but after the event, the rules committee summons the parties involved and decides whether a participant has indeed violated a rule and whether the participant is disqualified.

In Plan C tournaments, possible violations can also be examined by dispatching judges to observe in subsequent rounds.

Registration (A, B, C, D)

The registration chairperson is responsible for soliciting entrants. He or she mails to potential entrants flyers announcing the festival along with registration forms (Figure 4-6). When mail response is not adequate, the chairperson follows up with phone calls.

The registration chairperson is also responsible for collecting entry fees, photographs, and other entry requirements.

In some cases the chairperson is responsible for assigning entries a code. In competitive festivals, some entrants feel that judges will be influenced by the name of the school rather than the performance of the actors, particularly in cases where that school has won the past competition or several past competitions. Codes (like X, Y, Z, 25MM, 40ZZ) replace school names in programs and the judges' ballots, thus lessening the possibilities of prejudice.

In Plan C festivals, to handle registration of several different events, registration forms for each event (individual humorous, individual pantomime, group pantomime, etc.) should be color coded.

The registration chairperson schedules the entrants and in some cases mails back to the entrants confirmation of their entry along with their specific performance schedule (see Figure 4-7) and a festival information packet.

```
┌──────────────────────────────────────────┐
│        Report of Suspected Rule           │
│              Infraction                    │
│                                            │
│  School Code Number:_____      │
│                                            │
│  Room Number:_____         │
│                                            │
│  Category:_____           │
│                                            │
│  Reported by:_____         │
│                                            │
│  Date/Time:_____          │
│                                            │
│  Suspected Infraction:_____          │
│                                            │
│  _____          │
│                                            │
│  _____          │
│                                            │
│  - - - - - - - - - - - - - - - -           │
│                                            │
│  (for rules committee use:)                │
│                                            │
│  Judges:_____           │
│                                            │
│  Findings:_____           │
│                                            │
│  Action Taken:_____           │
│                                            │
│  _____          │
└──────────────────────────────────────────┘
```

Figure 4-5. Rule Infraction Report Form.   (Courtesy of DTASC.)

Judges (A, B, C, D)

The judges (evaluators) chairperson is responsible for obtaining the judges, or evaluators, needed for the festival. The number of judges will depend on the type of festival and the number of entrants.

```
  ┌─────────────────────────────────────────────────────────────────────┐
  │                  SCETA HIGH SCHOOL THEATRE FESTIVAL                   │
  │                          REGISTRATION FORM                            │
  │  (PLEASE PRINT OR TYPE)                                               │
  │      1.  _____     │
  │          Name of person to whom all correspondence should be addressed│
  │      2.  _____     │
  │          Street                    City                    Zip        │
  │      3.  _____                               │
  │          Telephone (including area code)                              │
  │      4.  _____     │
  │          Name of entering school                                      │
  │      5.  _____     │
  │          Street                    City                    Zip        │
  │      6.  _____     │
  │          Title of play                                                │
  │                                                                       │
  │          Playwright                Adaptor or translator              │
  │      7.  _____     │
  │                                                                       │
  │          Dates and times of local performances                        │
  │      8.  _____     │
  │          Name and address of theatre if different from participating school│
  │      9.  _____     │
  │          Name of director          School phone (including area code) │
  │     10.  Enclose five copies of maps to your school indicating freeway exits and│
  │          location of your theatre on campus.*                         │
  │     11.  Form letter will be sent at a later date to be signed by the appropriate│
  │          administrative officer giving your school permission to participate and│
  │          releasing the Festival and C.S.U.N.** from liability.        │
  │     12.  Please have black and white 8 x 10 glossy photographs available for newspaper│
  │          publication and photographs for the "all schools" display at Northridge.│
  │     13.  List below the names and addresses of local newspapers, TV, radio stations,│
  │          and drama editors.                                           │
  │     14.  The participating school agrees that all interpretations of regulations and│
  │          decisions of the Festival committee are final, including the selections of│
  │          participating schools, and that no recourse shall be initiated against the│
  │          Festival committee, SCETA, or the sponsors of the Festival.  │
  │                                                                       │
  │          _____                                 │
  │          Signed                                                       │
  │                                                                       │
  │          _____  _____                               │
  │          Title           Date                                         │
  │          Please send registration form, maps, and entry fee of $35.00 to:│
  │                     H.K. Baird                                        │
  │                     144 So. 1st Avenue      (Make check payable to SCETA.│
  │                     Covina, Calif.  91723    If not a member, you must│
  │                                              join SCETA.)              │
  │                                                                       │
  │          *One copy is sent to each judge.                             │
  │          **C.S.U.N.:  California State University, Northridge          │
  └─────────────────────────────────────────────────────────────────────┘
```

Figure 4-6. Festival Registration Form.

(Used by permission of the Southern California Educational Theatre Association.)

```
John Actor
1437 Broad Street
Santa Monica, California  90404


Friday, April 23


TIME                        EVENT                     PLACE

10:00 A.M.                  A & J Storytellers        Outdoor Theatre #5
                            Story Theatre

11:00 A.M.                  A & J Storytellers        Reader's Theatre
                            Story Theatre

12:30 P.M.                  A & J Storytellers        Outdoor Theatre #3
                            Story Theatre


Saturday, April 24

 1:00 P.M.                  A & J Storytellers        Reader's Theatre

 3:30 P.M.                  A & J Storytellers        Reader's Theatre


Sunday, April 25

 3:30 P.M.                  A & J Storytellers        Reader's Theatre


On Saturday, April 24, and Sunday, April 25, I intended that the story-
tellers might stroll around and gather their own small groups to tell
stories to.
```

Figure 4-7. Registration Confirmation and Assignment Used in a Plan D Festival.

(Used by permission of the Southern California Educational Theatre Association.)

The chairperson should be aware of a common tendency of entrants to accept decisions more readily when there are more judges for each round. For instance, entrants would prefer to be rated by five judges rather than three. But if some 50 sections are to be judged simultaneously (Plan C), an increase in the number of judges required can involve recruiting 100 extra judges!

Qualifications for judges should be set up within the festival rules; for example, a judge for a high school festival should be at least four years out of high school.

The judges chairperson should look for theater-knowledgeable people. Schools and theaters can each recommend several judges. High school drama teachers may judge junior high festivals, and college instructors may judge high school festivals.

The chairperson should also try to bring in VIPs as festival judges—the artistic director of a local resident theater, the manager of a television station, actors and actresses from the community, newspaper critics and editors, etc. Sometimes VIP judges may also serve as presenters of awards at the conclusion of the festival. If so, they should be advised in advance, and not on the day of the festival. A postcard invitation with a mail-back reply card attached (see Figure 4–8) is a handy way to recruit new judges and invite former ones.

The chairperson should keep a file of willing and capable judges, listing their names, addresses, and telephone numbers on three-by-five-inch or five-by-eight-inch cards. Such a file can shorten recruiting time for each successive festival.

A code is useful for making concise notes on the file cards. For example, as the returns come in, the chairperson should indicate whether or not each person is coming, along with the date the reply was received. The letter *R* would indicate that the judge sent regrets. After a few regrets from the same individual, the chairperson would know not to invite him or her again.

If any judges accepted the invitation and then did not participate, the chairperson would mark their file cards "NS" for "no show" and might not invite them the next year. Some judges chairpersons find it necessary to invite more judges than are needed to make up for the few no-shows. If there is a surplus of judges, some may be asked to observe the first rounds and then be held for use in later rounds, when other judges may be dismissed.

Those judges who have proven their dependability at prior festivals

*The Drama Teachers Association
of Southern California
would be honored to have you as a*

Judge

*at their 56th Annual Shakespeare Festival
(Hamlet, Much Ado About Nothing, The Winter's Tale)*

*on Saturday, April 24, 1976
8:30 o'clock in the morning*

*Beverly Hills High School
241 Moreno Drive
Beverly Hills, California*

*Please R.s.v.p.
before April 17*

☐ *I will be able to attend*

☒ *I will not be able to attend*

☐ *but wish to remain on list*

Are there any events you prefer not to judge?

_____

_____

Name   (Please Print)

_____

Address

_____

Figure 4–8. Postcard Invitation to Prospective Judges. The card was perforated so that the two sections could be easily separated. It was folded and stapled for mailing. The reverse side of the top part is addressed to the judge; the reverse side of the bottom part is addressed to the judges chairperson.

(Courtesy of DTASC.)

should be given a coded mark on their file cards (e.g., "X") so that the judges chairperson will schedule them for all the rounds. Those so coded should be programmed first, for all rounds. Unproven judges should be assigned only to preliminary rounds (when more judges are needed).

If a judge is assigned to several rounds in a Plan C festival, it is desirable that the rounds be in a variety of categories, to make participation more interesting. Instead of judging four rounds of individual pantomime, for example, the judge should be given one round of group serious, one round of individual comedy, one round of individual pantomime, and one round of group special event.

About ten days prior to the festival, a reminder note should be sent to all judges who have accepted the invitation, asking them to phone in last-minute cancellations (see Figure 4–9). It is a good idea to enclose a rough map showing how to get to the festival, with a note on where to park.

Upon arrival at the festival, each judge should be greeted by the judges chairperson and presented with the festival rules pertaining to judging (see Figure 4–10), an envelope containing ballots and evaluation forms, a nametag, and an identification ribbon. The judges chairperson should then address the judges as a group, thank them for their participation, and review the procedures with them.

Some method should be set up for getting feedback from judges. Either they should be provided with a festival evaluation form (see Figure 4–21) to encourage their suggestions, or they should be debriefed orally by the judges chairperson. Example: At one Plan C festival, judges felt that it was too difficult to render evaluations in the improvisation category. They did not feel comfortable in applying the rules. As a result, the category was dropped in subsequent festivals. Perhaps the rules should have been changed or clarified.

In some cases there will be honoraria for the judges, ranging from travel and hotel expenses to a free lunch pass. The judges chairperson should take responsibility for distributing such honoraria.

Tabulations/Evaluations (A, B, C, D)

The tabulation chairperson is responsible for tallying the ballots of the judges during a competitive festival. The chairperson should design the judges' ballots (Figure 4–11) and prepare tally forms (Figure 4–12) in advance so that ballots may be quickly processed at the end of each round.

THE DRAMA TEACHERS ASSOCIATION OF SOUTHERN CALIFORNIA

Thank you for accepting our invitation to judge at the 56th
annual Shakespeare Festival to be held on Saturday, April 24, 1976.

Enclosed please find a map to Beverly Hills High School, located
at 241 Moreno Dr., Beverly Hills, California.

Please plan to arrive by 8:30A.M. and report to the library.

If for any reason your plans change and you cannot attend,
please call me at Burbank High School, 555-3138, and leave a
message, or in the evening at my home number 555-6904. (Area
code 213)

Again thank you for taking the time to make our festival a
worthwhile experience for our students.

Deane Wolfson

Deane Wolfson
3rd Vice-President
DTASC

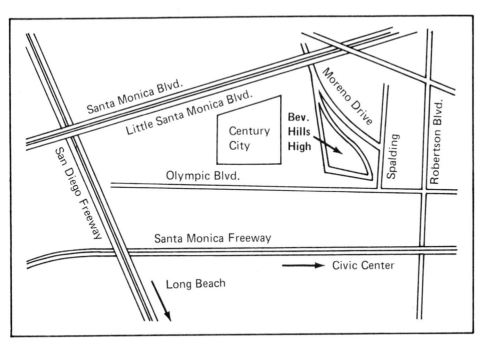

Figure 4-9. Reminder Note. This is sent to judges about ten days prior to the festival. A
map and parking instructions can be helpful.   (Courtesy of DTASC.)

SHAKESPEARE FESTIVAL - INSTRUCTIONS TO JUDGES

1. Room chairpersons will list the code numbers of contestants on the blackboard in the order in which they are to perform. PLEASE COPY THESE CODE NUMBERS, IN ORDER, ON YOUR BALLOT. Note the character name, if you wish.

2. Room chairpersons will time each performance and will stop the performers at the expiration of the allotted time. Contestants must stop when time has expired whether they have finished or not. Please evaluate each performance on the basis of its quality, even if performance has been stopped. DO NOT DISQUALIFY ANY CONTESTANTS. (It is assumed that an unfinished performance may have an effect upon its quality and upon your rating.)

3. PLEASE DO NOT CONFER with other judges or others in the room before marking and sealing your ballot. We want your private judgment.

4. Please do not announce your ratings to ANYONE. Winners will be announced in the assembly at the close of each round.

5. Please report to the chairperson of judges any attempt by students, teachers, or parents to influence or dispute your judgment.

6. At the close of each round, give your SEALED AND SIGNED ballot to the room chairperson, who will deliver it to the Tabulations Room.

7. Please stay available in the judges room in case of questions and we need to find you.

FESTIVAL RULES

*All selections are to be memorized.
*Students may portray more than one character and may play characters of the opposite sex.
*No props are to be used.
*Classroom furniture, such as tables and chairs, may be used with no limitations.
*Clothing worn may be used (i.e., hands in pockets) but may not be removed or put on during the scene.
*A memorized introduction is recommended but not required.
*Introductions may be either dramatized or narrated.
*Directors, parents, and students may not discuss performances with judges or attempt to influence decisions.
*Protests or questions must be handled by the Rules Committee. This committee can be contacted by room chairperson.

RULES FOR SPECIAL SCENE - WINTER'S TALE

*This scene must be done exactly as cut. No deletions or changes of any kind will be allowed.
*No introduction at all may be given, not even the title of the play.
*This scene will not be timed.
*All other general festival rules apply to the special scene.

VIOLATIONS OF RULES

Please report any suspected violation of rules to the Rules Committee as soon as possible. DO NOT DISQUALIFY CONTESTANTS! Only the Rules Committee may disqualify an entry.

PLEASE SIGN YOUR COMPLETED BALLOT!

Figure 4-10. Rules for Judges. These should be an abbreviated form of the complete festival rules. They should be reviewed orally before the festival. (Courtesy of DTASC.)

126

```
                        BALLOT

Drama Teachers Association of Southern California

Event: VI    Section: ‾‾‾    Room Number: 212

Round (Circle one:)   I    II    Semi-final    Final
```

Order	Code Number	Notes	Placement
1	HH	C	6
2	C	A	2
3	VV	A+	1
4	BB	B−	5
5	T	B+	3
6	A	B	4
7	P	EXCESSIVE SHOUTING	
8	LL	DROPPED LINES	
9			
10			
11			
12			

Winners' code numbers: only six places are to be listed,
other performances need not be rated.

First place: VV

Second place: C

Third place: T   Please do not list ties
                              for any places! Ties must
Fourth place: A   and will be broken by
                              tabulation!
Fifth place: BB

Sixth place: HH

Judged by: CAROL KATO   *Carol Kato*
           (Please print your name.)

Please give this ballot, in a sealed envelope, to the
room chairman who will deliver it to tabulations. Thank
you!

Figure 4-11. Judges Ballot for a Class C Festival.   (Courtesy of DTASC.)

127
```
```

TALLY

Event: __VI__   Section: __—__   Room Number: __212__   Round: __F__

| Code | Judges | | | | | | | Total | Place | Sweep |
	1	2	3	4	5	6	7			
HH	6	7	7	3	7	6	6	42		
C	2	3	7	5	6	7	3	33		
UU	1	1	5	6	4	4	1	22	2	4
BB	5	4	6	4	7	7	7	40		
T	3	2	4	1	1	2	4	17	1	6
A	4	7	1	2	2	5	5	26	3	2
P	7	6	2	7	5	3	7	37		
LL	7	5	3	7	3	1	2	28		

Figure 4-12. Tally Form for a Plan C Festival. The placements awarded to an entry by each judge are totaled, and the entry with the least number of points is awarded first place in the place column. If a sweepstakes trophy is to be awarded, winning entries are given sweepstakes points. First place in a group event (one in which two or more actors participate) wins six sweepstakes points; second place, four points; and third place, two points. In an individual event (one in which a single actor participates) first place gets three points toward sweepstakes, second place gets two points, and third place gets one point. In Event VI, Group T took first place, Group UU took second place, and Group A took third place. Since this was a group event, Group T earned six points toward the overall festival sweepstakes.   (Courtesy of DTASC.)

Last-minute, roughly drawn tally sheets can lead to confusion in adding the judges' votes.

The chairperson recruits a tabulation committee to work during the festival.

The tabulation chairperson may also distribute a summary of votes (Figure 4–13) to interested teachers immediately following the festival so that they may see how their students fared in various rounds. Sometimes it

---

FINALS

Event II

UU	20 7757776	C 20 777 2775	
BB	20 7475674		
R	25 5777777		
X	20 1113227	②	
CC	20 3521111	①	
P	20 4267352	③	
K	20 7336747		
LL	20 6644537	④	
P	25 7777777		
C	25 2777463		

Event IV

LL	40 4777376
E	40 3121433 ①
X	45 2734224 ③
W	40 1242542 ②
LL	45 7567717
Z	40 7677777
CC	45 7415171 ④
OO	40 7776777
C	40 5353655
WW	40 6777767

Event VI

HH	6773766
C	2375673
UU	1156441 ②
BB	5464777
T	3241124 ①
A	4712255 ③
P	7627537
LL	7537312 ④

Event III

C	30 4277727	P 302672475	②
L	30 3376754	P 357777177	
YY	30 7771277	JJ 301417577	①
RR	35 7124776 ④	DD 307735667	
ZZ	30 6553771 ③		
C	35 7777313		
GG	35 7747732		
LL	305767747		

Event V

LL	1421111 ①
CC	6566544
Y	5674256
P	2374465 ③
RR	7757172
M	4242677 ④
B	7757777
WW	3113332 ②

Event VII

XX	2115345 ②
LL	4242231 ①
L	7437456
CC	7564667
E	3376777
Y	5623122 ②
G	1751513 ④
A	6777774

Figure 4–13. Duplicated Summary of Votes. This may be distributed to teachers after the final rounds of a Plan C festival to allow the teachers to point out to their students just how subjective the judging was. Note, for instance, that in Event VII Entry LL was judged best by only one judge, but came in first; Entry XX was judged best by two judges, but came in second; and Entry G was judged best by three judges, but came in fourth! Because there was a tie for second place, no third place was awarded.   (Courtesy of DTASC.)

is desirable that teachers show these results to their students so that they may see just how subjective the judging was. (Example: An entry that does not even take third place in the final rounds of a Plan C festival may have had several first place votes from judges in earlier rounds.)

It is desirable that the tabulations room be near the stage or room where the winners of rounds are to be announced. This can eliminate some footwork.

In noncompetitive festivals (Plan D) an evaluations chairperson may be appointed to design evaluation forms (Figure 4–14), supervise the collection of the forms from judges or evaluators, and distribute the forms to the participants. At children's festivals, children may be asked to serve as evaluators, in which case evaluation forms should be especially prepared for them (see Figure 4–15). If oral critiques are held, the evaluations chairperson is responsible for scheduling and moderating the sessions.

Programs (A, B, C, D)

It usually takes at least two months to write, rewrite, proof, and publish a festival program. The following items should be included:

1. Statement of the festival's philosophy

2. History of the festival or the host institution

3. Statement of the festival's theme

4. Schedule (see Figure 4–16, Plan C, and 4–17, Plan D)

5. Map of grounds and room maps of the larger buildings

6. List of officers of the producing association and festival committee chairpersons

7. List of participating schools, theaters, etc.

8. Program of events with room assignments for Plan C (see Figure 4–18)

9. Background information on plays and playwrights whose works are to be presented

10. Background information on groups participating, with synopses of the works they will present (see Figure 4–19, Plan D)

11. Page with blanks on which to record names of festival winners (see Figure 4–20) (*List continues on page 141.*)

```
┌─────────────────────────────────────────────────────────────────────┐
│                                                                     │
│         FOURTH ANNUAL CHILDREN'S THEATRE FESTIVAL                    │
│         California State University, Los Angeles                    │
│                                                                     │
│            Reviewer's Evaluation and Critique                       │
│                                                                     │
│  Reviewer_____ Production_____    │
│                                                                     │
│  Date and Time Reviewer saw production_____   │
│                                                                     │
│  Style of Production_____   │
│  (formal, audience participation, musical, improvisational, educational, other) │
│                                                                     │
│  Please rate and/or comment on the following aspects of the production.  Suggested │
│  ratings are:  excellent, very good, good, adequate, needs improvement. │
│                                                                     │
│  1.  ENTIRE PRODUCTION                                              │
│                                                                     │
│       a.  Overall rating of relative success                        │
│           of production                         _____     │
│       b.  Audience response                     _____     │
│       C.  Consistency of style                  _____     │
│  Comments:                                                          │
│  _____  │
│  _____  │
│  _____  │
│  _____  │
│  _____  │
│  _____  │
│  _____  │
│                                                                     │
│  2.  DIRECTING                                                      │
│                                                                     │
│       a.  Appropriateness of production concept  _____    │
│       b.  Development and execution of production                   │
│           concept                                _____    │
│       c.  Development of ensemble                _____    │
│       d.  Casting and role development           _____    │
│       e.  Blocking and design of space           _____    │
│       f.  Respect for and ability to control and                    │
│           entertain an audience of children      _____    │
│  Comments:                                                          │
│  _____  │
│  _____  │
│  _____  │
│  _____  │
│  _____  │
│  _____  │
│  _____  │
│                                                                     │
└─────────────────────────────────────────────────────────────────────┘
```

Figure 4-14. Evaluation Form for a Plan D Festival.

(Used by permission of the Southern California Educational Theatre Association.)

3. ACTING

    a. Development of characters   _____
    b. Clarity of speech   _____
    c. Control of movement   _____
    d. Ability to relate to other actors and
       the audience   _____
    e. Illusion of the first time   _____
    f. Flexibility   _____

Comments:

_____

_____

_____

_____

_____

_____

4. DESIGN ELEMENTS

    a. Overall reaction   _____

Sets_____   Costumes_____

Lights_____   Makeup_____

Sound_____   Props_____

Comments:

_____

_____

_____

_____

_____

_____

5. SCRIPT

    a. What age child is the script appropriate for?   _____
    b. Consistency of style of script   _____
    c. Integrity and validity for an audience of
       children   _____

Comments (particularly appropriate if script is original):

_____

_____

_____

_____

_____

_____

Figure 4-14. (*continued*)

SOUTHERN CALIFORNIA

CHILDREN'S THEATRE FESTIVAL, 1976

California State University, Los Angeles

JUNIOR REVIEWER'S PLAY EVALUATION FORM

Reviewer_____ Production_____

Date and time reviewer saw production_____

1. The first questions are about how you liked the play. (Circle your response.)

   Did you like the play?   Yes No Parts of it

   Was the play interesting?   Yes No Parts of it

   Was the play fun to see?   Yes No Parts of it

   Could you follow the story?   Yes No Pretty well

   Would you like to see this play again?   Yes No

2. Circle the comments below that describe the way you felt about the play.

   Great!!   Pretty good   Too noisy   Too fast

   Exciting   Dull   Too violent   Too long

   OK   Scary   Too slow   Too boring

   Hard to understand   Easy to understand   Part good,part bad   Too scary

3. Give short answers to the following questions about the play.

   What did you like best about the play?

   What did you like least about the play?

   What did you learn from this play?

Figure 4-15. Evaluation Form for Use by Children at a Children's Festival.

(Used by permission of the Southern California Educational Theatre Association.)

4. What age kids do you think this play is best for?

    (Circle one age group)   3 - 6   6 - 9   10 - 14

    Would this play be fun for grownups, too?   Yes   No   I don't know

5. Please answer the following questions about the actors and the acting.
    (Circle your response)

    Did the actors have fun?   Yes   No   I don't know

    Were the actors nervous?   Yes   No   I don't know

    Did the actors have lots of energy?   Yes   No   Some of them

    Were the characters believable?   Yes   No   Some of them

    Could you hear the actors well enough?   Yes   No   Some of them

    Could you understand what they were saying?   Yes   No   Sometimes

    Which character did you like best?_____

    Why?

    Which character did you like least?_____

    Why?

Figure 4-15. (*continued*)

6. If this was the kind of play where the actors ask the audience to answer
   questions or do things on the stage, please answer the following questions.
   If it wasn't, skip #6 and go on to #7.

   Did the actors talk <u>to</u> the audience?   Yes   No   Sometimes

   Did the actors listen to the answers the   Yes   No   Sometimes
      audience gave?

   Do you think it was a good idea for the   Yes   No   I don't know
      actors to ask the audience's help with
      this particular play?

7. Please answer the following questions about the scenery and costumes.
   (Circle your response.)

   Was the scenery practical for the play?   Yes   No   I don't know

   Did you enjoy looking at the scenery?   Yes   No

   Was the scenery easy for the actors to   Yes   No   I don't know
      work with?

   Did the scenery take away from the play?   Yes   No   I don't know

   Did you enjoy looking at the costumes?   Yes   No

   Were the costumes easy for the actors to   Yes   No   I don't know
      work in?

   Do you think the scenery and the costumes   Yes   No   I don't know
      went well together?

8. Is there anything else you would like to say about this play?

Figure 4-15. (*continued*)

```
          FAIRFAX HIGH SCHOOL
          7850 Melrose Avenue
          Los Angeles

          NOVEMBER 15, 1975
```

 **SCHEDULE FOR THE DAY**

```
8:00 a.m. .... Hospitality in Library for directors and judges

               Judges meeting in Library

               Rules committee meets in Library

               Room Chairmen meeting in Student Cafeteria

               General registration and distribution of programs
               in foyer of auditorium. (Each school must be
               registered by its director who will receive programs.)

8:30 a.m. .... Assembly in auditorium

               General announcements by festival chairperson,
               Mr. Alan R. Josefsberg

9:00 a.m. .... Round 1.  (Participants proceed to assigned rooms
               as indicated in festival program.)

10:25 a.m. ... Round 2.  (Participants proceed to assigned rooms
               as indicated in festival program.)

11:45 -- 12:15 ... Luncheon

12:15 p.m. ... All participants will meet in the auditorium for
               the announcements of the semi-finalists

12:30 p.m. ... Semi-final round.  (Semi-finalists as announced
               in the auditorium will report to assigned rooms.)

1:00 p.m. .... Improvisational Workshop in amphitheater during
               semi-final and final rounds

1:45 p.m. .... All participants will meet in auditorium for
               the announcements of the finalists

2:00 p.m. .... Final round.  (Finalists as announced in the
               auditorium will report to assigned rooms.)

3:15 p.m. .... Awards assembly

               Presentation of guests

               Presentation of awards
```

Figure 4-16. A Festival Schedule. Four rounds are scheduled during one day.

(Courtesy of DTASC.)

Figure 4-17. A Festival Schedule. This shows one day of a three-day schedule.

(Courtesy of DTASC.)

EVENT 2 -- GROUP PANTOMIME

Semi-finals in Rooms 110, 112, 114

Finals in Room 112

Section 6		Round 1	Round 2
AAA	20	. . 110	. . 110
MMM	20	. . 110	. . 111
SS	20	. . 110	. . 112
S	20	. . 110	. . 112
B	20	. . 110	. . 114
R	20	. . 110	. . 115
CC	20	. . 110	. . 110
TT	20	. . 110	. . 111
Z	20	. . 110	. . 113

Section 7		Round 1	Round 2
N	20	. . 111	. . 113
LLL	20	. . 111	. . 114
FFFF	20	. . 111	. . 115
BB	20	. . 111	. . 114
JJ	20	. . 111	. . 113
K	20	. . 111	. . 112
SSS	20	. . 111	. . 115
A	20	. . 111	. . 111
Y	20	. . 111	. . 110

Section 8		Round 1	Round 2
H	20	. . 112	. . 111
C	20	. . 112	. . 112
YYY	20	. . 112	. . 114
RRR	20	. . 112	. . 113
TTT	20	. . 112	. . 110
NN	20	. . 112	. . 112
XX	20	. . 112	. . 111
JJJ	20	. . 112	. . 112
F	20	. . 112	. . 110

Section 9		Round 1	Round 2
EEEE	20	. . 113	. . 113
EEE	20	. . 113	. . 115
ZZZ	20	. . 113	. . 110
PPP	20	. . 113	. . 113
LL	20	. . 113	. . 115
NNN	20	. . 113	. . 114
UU	20	. . 113	. . 115
E	20	. . 113	. . 111
UUU	20	. . 113	. . 110

Section 10		Round 1	Round 2
AAAA	20	. . 114	. . 110
L	20	. . 114	. . 115
HH	20	. . 114	. . 112
J	20	. . 114	. . 115
AA	20	. . 114	. . 114
BBB	20	. . 114	. . 111
OO	20	. . 114	. . 111
X	20	. . 114	. . 110
OOO	20	. . 114	. . 113

Section 11		Round 1	Round 2
ZZ	20	. . 115	. . 112
GG	20	. . 115	. . 114
CCC	20	. . 115	. . 114
CCCC	20	. . 115	. . 113
DD	20	. . 115	. . 114
P	20	. . 115	. . 113
U	20	. . 115	. . 112
DDDD	20	. . 115	. . 111
FFF	20	. . 115	. . 115

Figure 4–18. Room Assignments for First Two Rounds of Plan C Festival. These rounds are scheduled in advance, letting entrants know in which rooms they will perform. Room assignments for later rounds are announced as judges eliminate entrants from competition.

(Courtesy of DTASC.)

THE TWELFTH NIGHT REPERTORY CO.

12732 Moorpark Street Studio City, Calif. 91604 (213) 760-2112

GREEK MYTHOLOGY

On October 18, 1974 we first presented GREEK MYTHOLOGY to Vintage Street School, in Sepulveda. The performance was for the Los Angeles City Schools Principal's Cultural committee. This committee rated GREEK MYTHOLOGY as "Excellent," and we began a massive tour of the Los Angeles City Schools.

This tour resulted in establishing Twelfth Night as a major source of educational theatre in Los Angeles. We played GREEK MYTHOLOGY to over 75,000 youngsters during the 1974-1975 school year. It remains one of our most requested presentations. In December of 1974, members of the Office of Multicultural Education for the L.A. City Schools came and saw GREEK MYTHOLOGY. They were very enthusiastic about the potential of using this same theatrical format as a means of multicultural education, and they proceeded to help us secure a $30,000.00 grant from HEW for that purpose.

In short, GREEK MYTHOLOGY was the start of something very good for Twelfth Night.

THE CAST

STEVE MUNSIE (pantomimist) is a founding member of Twelfth Night, and was the first to perform in GREEK MYTHOLOGY. Although his role has been successfully repeated by Don Lewis and Michael Ross Oddo, much of GREEK MYTHOLOGY has always been Steve's inspiration. Steve has taught at ISOMATA (Idyllwyld School of Music and the Arts), an extension of USC.

SCOTT CATAMAS (narrator) first founded Twelfth Night in June of 1973. Scott has played many leads, directed, and produced numerous productions. He was the original narrator for GREEK MYTHOLOGY in 1974. Scott is the President of Twelfth Night.

AARON HASSMAN (musician) MA in educational psychology, BA in Theatre Arts, BA in Music. Aaron first joined Twelfth Night in January 1975. He is currently performing every day for us with his MUSICIAN'S SEMINAR program. Aaron also teaches Creative Dramatics and Creative Guitar to Los Angeles City School teachers (through the In-Service Workshop program).

GREEK MYTHOLOGY was written and produced by Scott Catamas.

The Twelfth Night Repertory Company is an independent, Non-Profit Organization.

Figure 4-19. Description of a Group Participating in a Plan D Festival. This information may be printed in the program or on a flyer distributed to the audience.

(Courtesy of the Twelfth Night Repertory Co.)

AWARD WINNERS

Event 1 – Individual Pantomime

_____
Third

_____
Second

_____
First

Event 2 – Group Pantomime

_____
Third

_____
Second

_____
First

Event 3 – Individual Humorous

_____
Third

_____
Second

_____
First

Event 4 – Individual Serious

_____
Third

_____
Second

_____
First

Event 5 -- Group Special Event

_____
Third

_____
Second

_____
First

Event 6 -- Group Humorous

_____
Third

_____
Second

_____
First

Event 7 -- Group Serious

_____
Third

_____
Second

_____
First

Event 8 - Group Improvisation

_____
Third

_____
Second

_____
First

Sweepstakes Trophy

_____
Third

_____
Second

_____
First

Figure 4–20. A Page for Listing Award Winners in the Program. (Courtesy of DTASC.)

12. Decoration (an artistic cover design can make the program a valuable souvenir; designing a children's theater festival program as a coloring book is a clever idea)

13. A tear-out feedback form, addressed to the festival producer, that will encourage constructive criticism (see Figure 4-21)

14. Acknowledgments

Most of the items listed are self-explanatory, but a few need further comment.

The artwork for the program cover might take more time than the other items. The program chairperson should recruit an artist well in advance of other production work on the program.

The program chairperson should tell other chairpersons (registration, room chairperson) the deadline for submitting information for the program. Late entries are a major problem for the program chairperson; therefore, a definite deadline should be determined at the first planning meeting.

Illegible names and partial names on registration forms also create problems for the program chairperson. He or she should remind the registration chairperson to insure that the forms ask entrants to print clearly and to submit complete names.

After cost, proximity is the most important factor in selection of the printer, because the program chairperson will have to visit the printer often. An ideal arrangement is for the program chairperson to work with the school printshop.

To determine the number of programs to be printed, the chairperson should add the estimated number of entrants, judges, festival workers, expected audience, and guests, and then add a large number of extras. It is better to order too many than not to have enough.

Publicity (A, D)

The publicity for a festival requires all the effort that would be expended on a single production (see Chapter 5) and then some. The publicity chairperson should devise a schedule of publicity releases starting five weeks before the festival and building to a peak the weekend before the festival. (Some large annual festivals start their publicity work nine to twelve months ahead of the festival date.) The chairperson should attempt

```
                      FESTIVAL EVALUATION FORM

      What did you like best about the festival?
      _____
      _____
      _____
      _____
      _____
      _____
      _____
      _____


      What could we do to make it better or different?
      _____
      _____
      _____
      _____
      _____
      _____
      _____
      _____


      Were you well provided for in terms of facilities and courtesy?
      _____
      _____
      _____
      _____
      _____
      _____
      _____
      _____
      _____


      ____ I am willing to work on a committee for next year's festival.
      ____ I would like to serve as a reviewer for next year's festival.
      ____ I would like to be invited to bring a production next year.
      What day or days did you attend the festival?_____
      In what position did you attend the festival? (Circle one) Producer, Director,
      Reviewer, Performer, Audience member, Other_____

      Name_____  Position_____
      Address_____  City_____ Zip_____
      Home Phone_____  Office Phone_____
```

Figure 4-21. Festival Evaluation Form.

(Used by permission of the Southern California Educational Theatre Association.)

142

to obtain coverage from all media in the area of the festival and all media in the areas of prospective audiences. Releases to junior high, high school, college, and teacher organization newspapers will be especially useful (see Figure 4-22).

The publicity chairperson might issue releases on the following subjects (separately or in combinations):

1. Dates, places, chairperson, and intended audience for the festival
2. History of the festival
3. Judges named for festival
4. Participants listed for festival
5. VIPs planning to attend festival
6. Trophies, scholarships, and future competitions announced for festival winners
7. Winners selected and trophies presented

Sometimes it is better to divide the work of the publicity committee between two or more people. For example, the publicity chairperson can handle all public relations (face-to-face and telephone contacts) while the deputy or assistant chairperson handles all written releases to the media.

All public relations contacts should be logged and copies of all media releases should be filed so that successive publicity chairpersons can build on the work of their predecessors.

Guests/Hospitality (C, D)

The guests, or hospitality, chairperson is responsible for guides. Ways to obtain guide services include the following:

1. The host campus is asked to provide guides from one of its service organizations (Honor Society, ROTC, etc.).
2. Each entering school is required to bring one student to serve as a guide.
3. Students in the drama department earn classroom points by serving as guides (usually on college campuses).

Children's theatre festival '76

The spring of 1973 marked the beginning of a rather special theatrical enterprise: Immaculate Heart College of Los Angeles hosted the initial outing of the Children's Theatre Festival.

Appreciative of the concept which launches the American College Theatre Festival, members of the Southern California Educational Theatre Association hoped to bring together a diverse group of performers specializing in entertainment for children. It was of equal importance to provide good examples of Children's Theatre fare being produced throughout Southern California, and to present such programs at a reasonable cost to Southland families. An opportunity for children's theatre artists to meet and see one another's work (and a chance to broaden the audience for such artists) was also of special interest to festival planners.

The gathering at Immaculate Heart joined a dozen producing companies and an enthusiastic audience nearing a thousand people. The 1974 Festival held at Cal Poly, Pomona doubled the 1973 attendance and last year's festival, produced at California State University, Northridge, drew an audience of over 8,000. Since the beginning of the festival, many innovations such as strolling players on the grounds, a playwrighting contest, and premiere performances of a number of original plays have been introduced to the weekends activities.

Children's Theatre Festival '76 will be presented on Friday, April 23rd; Saturday, April 24th; and Sunday, April 25th at California State University, L.A. Over forty companies of performers will provide entertainment on Friday from 9:00 a.m. to 2:00 p.m. and on Saturday and Sunday from 10:30 a.m. to 5:00 p.m. Admissions will be $2.00 for adults, $1.00 for children. Families are again encouraged to picnic in a lovely campus setting — refreshments will be available at convenient locations — while enjoying the most diversified theatrical afternoon available at the price.

New representation in this years festival of educational, professional and community theatre groups will include a presentation of **Colonel Montana** by the Improvisational Theatre Project from the Mark Taper Forum; San Francisco's Magic Carpet presenting the critically acclaimed production of *Kid's Writes: Multicultural Mythology* produced by The Twelfth Night Repertory Co.; the L.A. Mime Company; a zany production of *Castle Hassel At Rainbows End* presented by the Trobadoor Puppets; and an exciting production of *Winnie-the-Pooh* produced by the University of Nevada.

Musical theatre, always a part of the festival, is represented this year by productions such as *H2O Where Are You?* produced by the Space Place Players in conjunction with the California Museum of Science and Industry and *Sacramento Fifty Miles* from Bakersfield College.

Among returning favorites are Betsy Brown in *Carnival of the Animals*, A salute to Orange County from the talented South Coast Repertory, John and Pam Wood as *J. P. Nightingale*, and *Macaroni Feathers* by McKerrow and McClelland produced by San Diego State University.

An exciting line-up, and only a part of all the entertainment to be staged in the theatres and on the lawns of the Cal. State L.A. campus.

Executive producer Pam Woody of the Cal. State L.A. faculty is busy collecting a distinguished group of theatre experts to act as production reviewers; for, though the festival remains a non-competitive event, a basic part of its philosophy is the improvement of quality and communication in children's theatre. However, the most expert of opinions may be provided by a panel of junior reviewers also being assembled. This year we will agains ask young people of the general age of the festival audience to express their thoughts and preferences to the performance companies and to the festival committee.

Plays, improvisational adventures, creative dramatics, clowns, strolling singers and dancers: a lively two-day presentation of theatre arts for children. Sponsored by the Southern California Educational Theatre Association, the 1976 Children's Theatre Festival presents its fourth annual gathering — a reflection of the unprecedented growth in theatre for children in California.

Further inquiries may be directed to Pam Woody at (213) 224-3342 or 224-3350, or to:

The Children's Theatre Festival
c/o California State University, L.A.
5151 State University Drive
Los Angeles, California 90032

Figure 4–22. A Festival Publicity Release Placed in a Teachers' Newspaper.

(Used with the permission of United Teachers–Los Angeles.)

The guest chairperson briefs the guides before the festival, explaining the layout of the host campus and taking them on a quick tour of important locations. Each guide receives a map to keep, some handout maps, and an identifying ribbon.

The guest chairperson might want to establish an information (and lost-and-found) booth, at the main entrance or in the central corridor, to which guides can direct people whose problems they can't resolve.

The guest chairperson should have ready emergency information—phone numbers for police, fire, and ambulance.

The guest chairperson is also responsible for personally greeting and hosting VIPs.

For a Plan D festival, the hospitality chairperson might also want to plan social events for participants (such as a welcoming cocktail party). If many of the festival participants are from out of town, the hospitality chairperson might provide a memo to each on accommodations, entertainment, and points of interest in the vicinity of the festival.

Facilities (Technical Director) (A, B, C, D)

Generally, the responsibility of the facilities chairperson (or technical director) is to insure that the participants can perform comfortably in the space assigned to them.

For a Plan D festival, the facilities chairperson drafts stage plans or floor plans for every production area of the festival. He or she consults with the technical director of each entry to insure that the stage or room scheduled for use by that entry can accommodate its scenery and lighting requirements.

It is best to set up separate appointments with each technical director to inspect the site before the festival and review the production requirements. Arrangements can be made for any necessary adjustments to the allotted facilities. Sometimes this will simply mean finding an extension cord. But in other cases more serious measures may be needed. For example, background flats that won't fit through the door to the stage area may require rescheduling of two presentation areas.

If entrants will have to travel a great distance to participate and technical directors cannot inspect sites in advance, the facilities chairperson must make special efforts to insure that complete floor plans are reviewed through the mail. Incoming groups should be advised of the height of the playing area, the diagonal length of the largest door (for entering scenery), the number and capacity of electric outlets and their distance from the playing area, and any other limiting factors.

Another especially important function of the facilities chairperson is checking with the host campus early in the planning stage to insure that there is adequate seating capacity for the expected participants and audience. For a Plan C festival, for example, there must be enough large rooms to accommodate the group events.

The facilities chairperson is also responsible for negotiating with the supervisor of the host campus for any special requirements—space, telephones, custodian time, etc. Therefore, it is convenient for the chairperson to be on the staff of the host school.

The chairperson, the festival producer, and the supervisor of the host campus should also discuss facility problems that arose during past festivals to determine how to prevent similar problems during the current festival.

Example 1: A home football game and a high school Shakespeare festival were scheduled at the same time. No conflict was expected, but the blare of the public address system from the field drifted through the open windows on that hot day and interrupted every Shakespearean scene. Can the host campus be persuaded not to schedule any event other than the festival? If an athletic event must be scheduled, can the volume of the public address system be limited?

Example 2: On the weekend of a three-day children's theater festival, the host state college also scheduled national debate finals, a national piano competition, and a gymnastics event. The resulting parking situation was impossible. Many people who might have attended one of those events were discouraged when they could not find parking within three city blocks of the campus. Can the facilities chairperson convince the campus supervisor to limit the number of events scheduled? Can a separate parking area be set up for the festival with large signs at the theater directing drivers to the lot and a shuttle bus to run drivers from the lot to the festival?

The chairperson should insure that notes are written to the faculty and staff of the host campus, letting them know that guests will be on their campus and in their rooms.

Room Chairperson (C)   The festival room chairperson sees that the host custodian unlocks the schoolrooms on time. The festival room chairperson organizes student room chairpersons to serve in each room to monitor and time events.

Usually each entering school is required to bring along with its participants two or more students to serve as room chairpersons. They insure that the judges and participants are present, time events, and supervise the running of the festival within each room.

The festival room chairperson should brief the student room chairpersons just before the festival by orally reviewing a written handout (Figure 4-23). He or she is also responsible for distributing stopwatches, instructing students in their use, and recovering them. The festival room chairperson should number the stopwatches and have the room chairpersons sign for them.

Stage Crew (Stage Manager) (A, B, C, D)

The stage crew chairperson, or festival stage manager, is responsible for the stage and backstage areas before, during, and after the festival. He or she insures that the stage, lighting equipment, and scene changing facilities are ready. The chairperson also meets with the technical directors and stage managers of each entry to insure efficient use of the stage.

In a Plan C festival, the stage is used primarily for the presentation of trophies and sometimes for the performance of winning entries. Another important use of the stage in a Plan C festival is the announcement of winners of the preliminary rounds. The use of an overhead projector for this is highly recommended. So much screaming and yelling follows the announcement of each preliminary winner that the reading of the entire list will be delayed without the use of a projector. With a projector, winners and their room assignments for the next round can all be projected at once. The projector operator is warned to wear ear plugs!

Associate Producer or Reviewers (D)

In festivals where groups are invited to perform, the festival producer might insist that the group's work be seen and evaluated prior to a formal invitation. In this case, an associate producer may recruit commit-

INFORMATION FOR ROOM CHAIRPERSONS

8:00 - 8:30	Registration	
8:30 - 8:45	Assembly	
9:00 - 10:20	Round 1 - Prelim	
10:25 - 11:45	Round 2 - Prelim	
11:45 - 12:15	Lunch	
12:15 - 12:30	Assembly - Semi-finalists Announced	
12:30 - 1:40	Semifinal Round	
1:40 - 1:55	Assembly - Finalists Announced	
1:55 - 4:00	Final Round	
4:00 - 4:30	Awards Assembly	

Important Rooms

Room Chairpersons	- Room 52
Judges	- Library
Tabulations	- Faculty Lounge
Rules	- Cafeteria

1. Report to Room 52 on Saturday at 8:00 to get instructions and materials which will include program.
2. Go to your assigned room.
3. List code numbers for the entrants on the board.
4. Check to see that all entrants are there by calling numbers.
5. Be certain to start each round at the time indicated, if possible. If late entrants arrive they may perform when others are finished. Cross out code numbers of entrants who do not participate.
6. Check to be certain that the indicated number of judges is present. If not, send a runner to the library. (Preliminary round --- 3 judges; semifinals --- 5 judges; finals --- 7 judges.)
7. Explain that if anyone feels there has been a rules violation he or she should speak to the room chairperson as soon as the scene in question has finished. Send a runner with a rules infraction slip to the cafeteria. A member of the rules committee will review the situation and determine whether it has been disqualified. Important: no judge or room chairperson can disqualify a scene for any reason.
8. There is to be no talking during scenes and no applause or comments which could influence the judges. You may ask anyone who misbehaves to leave the room.
9. Time each scene from the moment the players begin. (Individual pantomime, group pantomime, individual humorous, and individual serious --- 5 minutes; group special event, group humorous, and group serious --- 9 minutes; improvisation --- 5 minutes.)
10. If a scene runs over, you must say "time," and stop the scene. The entrant is to be judged on what was performed, not penalized for running over time.
11. At the end of the round, try to hold people in the room until the end of the time period to avoid noise in the halls.
12. When judges have finished voting, take their ballots immediately to the tabulations room.
13. Thank judges and participants and proceed to your next assignment.
14. At the end of the final round, or before if you do not have an assignment, return your stopwatch to Room 52.

Thank you!

Figure 4-23. Room Chairperson's Briefing Form.

(Courtesy of DTASC.)

tee members (reviewers) to preview, individually or as a committee, the work of prospective entrants.

Food/Refreshments (A, B, C, D)

The food/refreshments chairperson is responsible for food services at the festival. In some cases service will be limited to providing coffee and doughnuts for the judges and festival staff. In other cases, the host campus cafeteria will be set into operation to provide lunch for all participants in the festival. In still other cases, the chairperson might supervise a string of concessions for from one day to a week.

At one large, three-day children's festival, the food chairperson decided to sell a box lunch of sandwiches, potato chips, and fresh fruit to the audience and provide the same, free, to participants, workers, and judges. The price was kept low. The overall cost of the food program was not entirely covered by sales. But most felt that the program, though simple, was adequate and desirable.

In all cases the chairperson is advised to confer with the supervisor of the host campus cafeteria and to check on local government regulations concerning food services.

Business Manager/Trophies (A, B, C, D)

It is desirable that the treasurer of the organization sponsoring the festival serve as the business manager of the festival. The business manager is responsible for all income and expenditures. He or she approves payment of all expenses, makes out the checks, and receives income from the registration chairperson and the food/refreshment chairperson (assuming a profit from concessions).

The business manager submits a written report on the festival's finances (Figure 4-24) at the critique following the festival.

The business manager may be given the additional responsibility of obtaining trophies, or that duty may be assigned to a separate chairperson.

Consideration should be given to awarding special trophies to individuals who have worked especially hard in mounting the festival over a period of years and to the individual or institution that hosts the festival.

```
                              DTASC
                        Financial Statement
                       September 20, 1975

Balance--February 1, 1975                                    $3129.53
      (Last Financial Statement)

Receipts

          Entry Fees--Shakespeare Festival

               Sr. High    $1819.00
                            1024.50
                                                             2843.50
                       TOTAL BALANCE & RECEIPTS TO DATE      $5973.03


Expenses
            General
                Coffee & Food Services
                        (Planning Meetings)      77.45
                Art Work & Printing             221.64
                Programs                        849.54
                Queen's Costume Rental (Jr. & Sr.)  100.00
                Trophies & Ribbons              923.53
                High School Theatre Festival (SCETA)1000.00
                Rental, CTA Auditorium           37.50
                Postage, Supplies, Phone        146.60
                                                             $3356.26

            Shakespeare Festivals--Facilities, etc.
                Sr. High
                    Judges Inv. & Postage      65.00
                    Postage, Fest. Question.    8.20
                    Luncheon & Food Services  196.18
                                                269.38

                Jr. High
                    Lunches & Food Services   173.36
                    Custodial                 105.28
                    Photography                52.84
                    Supplies                   11.00
                                                342.48
                                                             611.86
                       TOTAL EXPENSES TO DATE                $3968.12


Balance in Bank, September 20, 1975

        Savings   $2000.00
        Checking      4.91
                                                             $2004.91
(TWO SCHOLARSHIPS AWARDED, BUT NOT PAID AS YET.)
```

Figure 4-24. Festival Financial Statement.   (Courtesy of DTASC.)

150

TO COMPETE OR NOT TO COMPETE

Many teachers with whom I've spoken resent competitive festivals. They state that they don't want to put their students in pressured situations. Some feel that competition is alien to art. Some say they don't want to attend festivals where year after year the same few schools win trophies both in events and in the festival sweepstakes (most points earned by a school in all events). Some feel that returning from festivals year after year without trophies reflects poorly on their teaching, and others say that they simply don't have the student talent to make their schools competitive. It feels good to win and it feels bad to lose, and at every competitive festival there are many more losers than winners.

On the other hand, those who favor competitive festivals say that they merely reflect our society. Our students live in a world of Olympic Gold Medals, Emmys, Tonys, Obies, and Oscars. Outstanding talent should be rewarded. Students must learn to win and to lose, to live with success and failure, to rise above setbacks, and, most important of all, to rise above accolades. The first time students go to an open reading at a community theater, they will be competing. Why shouldn't we prepare them?

Some teachers find that their students, particularly the shy and the overconfident, benefit enormously from the experience of competitive work.

"I love to take my students to festivals," one drama teacher told me. "They get off their high horse when they see so much talent at other schools. They go with such exaggerated ideas of their own importance and they return with such wondrous humility."

Festivals can also be run on a noncompetitive basis. Instead of trophies, all entrants get medals for participation. Instead of points, judges render evaluations that are forwarded to the students' teachers. Following the festival, each teacher reviews the evaluations and decides which items would be useful for the students. This takes massive amounts of paper shuffling and sorting. Participants still gain the major rewards of a festival—playing in a different environment to a different audience, sharing experiences, and measuring their own work against the work of others. But there are no winners or losers.

Drama teachers should make their feelings on the matter of competing known to festival planning committees. Festival planners must be responsive to the majority of their constituents. If teachers simply return their registration forms with a statement that they are not entering this year, the festival is likely to continue as it always has. But if they state their reason for declining, they may get some response.

If you are going to compete, prepare your students for it. Tell them how you feel about competing. Ask how they feel about it. Discuss what behavior they expect of themselves during and following the festival. Ask what they expect to gain by competing, and follow-up afterward by asking if they got out of it what they expected.

One teacher has his entrants present their work to an audience of parents the night before the festival. Another drama teacher has his entrants tour selected classrooms to present their work during the week before the festival. Both systems give the students extra experience and get them up for the festival.

CONCLUSION

Festivals do not just happen. The major factors contributing to their overall success are painstaking planning and careful problem solving. With these and a few years of experience, your festival should run smoothly and effectively.

CHAPTER FIVE

Publicity

How can we encourage students to attend performances?

How can we increase box office receipts to meet production costs?

How can we gain the support of the community?

These are three questions that most drama teachers must face. The answer to all three is publicity and a product so good that it will inspire students and community members to return to the next production.

Good publicity is easier to achieve than a good production. Therefore, drama teachers must emphasize good production, avoiding time-consuming involvement in publicity. The less work drama teachers do on publicity the better!

To generate effective publicity while doing little work they must be well organized, obtain the cooperation of fellow faculty members, and delegate authority while retaining responsibility for the overall effectiveness of the publicity campaign.

It can be done, and here's how.

Two tools are used: a campaign outline and a fact sheet.

The outline (Figure 5–1) lists all possible techniques that the drama teacher might employ in the campaign. It names the individuals responsi-

```
┌─────────────────────────────────────────────────────────────────────┐
│                                                                       │
│       PUBLICITY CAMPAIGN FOR                  Today's Date_____    │
│                                                                       │
│       _____                   Opening Date_____    │
│                                                                       │
│                                         responsible │ due  │ release   │
│                                                      │ date │ date      │
│                                                                       │
│           fact sheet                                                  │
│   PICTURES                                                            │
│           8 x 10s of leads                                            │
│           rehearsal, no costumes                                      │
│           rehearsal, costumes                                         │
│           production (history, scrapbook)                             │
│   NEWS RELEASES                                                       │
│           school paper                                                │
│           other schools                                               │
│           local throwaway                                             │
│           major newspapers                                            │
│           monthly school newsletter                                   │
│           daily bulletins                                             │
│           public address announcements                                │
│           alumni magazines                                            │
│           radio/TV                                                    │
│   ART WORK/PRINTING                                                   │
│           posters, internal (classrooms, bulletin boards)             │
│           posters, external (stores in community)                     │
│           handbills                                                   │
│           banners                                                     │
│           paper badges                                                │
│           drama display case                                          │
│           tickets                                                     │
│           ticket control books                                        │
│   LETTERS OF INVITATION                                               │
│           flyers                                                      │
│           PTA (other groups: Lions, Rotary)                           │
│           individual parents                                          │
│           neighboring school drama classes                            │
│           special interest group                                      │
│           reviewers (include passes)                                  │
│           student clubs, organizations                                │
│   PREVIEW SCENES                                                      │
│           visits to classes                                           │
│           classes invited to drama room                               │
│           public places (malls, shopping centers)                     │
│   WORD-OF-MOUTH CAMPAIGN                                              │
│   TICKET SALES BY STUDENTS                                            │
│   SPECIAL PUBLICITY PROJECTS, PROMOTIONS                              │
│                                                                       │
└─────────────────────────────────────────────────────────────────────┘
```

Figure 5-1. Publicity Campaign Outline.

ble for each aspect of the campaign. It also gives the dates when each aspect will be completed and the target dates for publication of releases.

Let's assume that you are a drama teacher planning a production. Using the campaign outline, you select the publicity methods that you feel will be best for a particular production. You then determine who can be called on to do the work. As in all other phases of theatrical production, many hands make light work. Students can often carry out publicity work with minimum guidance.

For some aspects it is necessary to obtain the help and cooperation of the art production teacher, the design teacher, the printshop teacher, the journalism teacher, the administrator in charge of community relations, and the secretarial staff. All other volunteers are welcome.

Tailoring your publicity campaign should take just a few minutes. Evaluate your situation. Are the students required to attend your performances? Or is attendance voluntary? Are students already theater-oriented, or do they need to be persuaded to attend? Is this particular production popular? Will it draw because of title alone? What methods of publicity have proven successful before? What methods do you think will be ineffective here? What is the main purpose of your publicity? To obtain box office? To boost cast morale? Or is its most important goal to bring your program to the attention of the tax payer, the community, and the board of education?

After evaluating the questions above, check off the methods listed in Figure 5-1 that you will want to use for your next production.

Now decide whom you can get to do the work.

It takes salesmanship and tact to secure the cooperation of fellow faculty members. Once you have their support, however, they can repeat publicity procedures every semester without close supervision, thus relieving you of considerable work.

Example:

Once each semester, the teacher in charge of the art production class will know that you have a standing order for five banners. The teacher knows the sizes and where they are to be hung. All he or she needs from you is the fact sheet (Figure 5-2) and the desired completion date. Always give your co-workers ample time to do the work you expect of them. Of course, you never forget to acknowledge their work in the program. Thank-you notes signed by the whole cast don't hurt either, and occasionally you send a note to the principal expressing your gratitude for the support of fellow faculty members.

```
                                                  Carol Scherkenback
                                                  Publicity Director
                                                  555-1212 Ext. 40


          THE GLENVILLE PLAYERS
               present

     YOU CAN'T TAKE IT WITH YOU
               May 1976

                              FACT SHEET


     What        You Can't Take It with You

                 by Moss Hart and George S. Kaufman

                 51st production of the Glenville Players

     When        Thursday,   May 19, 1977    8:15 PM
                 Friday,     May 20, 1977    8:30 PM
                 Saturday,   May 21, 1977    8:30 PM

     Where       Glenville High School Auditorium, 9005 Cynthia Ave.,
                 Los Angeles

                 Ample parking is available in school parking lots.

     How Much    Admission:  Students $1.00, Adults $2.00

                 Call 555-1212 Ext. 40 for reservations.

     Who         Cast        The Glenville Players

                             Penny              Ruby Meyers
                             Essie              Diane Abram
                             Rheba              Jo Stewart
                             Paul Sycamore      Richard Meyers
                             Mr. DePinna        Joe Kilasinski
                             Ed                 Jim Packard
                             Donald             Ray Elias
                             Grandpa            Ben Brodow
                             Alice              Bev Connolly
                             Henderson          Lawrence Dumespotz
                             Tony Kirby         Herb Grossman
                             Gay Wellington     Sue Hummeland
                             Mr. Kirby          Mark Legas
                             Olga Katrina       Juliette Brodow
                             J-Men              Rog Emery
                                                Don Ruehle
                                                Paul Martin


                             Student Director   Becky Leggett
                             Faculty Advisor    Mr. Eugene C. Davis
```

Figure 5-2. Fact Sheet.

Sometimes you may assign several tasks to a class or committee of students and allow them to choose individual students to carry out specific duties. A journalism class, for instance, might be called upon to handle all newspaper, radio, and TV releases.

To make sure that all publicity materials have correct information, you should personally write out the fact sheet and insure that it is reproduced and distributed to all those concerned before any publicity tasks are undertaken. This basic tool should give the essentials that will appear in all publicity releases (the *what, when, where, how much,* and *why*)—title of production, author's name (correctly spelled!), dates of production, curtain times, place (address of the school), parking information, phone number to call for reservations, phone number of person responsible for publicity, and any other information you feel is absolutely essential.

It is very important that these basic facts be correct from the outset. Changes in date of production, for example, can cause a lot of wasted effort in publicity work.

THE RELEASE FORMAT

In your basic release (Figure 5-3) try to get your who, what, where, and when into the first sentence of the first paragraph. Keep that first sentence under twenty-five words if possible. Assume that the editor might have room for only the first paragraph. Put the most important information first and the least important last. This is called pyramid style.

Keep all of your paragraphs short and stick to the facts. No editorial comment; don't tell how good your production is going to be.

Type all releases double-spaced.

Mimeographed releases may gain some attention from the editors of school papers, but for best results from other papers, send an original release tailored for the specific paper, including a line such as "exclusive to the *Los Angeles Post.*" Some editors consider it an insult to receive mimeographed or carbon releases.

Keep on hand a scrapbook of all past publicity releases and the clippings that resulted from them. It is much easier for students to write releases if they can use prior releases as models to get the format and the rhythm.

Carol Scherkenback
Publicity Director
The Glenville Players
9005 Cynthia Ave.
Los Angeles 90069
555-1212 Ext. 40

FOR IMMEDIATE

RELEASE

EXCLUSIVE TO THE LA POST

You Can't Take It with You, by Moss Hart and George
S. Kaufman, will open Thursday night, May 19, at Glenville
High School auditorium. Curtain time is 8:15 p.m.

Two other performances are scheduled on Friday, May 20,
and Saturday, May 21, at 8:30 p.m.

Tickets are $1 for students and $2 for adults. Ample
parking is available in school lots.

Becky Leggett is the student director and Mr. Eugene
C. Davis is faculty advisor.

This Broadway comedy is the 51st production of the
Glenville Players.

Call 555-1212 for reservations.

Figure 5-3. Basic Release.

Well-established patterns for releases to various media will soon develop. Example (school newspaper):

Timing	Content
Six weeks prior to opening	Initial announcement—title, type of play, dates, props needed
Five weeks prior	Staff and crew assignments
Four weeks prior	Supporting cast members
Three weeks	Leads
Two weeks	Rehearsal pictures, not finished costumes but approximate
One week	Rehearsal pictures, costumes
Week of opening	Student director interview
Week after opening	Review or comment on opening night

This schedule works well at one large metropolitan high school. It may not work at your school.

Many short mentions in any media tend to reinforce. They are preferable to a single long piece.

The throwaways (free advertising papers) that circulate in the immediate neighborhood of the school can be especially useful. They will often use the "local interest" release, the story that starts, "Harry Smith, son of Mr. and Mrs. Austin Smith of Bell Street, will play the eccentric grandfather when Kennedy High presents *You Can't Take It with You.*"

HANDLES

Sometimes it is easier to publicize human interest aspects of a production rather than the production itself. These items, or handles, are found by carefully examining cast biographies and the history of the play's previous productions. You can also actively solicit special interest material and rehearsal anecdotes from cast, staff, and crew.

Example:

A cast member tells you that her mother played the same role when it was presented years ago (or in the play version of the musical, or at another school, or in the Broadway production). You now have the makings of a human interest story that can help to publicize the play.

At other times the publicist creates an item that will grab the reader's attention.

Celebrity tie-ins are the handles that usually get the biggest play. A celebrity need not be a glamorous movie star. He or she can be anyone your readers will want to read about—a popular teacher, an outstanding student athlete, a very popular student, a well-known alumnus. The tie-in may be direct or remote. The direct tie-in is the celebrity's participation in the production, doing a role, a walk-on, or any backstage work. Stories about a celebrity who is directing a play or contributing a prop can usually find easy placement.

The more remote tie-ins are the "Homecoming queen buys first tickets" or "TV actor sends telegram to cast" stories.

Celebrity walk-ons can be fun and mutually beneficial. They demonstrate the celebrity's interest in the welfare of the school, which can be good PR for the celebrity. Sometimes you can get good publicity mileage out of keeping the celebrity's name a secret until he or she actually appears on stage.

Look for the special audience members who might be attracted to your play, and appeal directly to them in your release copy. "Union members will be very interested by the playwright's insight into both sides of the strike." "People of Irish descent will recognize . . . ."

If your play has themes relevant to current events, make that clear in your copy. Sometimes you may even want to pick your play or determine its production dates to take advantage of holidays or current events, such as a political play around election time or a religious play around Easter.

SPECIAL EVENTS

Special events or promotions may be held in conjunction with the production of a play.

Example:

You and members of your drama class decide to raise funds to enable your production to travel to a statewide festival. To do this you stage a dance marathon attempting to break the record in the *Guinness Book of World Records.* Students raise money by getting sponsors to pay them $1 per hour for every hour that they dance. You pull out all of the publicity stops in obtaining coverage for the attempt at record breaking—and the opening of your play. Be sure to publicize the amount of money needed to reach your goal.

Give your event a name, such a Dramathon. Avoid the use of the word *promotion* in your releases. Send letters of invitation to the city editors of newspapers and the assignment editors of radio and TV stations. Include the statement, ''The photographic possibilities will be especially good. We urge you to cover the Dramathon.''

This type of promotion can generate a lot of spirit among your group; they feel that they have all worked as a team to attain a worthwhile goal, even if they cannot all be playing leads in the production.

Read critically the publicity generated by other school theaters and professional theaters and movies. Keep a list of the handles and promotions that they use. After a few semesters, most of the handles and promotions on your list will be forgotten by the public and ready for recycling.

PHOTOGRAPHS

Photographs for both newspaper releases and TV use can be very valuable because they catch the eye and often have more punch than a lengthy release.

To get good publicity shots, run the cast through an emotional high-point or an interesting point in the script. Then freeze them. Tighten them together with little room between heads and no room between shoulders. Try to get an emphatic emotion on each face even if the actors have to exaggerate the emotional level called for in the scene. Sometimes it is even necessary to invent business to produce a visually interesting photo. Makeup and costumes help, as do interesting props or unusual set pieces.

Try to hold the number of people in the photo to three if you expect to have their names in the caption.

Short captions should be typewritten. Turn your release stationery upside down and write your caption at the very top. Tape the release to the back of the photo so that the caption can be folded over the front of the picture. This method insures that the picture won't get separated from the caption and that an editor can reach you if he needs further information.

The caption should read well enough to stand by itself without the story. Try to get the who, what, where, and when into the caption.

Taking interesting publicity shots is an art. Study the best pictures you see in your newspapers publicizing other plays and movies. Then imitate their best features. Note that there is no dead space in the best ones. Sometimes cropping a picture can help. But if you have two or more people in a picture, you can't crop the space between them, so you must be careful when you pose them.

RADIO AND TV RELEASES

Don't be afraid to ask for radio and TV time to promote a school play. Don't be intimidated by the high cost of radio and TV advertising. You don't want to pay for advertising. You are looking for public service time, and most radio and TV stations will be cordial at least in considering your request. If you don't request, you won't get; the stations will not reach out to encourage you.

If you apply with your materials in readily usable form you are likely to get good results.

Radio and TV releases must be shorter and snappier than newspaper releases. The public service director of a TV station is likely to give more favorable attention to a ten-second spot than to a rewrite of a two-page release you submitted to the school paper. TV releases should be accompanied by good visual material, preferably in the form of a 35 mm glass-covered slide. (The heat generated by the film chain makes it impossible to use the ordinary cardboard mounts supplied by your film processor.) When you submit a slide you don't have to worry about the ratio required of other visual material.

If you submit a photograph or artwork, it should be at least six inches high by eight inches wide, and anything larger should be in the same 3:4 ratio. If you submit an eight-by-ten-inch photograph, be sure that it can be cropped to a usable 3:4 ratio picture. Photos should be on matte print rather than glossy to prevent glare; the station can spray a glossy if necessary, but that's just one more step for the public service director.

What can you get into a ten-second spot? "Don't miss the Glenville High production of *You Can't Take It with You.* The Moss Hart-George S. Kaufman classic opens Friday." Just those few words, combined with a slide of the logo and title plus the visual message "Tickets $2.—Free parking," might readily be accepted by a public service director as a station break announcement. This could not possibly serve as your total publicity campaign for a production, but it could be a significant addition to other publicity methods.

Some radio stations air cultural events calendars and welcome dates of school plays. To get more than a listing, contact radio talk show hosts and disk jockeys. Point out to them that your students are listeners. Submit releases in short, snappy format and request student interviews whenever possible.

Contact radio and TV people in person. Over the phone you may get rejected because an editor or public service director can't show you how to revise your copy. Editors can't be sure of what they'll get if they give you a telephone go ahead; they might be creating work for themselves. But if you take in your copy, an editor may respond by helping you on the spot to reshape your material. Learn by the experience and always thereafter submit material in that format. Write the editor's name on your file copy of the release and next time you submit a release, address it to his or her personal attention.

FLYERS, HANDBILLS, AND POSTERS

Flyers and handbills can sometimes be more effective than releases and pictures. Colleges lean heavily on the flyer as the major instrument of their publicity campaigns. If they can be run off in your school printshop and addressed by students, they may be the best value for your publicity dollar.

A flyer is folded and sent through the mail. A handbill is unfolded and posted. The same material may be used for both.

You may choose to have talented, imaginative students create an eye-appealing logo for your play, or you might want to use the logo associated with the play during its Broadway production or national tour. The logos are usually available from Package Publicity Service, Inc., 1564 Broadway, New York, New York 10036, for a small fee.

Try this. Design the cover of your program so that you can use it as a flyer/handbill. It might save you time and money.

A guest book in the lobby is the best source of a mailing list for future productions. (See Chapter 3 for more information on mailing lists.)

If flyers in envelopes or address-labeled flyers are too expensive, you might want to try postcards. They can be addressed in homerooms by students and mailed to parents. Asking students to carry home materials does not achieve the same impact.

Look for opportunities to stuff flyers into other official school mailings. This requires the approval of the principal but may cut your postage budget.

Call on your art department for posters, hand painted or silk-screened, to be placed on bulletin boards in the school and in store windows in the community. Students might want to do treatments of the play's Broadway logo or create their own eye-catchers.

WORD OF MOUTH

Get the students out on the campus to spread the word. If possible, get them out in costume wherever students gather—in the cafeteria during lunch and on the quad between classes. Even if the costumes are not appropriate to the show you're doing, they can attract attention and create talk. If possible, have students either sell tickets or give something away—perhaps a small paper badge with the name of the school play. (The students would ask, "Will you help us publicize our play by wearing this for the next two days?") I especially like a fortune cookie giveaway during lunchtime. The fortune, of course, reads, "You are going to see a marvelous play this weekend—*You Can't Take It with You.* Tickets $1."

PUBLICITY CHECK

Periodically you might want to hand out a questionnaire to your audience to determine what publicity method is most effective for you:

(Check one:)

I first decided to attend this performance because of

A.   Personal invitation

B.   Newspaper story

C.   Newspaper picture

D.   Radio announcement

E.   TV announcement

F.   Flyer I received in the mail

G.   Poster or handbill I saw

H.   Other (please specify):

Review the results to determine where greater emphasis might be useful in your next campaign.

A FINAL WORD—ENTHUSIASM!

There is no substitute for enthusiasm in placing publicity materials. Your release might be in just the right format and style for the intended media. Your timing might be excellent—that happy coincidence of your walking through the door just as an editor scratches his head not knowing how to fill twenty column inches. But it might all be lost if you don't sell—show enthusiasm. Walk in not begging a favor, but performing a virtuous, considerate, ethical, and charitable act. "Hey, have I got something terrific for you! Our next play is going to be a real winner—the best ever! And everyone who hears about it from you will absolutely love you for it!" If not these words, the music. Sometimes you can't get the enthusiasm to leap out from the paper release. That's why personal contact is so important. Get out of your school to meet the editors of the media whose cooperation you want. It may require some extra time and work in the beginning, but it will pay off in the long run with the publicity you want to keep your audience packed, your bank balance favorable, and your community supportive.

CHAPTER SIX

Accounting Needs

Up-to-date financial records are essential for efficient operation of a theater department. These include budgets, income forecasts, periodic reports of income and attendance, summaries, and requisitions, purchase orders, and invoices.

THE BUDGET

The purpose of a budget is to insure that you do not spend more than you have or spend unwisely. At the educational level a budget has another important use—to introduce students to the realities of theater economics.

Usually the theater budget at a college is controlled by a business manager or the department chairperson, who is in turn responsible to the college's business office. At the high school level, the drama teacher alone may be responsible for the budget, or the teacher may share the responsibility with the school's financial manager or a vice-principal. In this book, the person responsible will be called the business manager.

The first step in preparing the budget is to brainstorm *all* the areas (or categories) of expenditures.

The following general list of areas is offered merely as a starting point. Add to it any areas of expenditures that are peculiar to your production. (Code numbers are assigned to categories for accounting purposes as described later in this chapter.)

1010   Scenery
        1011 Lumber
        1012 Muslin/Fabrics
        1013 Paint
        1014 Hardware
        1015 Rigging
        1016 Electronics
        1017 Tools

1020   Props
        1021 Lumber
        1022 Paint
        1023 Purchases
        1024 Rentals

1030   Lighting
        1031 Color Media
        1032 Lamps
        1033 Cable
        1034 Rental

1040   Audio
        1041 Tapes/Discs
        1042 Recording Supplies
        1043 Construction
        1044 Rental

1050   Costumes
        1051 Materials
        1052 Costumes
        1053 Construction
        1054 Accessories
        1055 Rental
        1056 Cleaning

1060 Makeup
    1061 Supplies
    1062 Wigs
    1063 Rentals
    1064 Purchases
1070 Scripts
    1071 Royalties
    1072 Purchase
    1073 Rental
    1074 Reproduction
    1075 Shipping
1080 Publicity
    1081 Printing
    1082 Postage
    1083 Labor
    1084 Photography
    1085 Display
    1086 Banners
    1087 Newspaper Advertising
    1088 Miscellaneous
1090 Tickets/Programs
    1091 Printing
    1092 Postage
    1093 Office Materials
    1094 Labor
1100 Design Fees
1200 Petty Cash
1300 Transportation

If you have mounted a production in the past, you may start with the areas of expenses of your last show and add additional areas. Example: The last show was modern dress with no costume budget. This show requires extensive costumes. So you would add all of the areas related to costumes to your list.

When you have determined your areas, you are ready to start setting down cost estimates for each area. Here are some general rules.

1. Go to the sources for the figures. Don't estimate a costume budget, for instance, without consulting your costume designer. And don't accept the designer's figures unless he or she has recently checked the cost of

rentals and supplies. Prices change too frequently to make costume estimates (or any other estimates) only on the basis of what costumes for the last show cost or what the average costume budget was for all shows last season. Prices have been known to rise so fast between the time a supplier submits an estimate and the time the supplier sends the invoice that you find a surcharge added to the invoice.

2. Review estimates at staff meetings to get the benefit of the entire staff's thinking. Example: The technical director may not know the cost of yardage for costumes, but he or she might remember that another college did a Roman era costume show within the last four years. Why not rent some of the costumes, if available, rather than make them all?

3. Demand student involvement in making cost estimates for productions. It makes the students aware of the cost of materials they are working with. At the least, it will make them less wasteful. Too often student-artists adopt the attitude that they can't be bothered with the materialistic aspects of theater. Then, when they leave their educational environment and are confronted with the reality of paying for a production, they suffer shock. Appoint a student business manager to work with you on finding ways of holding down expenses. Insist that student budget forms be submitted in advance of all student productions. (See Figure 6–1.)

Be constantly alert for bargains. Investigate closeouts and shutdowns of theater businesses and related entertainment enterprises. Investigate state agencies that dispose of surplus (including army and navy property) to nonprofit organizations. Schools have purchased used tent canvas at two cents per running yard and used it to build flats. Used netting and parachutes have been used for scenic effects. Even lamps and projectors are sometimes available.

Offer advertising consideration rather than money for some of the things you need. Sometimes a courtesy mention in your program can be traded for items you need.

INCOME FORECASTS

In forecasting income, the business manager must evaluate many variables—the drawing power of the play's title, the effectiveness of publicity, the aggressiveness of ticket-selling campaigns, the reviews, and

SCENERY	Est.	Expend.	Net	Net Totals
Lumber	50.—			
Muslin	10.—			
Paint	10.—			
Rental				
Stock	30.—			
Totals	100.—			

COSTUMES	Est.	Expend.	Net	Net Totals
Construction	50.—			
Rentals	150.—			
Accessories				
Cleaning				
Stock				
Totals	200.—			

PROPS			
Lumber			
Paint			
Purchases			
Rentals	25.—		
Stock	10.—		
Totals	35.—		

MAKEUP			
Supplies	10.—		
Rentals (Wig)			
Purchases (Wig)			
Stock			
	30.—		
Totals	40.—		

LIGHTING			
Lamps			
Cable			
Color Media	26.40		
Rental			
Stock			
Totals	26.40		

MANAGEMENT			
Royalties	200.—		
Scripts	50.—		
Shipping	—		
Rental (Scripts)	—		
Design Fees	25.—		
Printing	145.—		
Mailing	25.—		
Labor	170.—		
Photography	60.—		
Displays	—		
Banners	18.72		
Ticket Printing	50.—		
Totals	743.72		

AUDIO			
Tapes & Discs	20.—		
Construction			
Rental			
Recording Sup.			
Stock			
Totals	20.—		

TOTALS
Estimates 1165.12
Expend.
Net Diff.

Figure 6-1. Student Budget Form. If an item is used from stock, it must still be charged to a specific production.

even the weather. With so many uncontrollable variables, the business manager can only average past performances over a three-to-five-year period (when possible) to make a ball park guesstimate of income from ticket sales. Then he or she adjusts for any recent changes, such as more performances or an increase in the price of tickets.

The general areas of income other than ticket sales are season tickets, subsidies, rentals of the theater's equipment and costumes, program advertising, and concessions.

The projected income for a production might look like this:

Projected ticket sales: (@ $2 and $3)	1,760	$ 4,520
Actual season tickets: (@ $8/4 productions)	133	266
Actual subsidy		1,000
Actual rentals		---
Projected program advertising		200
Projected concessions		150
Other		---
TOTAL		$ 6,136

Subsidy funds may come from a variety of sources. With the funds come control measures from the source. A state will specify audit procedures for its funds and stipulate how the money may be spent. For example, it may provide a formula for the percent to be applied to classwork as opposed to production work.

If the subsidy comes from a student body fund, the general manager will determine audit procedures. Censorship may come from anyone who controls, or believes he or she controls, student body funds.

Renting your equipment to other groups can be a very good source of income, but in some cases state rulings will preclude the rental of any items that were made with materials purchased with state funds.

Concessions may be run by the student drama society, the faculty wives' association, or any other interested group. Harness the students' imagination in making the concession relevant to the play. But anticipate inspection by the Department of Public Health if you intend to sell any food that is not completely wrapped, including coffee.

The forecast of income should be discussed at the staff meetings along with the expenses, and everyone should be encouraged to contribute ideas on how income can be increased and where additional sources of income should be sought. Obviously, if your projected expenses are greater than your projected income, it is time to reevaluate and plan changes.

When both projected expenses and projected income have been discussed, there should be a formal acceptance of the budget—either the vote of the staff or the signature of the head of the department—which will authorize the business manager to disburse funds for that production.

Once the budget has been approved, all members of the staff should receive a copy (see Figure 6-2) and instructions on how and when to submit requisition forms (discussed later in this chapter) to the business manager.

PERIODIC REPORTS OF INCOME AND ATTENDANCE

The box office and the business manager are responsible for periodic reports of income and attendance (beyond box office reports discussed in Chapter 3). Before the opening, the reports are prepared weekly. After the opening, daily reports are prepared. These reports show the administration how well the production is doing financially (see Figure 6-3). Notes should be made on these reports, explaining how the weather, competing campus activities, and other factors are influencing attendance. (Weather insurance is sometimes worth considering. The business manager would have to consider the effects of inclement weather on attendance at past shows and then weigh the potential loss against the premium cost.)

In cases where the production will run more than one week, the income and attendance reports can serve as a basis for a decision to increase or decrease publicity, to change box office hours, etc. You may extend box office hours if you feel it will increase sales, but do not decrease your hours. The very best of customers will be upset if they arrive at the box office and find it closed. Strive for consistent hours year after year if at all possible.

At some universities the amount of subsidy to the theater department

PRODUCTION BUDGET

ASSOCIATED STUDENTS　　　　　　　　　　　　　CALIFORNIA UNIVERSITY

Item	Line Item	Comparable Production *	This Production	% Increase or Decrease	Comments
	INCOME				*COMPARED TO LAST YEAR'S ACTUAL TOTALS FOR BUTTERFLIES ARE FREE (ROUNDED OFF)
1.	Box Office	1640	1640	—	
2.	Season Tickets	450	475	+6%	
3.	Subsidy	—	—		
4.	Rentals	——	—		
5.	Program Advertising	100	100	—	
6.	Concessions	20	20	—	
7.	Other	—	—	—	
	EXPENSE				
8.	Scenery	420	450	+7%	INCREASED COSTS OF DURATEEN, MUSLIN AND OTHER MATERIALS
9.	Props	80	90	+13%	
10.	Lighting	110	95	−14%	
11.	Audio	15	5	−67%	
12.	Costumes	30	40	+33%	
13.	Makeup	100	40	−60%	
14.	Scripts/Royalties	410	385	−6%	
15.	Publicity	440	450	+2%	
16.	Tickets/Programs	230	250	+9%	
17.	Other	5	60	+1200%	ADDITIONAL SEATING BANKS, REUSABLE WHEN NEEDED.
	Total Income	2210	2235	+1%	
	Total Expense	1840	1865	+1%	
	Difference	+370	+370	—	

Student Chairperson (signature)　　　　Faculty/Staff Advisor (signature)　　　　Department Chairperson (signature)

Figure 6-2. Production Budget.

174

```
┌─────────────────────────────────────────────────────────────────┐
│                                                                   │
│              WEEKLY TICKET SALES REPORT                           │
│                                                                   │
│                THEATER DEPARTMENT                                 │
│                                                                   │
│   PLAY_____THEATER_____DATE_____    │
│                                                                   │
│   ____Students (I.D.)          @ $2.00_____                   │
│   ____Faculty and Staff (I.D.) @ $2.00_____                   │
│   ____Season Tickets           @ $2.50_____  (transfer from   │
│                                                    season accnt.)  │
│                                                                   │
│   ____Group Sales (25+)        @ $2.00_____                   │
│   ____Theater Students         @ $2.00_____  (transfer from   │
│                                                    accnt. #50981)  │
│                                                                   │
│   ____General Admission        @ $3.00_____                   │
│       _____Unsold                                                 │
│   ____Promotional Passes                                          │
│   ____Senior Citizen (Gold Card)                                  │
│   ____Theater Staff                                               │
│   ____Life Passes                                                 │
│                                                                   │
│                                                                   │
│   ____Total Tickets/Attendance    Total   $_____             │
│                                                                   │
│                                                                   │
│   Weather Factors:                                                │
│                                                                   │
│   Competing Campus Activities:                                    │
│                                                                   │
│   Competing Off-Campus Activities:                                │
│                                                                   │
│   Other Factors:                                                  │
│                                                                   │
│                                                                   │
└─────────────────────────────────────────────────────────────────┘
```

Figure 6-3. Weekly Sales Barometer.

is dependent on the number of students attending. In other cases, statistics showing student and community involvement in the theater's operations help to justify the theater's existence. (See Figure 6–4.) At some schools, student body cards are used for admission or reduced admission. The card is punched and the box office is reimbursed from student body funds. Then the drama department must account for how many students were admitted with student body cards. In Figure 6–4, the 50¢ sales might be those to students and the $1.50 sales those to all others. This would show the student/community ratio. Forms have to be tailored to display information that you need for your specific circumstances.

SUMMARIES (BALANCE SHEETS)

Within two weeks to thirty days after the closing of a production, a summary, or balance sheet (see Figure 6–5), should be prepared showing the total actual expenditures, income, and profit or loss.

The staff should analyze the summary to evaluate many factors: Did the production have the drawing power it was expected to have? Does the audience seem to want more of this type of production? If another such play is presented, must a loss be anticipated? Can such a loss be supported by an increased subsidy or by increasing other types of plays during the season? Should plays be scheduled so that they don't compete with home basketball games or other events? Was inability to park within a reasonable distance from the theater a reason for the lower-than-expected box office sales? Is greater effort needed in publicity? Should more attempts be made to educate the potential audience? What were the unexpected expenses and what steps should be taken to eliminate them in the future?

An analysis of the income and expenses of concessions, program advertising, and equipment rental may determine whether the effort involved is justified. If they require too much work for too little return, perhaps they should be discontinued.

A thorough discussion of the financial summary by the entire staff is highly recommended. The group effort of many minds can lead to improving the economic efficiency of production.

In educational theater, many costs related to the production are not

CSCLA THEATRE STATISTICAL ANALYSIS

Play: Number of Performances:

Dates: House Capacity:

	Friday	Saturday	Wednesday	Thursday	Friday	Saturday	Total
Attendance							
Percentage of Capacity							
Number of Ushers							

Total Ticket Sales: $_____   House Manager: Hours:
                                                                   Cost:
50¢ Sales: $_____
                                             Box Office Manager: Hours:
$1.50 Sales: $_____   Cost:

Complimentaries (cashed in):   Publicity Asst: Hours:
                                                                   Cost:
Number of Crew:
                                             Addressing: Cost:
Number of Actors:

Number of Mailers Printed: Cost:

Number of Mailers Mailed: Cost: (Post Office):

Number of Programs Printed: Cost: Signed _____

Number of Posters Printed: Cost: Date   _____

Number of Advertising Material Made: Cost:

Figure 6-4. Statistical Analysis Form Used at California State University, Los Angeles. This form shows how attendance compares to costs and other factors.

ASSOCIATED STUDENTS OF CALIFORNIA UNIVERSITY   CLOSING AUDIT DATE 10/28/77

PRODUCTION COST REPORT

GAMMA RAYS

Item	Estimated	Actual	Variance/Comments
Income			
1. Box Office	1640	1545.00	
2. Season Tickets	475	475.00	
3. Subsidy	—	—	
4. Rentals	—	—	
5. Program Advertising	100	120.00	
6. Concessions	20	27.85	
7. Other			
Expense			
8. Scenery	450	492.90	
9. Props	90	81.62	
10. Lighting	95	99.64	
11. Audio	5	4.18	
12. Costumes	40	53.00	
13. Makeup	40	32.86	
14. Script/Royalties	385	385.00	
15. Publicity	450	492.90	
16. Tickets/Programs	250	264.16	
17. Other	60	—	PLANS FOR ADDITIONAL SEATING CANCELLED
Total Income	2235	2167.85	
Total Expense	1865	1906.26	
Difference	+370	261.59	

Student Chairperson _____

Box Office   _____

Faculty Advisor   _____

Dept. Chairperson   _____

Figure 6-5. Balance Sheet, Single Production. The estimated figures are those shown on the production budget in Figure 6-2.

shown on the balance sheet—faculty salaries covering directing, design, and technical supervision; rental of the theater; upkeep and janitorial services; to mention just the major ones. Because these costs are not charged against productions, students get an inaccurate picture of the economics of theater even when they are encouraged to evaluate the summaries for their productions.

Exercises are therefore needed to help students see the cost of theater in other environments. Have selected students, particularly those interested in directing and producing, devise two budgets for the play that they have just presented—one for a 600-seat Equity theater (see Figure 6-6) and one for a 200-seat community theater with a mortgage on its property and a paid resident director (see Figure 6-7). What would tickets have to sell for in each situation if there were no grants, subsidies, or other income?

Annual summaries of the whole season's work should be analyzed at the close of each year so that the information may be used in planning the next year's work (see Figure 6-8).

REQUISITIONS, PURCHASE ORDERS, INVOICES

To keep track of funds and limit individual spending, a system of requisitions, purchase orders, and invoices is usually used.

It works this way. Assume that the technical director wishes to purchase color media for the coming year. He or she writes a request to you, the business manager, fully describing the materials needed, the date needed, the production or productions for which it is intended, the vendor, and the estimated cost.

You write out a requisition form and add the code assigned to that category of expenditures (i.e., color media 1031). You check previous amounts that you have logged against that code in your ledger. If the new amount is within the budget, you approve it. If it is not, you can deny that purchase. Or if there are compelling reasons why a budget override should be considered, you might refer the technical director to the department chairperson for clearance. The important point is that there is a check, and no staff member may spend funds without considering the overall budget.

			1 Pre-Production Rehearsals	2 Production	3 Production	4 Totals	
1		Rentals					1
2		Theater					2
3		Rehearsal Space					3
4		Office Space					4
5							5
6		Royalties					6
7		Script Rentals					7
8		Music Rentals					8
9							9
10		Salaries/Fees					10
11		Producer					11
12		Director					12
13		Set Designer					13
14		Lighting Designer					14
15		Costume Designer					15
16		Sound Designer					16
17		Box Office Personnel					17
18		Publicist					18
19		Business Manager					19
20		Production Assistants					20
21		Wardrobe Personnel					21
22		Accountant					22
23		Legal Advisor					23
24		Ushers					24
25							25
26		Principals					26
27		Characters/Support					27
28		Extras					28
29		Understudies					29
30							30
31		Conductor					31
32		Orchestra Members					32
33		Choral Director					33
34		Choreographer					34
35		Chorus/Dancers					35
36							36
37							37

Figure 6–6. Proposed Budget, Commercial. The student would be given the following instructions: Assume that our current production is to be rehearsed and produced in a commercial, union, 600-seat theater. It will run for the same length of time at 70 percent capacity. With no income other than ticket sales, what will we have to charge for each ticket in a non-scaled house in order to break even?

		Pre-Production Rehearsals	Production	Post-Production	Totals
1	Salaries/Fees (continued)				
2	Production Stage Manager				
3	Stage Manager				
4	Assistant Stage Manager (s)				
5					
6	Master Carpenter				
7	Master Electrician				
8	Property Master				
9	Sound Technician				
10	Other Crew				
11					
12	Secretary				
13	Custodial Staff				
14					
15	Fringe Benefits (as per Equity, IATSE, ATPAM, etc. contracts)				
16	Health				
17	Life Insurance				
18	Vacation				
19	Other				
20					
21	Set				
22	Rental				
23	Construction				
24	Flameproofing				
25	Lights				
26	Equipment Rentals				
27	Color Media				
28	Lamps				
29	Costumes				
30	Rental				
31	Construction				
32	Cleaning				
33	Makeup				
34	Purchase				
35	Rental				
36					
37					
38					
39					
40					

Figure 6-6. (*continued*)

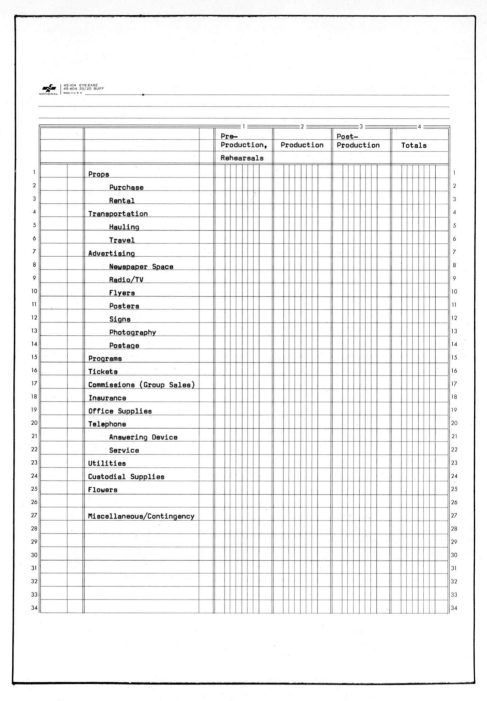

			1 Pre-Production, Rehearsals	2 Production	3 Post-Production	4 Totals	
1		Props					1
2		Purchase					2
3		Rental					3
4		Transportation					4
5		Hauling					5
6		Travel					6
7		Advertising					7
8		Newspaper Space					8
9		Radio/TV					9
10		Flyers					10
11		Posters					11
12		Signs					12
13		Photography					13
14		Postage					14
15		Programs					15
16		Tickets					16
17		Commissions (Group Sales)					17
18		Insurance					18
19		Office Supplies					19
20		Telephone					20
21		Answering Device					21
22		Service					22
23		Utilities					23
24		Custodial Supplies					24
25		Flowers					25
26							26
27		Miscellaneous/Contingency					27
28							28
29							29
30							30
31							31
32							32
33							33
34							34

Figure 6-6. (*continued*)

		Pre-Production, Rehearsals	Production	Post-Production	Totals	
1	Mortgage					1
2	Royalties					2
3	Scripts					3
4	Director					4
5	Set Construction					5
6	Hardware					6
7	Paint					7
8	Lumber					8
9	Fabrics					9
10	Hauling					10
11	Lights					11
12	Purchase					12
13	Color Media					13
14	Sound					14
15	Costumes/Makeup					15
16	Rental					16
17	Purchase					17
18	Cleaning					18
19	Props					19
20	Set Pieces					20
21	Music					21
22	Food					22
23	Publicity					23
24	Printing					24
25	Photography					25
26	Postage					26
27	Programs					27
28	Tickets					28
29	Hospitality					29
30	Building Maintenance					30
31	Phone/Utilities					31
32	Janitor Service					32
33	Contingency					33
34						34
35						35
36						36
37						37
38						38

Figure 6-7. Proposed Budget, Community. The student would be given the following instructions: Assume that our current production is to be rehearsed and produced in a 200-seat community theater with a mortgage and resident director. It will run for the same length of time at 90 percent capacity. With no income other than ticket sales, what will we have to charge for each ticket in a non-scaled house in order to break even?

ASSOCIATED STUDENTS OF CALIFORNIA UNIVERSITY

ANNUAL SUMMARY

MAJOR PRODUCTIONS 1977-78

	Gamma Rays	Macbeth	Idiot's Delight	Little Mary Sunshine	77-78
Income					
1. Box Office	1545				
2. Season Tickets	475				
3. Subsidy	—				
4. Rentals	—				
5. Program Advertising	120				
6. Concessions	28				
7. Other	—				
Expense					
8. Scenery	493				
9. Props	82				
10. Lighting	100				
11. Audio	4				
12. Costumes	53				
13. Makeup	33				
14. Scripts/Royalties	385				
15. Publicity	493				
16. Tickets/Programs	264				
17. Other	—				
Total Income	2168				
Total Expense	1906				
Profit/Loss	262				

Figure 6-8. Annual Summary.

Once cleared, the requisition form is forwarded to the purchasing office (business office) of the college, where a purchase order is written (see Figure 6-9). The purchase order is then forwarded to the vendor.

A call-in system may also be used to obtain purchase order numbers. The business manager is able to approve a purchase by the technical director and issue an order number over the phone. This may be helpful in expediting purchases, but it may lead to needless, impulse buying.

In small colleges and community theaters, the business manager may function alone, without the supportive business office. No requisition forms are used. The business manager approves purchases and forwards purchase orders as necessary.

The processing of paperwork takes time. Therefore, the business manager must encourage staff members to submit requisitions well in advance of the dates the materials are needed so that emergency procedures for obtaining materials won't be necessary.

Conditions for use are sometimes specified by the donor of funds (e.g., state funds). Business managers may be required to obtain three bids on any item over $100. This means spending a lot of time filling out forms just to spend the money. Business managers should therefore plan ahead. They should estimate their needs three to six months ahead and buy in bulk. They should apply unwieldy funds to major items of supply and use their other income sources for the smaller items.

Vendors submit invoices to the college business office showing the actual cost of the items ordered. The business manager must check the actual cost against his or her records and make corrections if the actual cost differs from the estimated cost.

When a vendor does not have invoice forms, it is convenient for the business manager to provide an invoice that the vendor may use (see Figure 6-10). The business manager should also provide invoices when renting props, set pieces, scenery, or costumes (see Figure 6-11).

For small items the expense of processing all of the above paperwork can be greater than the cost of the item purchased! To counter this situation, various types of blanket requisitions may be approved by the college business office. One type establishes charge accounts with some often-used vendors (e.g., printer, lumberyard). Another type of blanket requisition allows the business manager to write several purchase orders to several different vendors just as long as the orders do not exceed the total amount approved in the requisition (e.g., $750). Blanket requisitions decrease the amount of work done by the business office and vest greater discretion in the theater's business manager.

```
                    DRAMA PRODUCTION TRUST
                 DEPARTMENT OF SPEECH AND DRAMA
              CALIFORNIA STATE UNIVERSITY, LOS ANGELES
                    5151 STATE UNIVERSITY DRIVE
                   LOS ANGELES, CALIFORNIA  90032

                      Telephone:  224-3345

                   P U R C H A S E   O R D E R

                                              No. DPT-

          To:                                 Date:
```

Quantity	Unit	Description	Unit Price	Total Price

Authorized Signature:	Sub-Total
	Tax
	Total

Date Due:

Deliver to: Theatre 110A
             California State University, Los Angeles, 5151 State University Drive
             Los Angeles, California 90032

Figure 6-9. Purchase Order.   (Courtesy of California State University, Los Angeles.)

```
FROM:                              DATE:_____

                                   P.O.#_____

   _____

   _____

   _____

TO:

Drama Production Trust
California State University, Los Angeles
5151 State University Drive
Los Angeles, California 90032


                    I N V O I C E

Quantity        Description of        Unit        Amount
                Material or Service   Rate
_____
```

                              I N V O I C E

Quantity	Description of Material or Service	Unit Rate	Amount

TOTAL $_____

_____
Signature

Figure 6-10. Invoice Form Furnished to Vendors Who Do Not Have Their Own Invoice Forms.

(Courtesy of California State University, Los Angeles.)

```
CALIFORNIA STATE UNIVERSITY, LOS ANGELES
             5151 STATE UNIVERSITY DRIVE
               LOS ANGELES, CALIF.  90032
     DEPARTMENT OF SPEECH COMMUNICATION & DRAMA
              DRAMA PRODUCTION TRUST
                      INVOICE

TO:                                        DATE:
```

QUANTITY	UNIT	DESCRIPTION	Unit Price	Total Price

```
YOUR PURCHASE ORDER NUMBER:

PLEASE MAKE CHECKS PAYABLE TO:  DRAMA PRODUCTION TRUST
```

Figure 6–11. Invoice Supplied by Drama Department for Rentals of Its Costumes, Props, and Scenery to Others. (Courtesy of California State University, Los Angeles.)

188

Petty cash funds are necessary for purchasing small items in a hurry. Adequate records must still be kept. Cash register receipts for every item purchased with petty cash should be stapled or glued to a petty cash voucher and turned in to the business office when the purchaser is reimbursed.

All claims for funds to cover mileage expenses must also be submitted in writing (see Figure 6–12).

Regardless of the system used, it is the business manager's responsibility to keep accurate ledgers and maintain well-organized files of all invoices.

An effective method of filing is to label a folder with each budget category. Corresponding invoices, purchase orders, and requisitions may then be stapled together within the folder.

CONCLUSION

Open discussions of budget problems at staff meetings help any theater department to operate efficiently. Careful maintenance of financial records makes them readily available to staff members, allowing the staff to base decisions on reliable information. Encouraging students to understand the budgets for their productions as well as the economic problems of making theater in other environments is highly desirable. Now more than ever, show business is *know* business!

```
                    DRAMA PRODUCTION TRUST
              CALIFORNIA STATE UNIVERSITY, LOS ANGELES
                     5151 STATE UNIVERSITY DRIVE
                  LOS ANGELES, CALIFORNIA 90032

                  REQUEST FOR MILEAGE REIMBURSEMENT

                               ACCOUNT TO
                               CHARGE:  DRAMA PRODUCTION TRUST #3260
    NAME_____

                                    DATE:_____
```

Date	From	To	Total Miles	Amount	Remarks

Maximum reimbursement rate allowable is 14¢ per mile.

_____
Signature of Claimant

_____
Signature of Advisor

Figure 6–12. Mileage Reimbursement Form.   (Courtesy of California State University, Los Angeles.)

CHAPTER SEVEN

Educational Theater Organizations and Institutions

There are many regional and national organizations and institutions whose primary purpose is to support educational theater. These organizations offer a wide variety of goods, services, and opportunities that every theater educator should be aware of. Your organization should decide whether participation would be beneficial.

The following survey of a few of the organizations and institutions that can provide services to educational theater groups is only intended to sharpen your appetite. Investigate! Find out more about these organizations and others that can help you, or that you can help. Then get involved. Improvement of the theater is the common goal of all of the organizations. With your participation, perhaps you and they can reach that goal a little sooner.

The American Theatre Association (ATA)
1000 Vermont Ave., N.W.
Washington, D.C. 20005, (202) 628-4634

The American Theatre Association is an association of theater workers, students, teachers, individuals, and organizations involved in noncommercial theater. It promotes communication among theater people and with other theater organizations: commercial theater, federal and state agencies, international theater organizations, and agencies of the United Nations. ATA promotes research in the theater; publishes a variety of magazines, newsletters, and books; provides a placement service to individual and organizational members; and coordinates the work of eight divisions in nine geographical regions.

The divisions of ATA are the American Community Theatre Association (ACTA) (discussed in Chapter 14), the Army Theatre Arts Association (ATAA), the National Association of Schools of Theatre (NAST), the National Children's Theatre Association (NCTA), the Secondary School Theatre Association (SSTA), the University and College Theatre Association (UCTA), the University/Resident Theatre Association (U/RTA), and the American Theatre Student League (ATSL). One glance through *Theatre News,* ATA's newsletter, and you develop a sudden craving for alphabet soup.

Theatre News attempts to include information about the workings of all of ATA's divisions and regions. It is published ten times a year and distributed to all of ATA's 6,000 plus members.

ATA also publishes the *Educational Theatre Journal,* which has articles of special interest to college-university theater. It is distributed four times a year, in March, May, October, and December. Members of UCTA (remember?) receive it as one of their membership privileges. Primarily circulated in the United States and Canada, it also goes to over twenty foreign countries.

The *Children's Theatre Review* is published four times a year, in February, May, August, and November. It goes to members of NCTA.

The *Secondary School Theatre Journal* is published tri-annually—in November, January, and May—and goes to members of SSTA.

Other publications include the ATA Annual Convention Program, the ATA Annual Directory, and ATA mailing lists, as well as assorted books, pamphlets, brochures, and regional newsletters.

A national convention is held annually in a major city and features workshops, discussions, play presentations, dinners, and exhibits.

The American College Theatre Festival (ACTF)
John F. Kennedy Center for the Performing Arts
Washington, D.C. 20566, (202) 254-3437

The American College Theatre Festival is an annual program of the American Theatre Association. Each spring it takes eight productions, chosen from those presented by over 350 colleges throughout the United States, to the John F. Kennedy Center for the Performing Arts in Washington, D.C.

To select eight outstanding productions, the ATA uses the following system. The nation is divided into thirteen regions. Judges appointed by ATA visit the home theaters of the entrants. The judges invite three to eight productions to take part in a regional festival. Each of the thirteen regional festivals is judged by at least two judges from the ACTF central committee and one regional chairman from another region. On the basis of their appraisal, eight productions are invited to Kennedy Center.

ACTF estimates that in a recent year, 620,000 people saw festival productions in their home theaters, 40,000 attended regional festivals, and 18,000 saw the performances in Washington, D.C.

Several awards and scholarships are available to outstanding works at the regional and national festivals. An award of $2,500, sponsored by the William Morris Agency, Samuel French, and the Dramatists' Guild, goes to the best play written by a student. Tandem Productions, Inc., presents the Norman Lear Award of $2,500 for the best comedy play entered by a student. The David Library of the American Revolution sponsors awards of $2,500 and $1,000 for plays written on the subject of American Freedom. McDonald's Corporation sponsors the Lorraine Hansberry Playwriting Award of $2,000, which is presented to the student author of the best play on the black experience in America. A grant of $500 is also presented to the drama department of the college producing the play. The Irene Ryan Scholarship Award goes to the most promising young players in the regional and national festivals. Miss Ryan, remembered as Granny of the "Beverly Hillbillies," set up a $1,000,000 trust fund to provide these scholarships.

But the awards and scholarships are not necessarily the greatest rewards of participation. College theater people—students and teachers—have the opportunity to exchange ideas and to measure themselves against the work of others in their field.

The International Thespian Society (ITS)
3368 Central Parkway
Cincinnati, Ohio 45225, (513) 559-1996

Founded in 1929, the International Thespian Society works through troupes in high schools "to create an active and intelligent interest in theater arts and to advance standards of excellence in all phases of the theater arts."

Associate Thespians has recently been formed to serve junior high schools and elementary schools with grades one through eight.

ITS has a membership of close to one million, with over three thousand troupes in high schools throughout the world. There is a charter fee of fifteen dollars for new troupes. Forty thousand new members are initiated annually at a lifetime fee of three dollars.

ITS publishes *Dramatics,* an educational theater magazine, five times per year, bimonthly September through June. Single copies are one dollar, and annual subscriptions are five dollars. Student subscriptions are three dollars, and lifetime members of ITS may renew at three dollars even if no longer students. *Dramatics* features short plays, reviews of theater-related books, production reports from ITS troupes, news of ITS workshops and festivals, and articles on a wide variety of theater subjects. The advertising is also useful, as it carries information about goods, services, and opportunities of interest to theater-loving readers.

ITS maintains a lending library of more than 12,000 scripts and 2,000 books on theater, with emphasis on the needs of educational theater.

State conferences are held annually, and regional conferences are held every two years (on odd-numbered years). The conferences feature workshops on a wide variety of theater subjects and one-act play marathons, as well as dance, singing, pantomime, and semi- and fully staged versions of plays and musicals. Firms and organizations with goods and services of interest to high school dramatics programs are encouraged to exhibit.

As part of its motivational approach for teenagers, ITS offers certificates of membership and membership cards. It also sells a wide variety of esprit-building items including jewelry with masks, chenille letters, pennants, beanies, T-shirts, and stationery.

A royalty adjustment plan sponsored by ITS allows member troupes to apply through ITS to leading play publishers for a reduction in royalties. ITS claims that reductions are secured for 90 percent of those schools submitting application.

Scholarships helping Thespians to continue their theater education are awarded through the ITS regions. Recipients are chosen on the basis of scholastic excellence, financial need, interest, and meritorious work in theater arts.

The National Association of Dramatic and Speech Arts (NADSA)
Fort Valley State College, Box 579
Fort Valley, Georgia, 31030

The National Association of Dramatic and Speech Arts is primarily concerned with the promotion of black theater and rhetoric at the college level. Teachers and directors of high school speech and drama programs are also encouraged to join.

Founded in 1936, NADSA supports programs in theater and communicative arts at member institutions and provides acting and speech opportunities for students.

The membership fee for organizations is $35 per year. Individual members may participate for $15 (sustaining), $10 (regular), or $2.50 (student) annually.

NADSA operates in twenty states (through five geographical regions): (1) Southeastern: North Carolina, South Carolina, Georgia, Florida; (2) North Central: Ohio, Missouri, Kentucky, Tennessee; (3) South Central: Alabama, Mississippi; (4) Southwestern: Arkansas, Oklahoma, Louisiana, Texas; (5) Northeastern: Maryland, Virginia, West Virginia, Washington, D.C., Delaware, Pennsylvania.

The magazine *Encore* is published once a year, in April. It contains articles about black theater, plays, and rhetoric, as well as news and photo coverage of the activities of member colleges. The quarterly NADSA Newsletter features schedules of productions, news about members, and book reviews.

During NADSA's annual spring conference (in April), one-act plays, produced and directed by students, are presented. Workshops are held in costuming, lighting, makeup, acting, public speaking, debate, speech correction, and choric speech.

American Playwrights Theatre (APT)
1849 Cannon Drive
Columbus, Ohio 43210, (614) 422-4205

The challenging function of the American Playwright's Theatre (APT) is to produce new plays in college and community theaters throughout the land.

Organized in 1963, APT has produced *The Days Between,* by Robert Anderson; *And People All Around,* by George Sklar; *Ivory Tower,* by Jerome Weidman and James Jaffe; *Summertree,* by Ron Cowen; *The Night Thoreau Spent in Jail,* by Jerome Lawrence and Robert E. Lee; *Echoes,* by N. Richard Nash; *Jabberwock,* by Lawrence and Lee; and *The Last Meeting of the Knights of the White Magnolia,* by Preston Jones (see Figure 7–1).

Play scripts are submitted for consideration by literary agents, active members of the Dramatists Guild, the Eugene O'Neill Foundation, the Office for Advanced Drama Research, or subscribing theaters.

APT screens the scripts and circulates those it feels have potential to over 125 colleges and community theater subscribers. When 25 or more ask to produce the play, it is put into production.

The subscribers pay $50 annually as a fee to receive the promising scripts. If they decide to produce a play, they pay a royalty fee of at least $200. The minimum a playwright receives for any work produced at APT is therefore $5,000. If more than 25 ask to produce it, the initial earnings for the playwright are greater. The playwright also receives 5 percent of the first $2,500 in receipts, 7.5 percent of the next $2,500, and 10 percent of anything over $5,000 for each successful production. With this system, playwrights can earn respectable royalties without having their plays produced on Broadway.

There are other advantages for playwrights. They do not have to submit their plays to the hit-failure evaluation of the very few New York City-based critics. They do not have to cater to the philosophies of the Broadway producers. They can reach a larger audience than would normally see their plays if the plays were long-run hits on Broadway. They may attend regional productions of their plays and work on changes and refinements as the plays are mounted. And finally, they may still have a Broadway production when APT's exclusive rights terminate (within a year).

It seems that APT is reaching its goal (from APT bylaws):

> To serve a truly nationwide theatre by fostering cooperation between living American dramatists and the play producers of university, college and nonprofit community theatres, thereby enabling the best new works of substance and ideas to be presented first and nationally on the stages of America's educational theatres, which are both teaching laboratories and instruments of creative expression for the communities they serve. The ultimate objective is to enhance the quality of our national drama.

'Knights of White Magnolia' Opens

BY DAN SULLIVAN
Times Theater Critic

Not too long ago a new American play had to succeed in New York before anyone would take it seriously. Now the machinery is there to have a national hit without playing New York at all, as witness "The Last Meeting of the Knights of the White Magnolia."

Preston Jones' comedy about some good old Texas boys was first offered at the Dallas Theater Center. Then it was done at Washington's Arena Stage. Then it was picked up by the American Playwrights Theater, which isn't a theater but a way of getting new scripts around to some 200 member theaters across the country.

This winter such APT affiliates as the Cleveland Play House, the Seattle Repertory Company and the Alliance Theater of Atlanta are offering major productions of the play. Broadway will see it too, but its fate there won't determine whether the rest of the country will see it. We already have.

"We" now includes Los Angeles—Redlands, anyway. Crafton Hills College Theater offered the local premiere of "Knights" over the weekend, and it was worth the drive. The production was able, the play as true to West Texas as chicken-fried steak.

The time is 1962, the scene an upstairs room in the Cattleman's Hotel, Bradleyville (pop. 6,000). This is where the Knights of the White Magnolia meet every month for dominoes and "refreshments." The Knights—an offshoot of the

THE LAST MEETING OF THE KNIGHTS OF THE WHITE MAGNOLIA

A new play by Preston Jones, presented by the Crafton Hills College Theater, Redlands. Director Cliff Cabanilla. Costumes Melody Holcomb. Lighting Kurtis Van Sant. With Mike Martin, Art Crafts, John Maloney, Tony Murphy, Rich Swan, Bill Stice, Joe Keefe, Kevin McCarty and Dick Booth.

Klan—were big in Southern lodge circles for awhile but have not been having a lot of luck since the end of the war. In fact we learn that these are the last seven members.

Tonight, though, they are to initiate a new man. He is, alas, from Silver City (Bradleyville and Silver City don't get along) but otherwise he has all it takes to be a valued member of the brotherhood. That is, he is white and he wants to join.

Remember Amos 'n' Andy's Mystic Knights of the Sea? This group is no better organized and considerably less congenial. Bitch, bitch, bitch. "If he's from Silver City he's no damn good." "Now that's about a damn *nough*." If you crack up at the sketches on the Carol Burnett Show about the redneck family who can't stand each other, you'll crack up at this bunch.

But when they go through that ridiculous initiation ceremony ("Olin, yo're the Moon . . . Rufe, yo're the West Wind"), there is a sense of the dignity they are dimly seeking—a transcendence you don't find at Rotary. "Knights" isn't, as you were expecting, about

Figure 7–1. A Newspaper Review. Plays produced by the American Playwrights Theatre are reviewed throughout the nation, not just by a handful of reviewers based in New York City.

racism. It's about trying to believe in something that doesn't apply anymore and the hollow feeling when you give up trying. The hollowness to be filled with what? Like those Burnett sketches, "Knights" leaves you wondering about its people.

Cliff Cabanilla's cast at Redlands has a good age range and a real flair for rube comedy, faltering only when the play's serious underside must be examined. Rich Swan as the respectable grocer trying to hold them together is impressive all the way. But everybody has his moment—Bill Stice as the thirsty Skip, John Maloney as the complaisant Olin, Tony Murphy as the surly Red, Kevin McCarty as the new boy, Lonnie Roy, Mike Martin as Ramsey Eyes, who sweeps up, Dick Booth as Milo the Mama's boy, Art Crafts as the petulant Rufe and Joe Keefe as the doddering "Col." Kinkaid.

The physical production is so real it's embarrassing—that flickering plug-in cross by lighting designer Kurtis Van Sant, for instance. Final performances at 8:30 Thursday through Saturday, 410 Orange St., Redlands (714-794-2161). But we'll be seeing more of this fine little play.

Figure 7-1. *(continued)*

The Speech Communication Association (SCA)
5205 Leesburg Pike
Falls Church, Virginia 22041, (703) 379-1888

The Speech Communication Association is a nonprofit scholarly and professional organization. It provides services and opportunities for service to its membership: teachers and administrators, speech scientists and clinicians, media specialists, theater artists and craftsmen, communication consultants, students of the communication arts and sciences, and persons in business, industry, and government particularly concerned with communications. Its purpose is to "promote study, criticism, research, teaching, and application of the artistic, humanistic and scientific principles of communication, particularly speech communication."

Founded in 1914, SCA has 7,000 members in the United States and twenty foreign countries. Its ten internal divisions are (1) Community College Instruction, (2) Forensics, (3) Instructional Development, (4) Interpersonal and Small Group Interaction, (5) Interpretation, (6) Mass Communication, (7) Public Address, (8) Rhetorical and Communication Theory, (9) Speech Sciences, and (10) Theatre.

SCA publishes *The Quarterly Journal of Speech Communication*

Education (a quarterly emphasizing teaching methods and supervision of cocurricular activities), *Communication Monographs* (a quarterly of research reports), and *Spectra* (a bimonthly national newsletter). SCA also publishes an *Annual Directory* that includes biographical data on its members, rosters of degree-granting institutions, and checklists of books, equipment, and supplies. A *Directory of Graduate Programs,* put out biennially, explores 300 graduate departments, describing requirements, deadlines, financial aid, areas of concentration, etc.

SCA's placement service publishes a *Bulletin* that lists vacancies and assists in preparing and forwarding letters of application, folders, and credentials.

An annual meeting is held in major cities. It features research reports, exhibits, demonstrations, workshops, short courses, placement service, and social events.

The Puppeteers of America (P of A)
P.O. Box 1061
Ojai, California 93203

In existence since 1937, The Puppeteers of America is a nonprofit organization dedicated to the art of puppetry. It is open to anyone interested in puppets, from beginners and hobbyists to professionals. Dues are twelve dollars per year for adults, and there are several other classes of membership allowing full participation at reduced cost to groups, young people under fifteen, and retired members.

P of A publishes *The Puppetry Journal* bi-monthly ($1.25 per issue, $8 annual subscription, $5.25 to members). It contains articles on puppet techniques, puppetry in other lands, educational and commercial puppetry, reviews of puppetry-related books, and news of P of A's regional guild activities. An annual membership directory is also published.

Services offered include consultants, a puppet store (books, scripts, puppets, props, stages, etc.), national festivals (conducted annually since 1937), regional festivals, and workshops.

P of A is affiliated with the Union Internationale de la Marionette (222 E. 67th Street, New York, New York 10021), an international organization voluntarily uniting puppeteers from the entire world.

Theatre Collection, Library and Museum
of the Performing Arts
The New York Public Library at Lincoln Center
111 Amsterdam Avenue
New York, New York 10023, (212) 799-2200

New York's public library established its Theatre Collection as an administrative unit in September 1931, but major collections related to the theater had been donated as early as 1905.

The collection includes programs, playbills, photographs, clippings, letters, legal papers, manuscripts, promptbooks, costumes, and stage designs. The vast files of clippings from newspapers and magazines are arranged by title, actor, producer, designer, playwright, name of the theater, and subject. Programs and playbills number approximately one million; original drawings for costumes and scenery and pen-and-pencil portraits, including caricatures, run to several thousand.

Some of the major collections donated to the library are as follows: The Robinson Locke Collection of Dramatic Scrapbooks—800 bound volumes and over 2,500 portfolios of loose clippings, programs, holograph letters, and unmounted photographs relative to the American stage and screen 1870–1920; The David Belasco Collection of typescripts, photographs, original designs, and scrapbooks; The George Becks Collection of promptbooks and holograph scripts of plays produced in the United States and England mainly during the eighteenth and nineteenth centuries; The Hiram Stead Collection, covering British theater from 1672 to 1932, in 600 portfolios containing letters, autographs, and written copies of leases and documents relating to theatrical litigation, as well as a vast file of playbills and portraits; The Henin Collection, covering the Parisian stage of the eighteenth and nineteenth centuries, including original drawings for costumes and scenery; The Carl Van Vechten Collection, comprising theatrical portraits and annotated scrapbooks covering his theatergoing from the 1890s to 1950; The Vandamn Studio Collection of Theatrical Photographs, containing prints and negatives of stage productions and photographs of actors from the early 1900s to 1960, including many caricatures by Al Frueh, Al Hirschfeld, and Alex Garde.

A great number of smaller collections are centered on performing artists, designers, producing firms, managerial firms, theatrical associations, or photographers. *Vast* does not adequately describe the magnitude of this fine theatrical library and museum.

Although this is the only library cited in this chapter, there are many fine theater collections at public and college libraries throughout the world. Their range of services goes far beyond serving as a book depository. See what the library near you has to offer.

The National Theatre Conference
c/o Library and Museum of the Performing Arts
111 Amsterdam Avenue
New York, New York 10023, (212) 799-2200

Founded in 1925, the National Theatre Conference is a cooperative association of leaders of nonprofit theater—regional, community, and college. Membership of the conference is limited to one hundred, and members are admitted by invitation only. The conference meets annually in New York City to confer on matters pertaining to the welfare and development of the theater.

Check *Simon's Directory of Theatrical Materials, Services, and Information* for the names and addresses of other organizations concerned with educational theater.

PART TWO

Community Theater

CHAPTER EIGHT

Forming a New Community Theater Group

Community theater is theater made by members of the community for a local audience. The prime moving force is the enjoyment of making theater, not potential profits. Community theater provides for its members a recreational outlet for their creativity. Its function is to bring theater to an audience that might otherwise be without it.

It is a continuing enterprise. Although possibly started to present a single play, the theater provides a sense of community involvement and achievement that keeps the group together producing season after season.

At its best, community theater can offer its participants and audiences rewards all too frequently missing in other types of theater. One is the great satisfaction of belonging to a creative enterprise—the kind of satisfaction experienced in pioneer times in the United States when a neighbor's house burned down and the entire community donated time and labor to rebuild the house. That same sense of working together can still be observed backstage at many community theaters across our land. In how many other community enterprises can teenagers and grandparents work together to achieve a common goal? Long-established community theaters have a sense of family and tradition. They have social events (picnics, dances, award banquets). The members go as audience to school theater when one of their children is appearing. Ties are close and friendships endure.

Authentic enthusiasm radiates from the stage. Sometimes you find this in educational theater—high school and college. More often than not it's absent in professional theater.

Community theater has a freshness and first-time quality. Long runs on Broadway and touring companies usually have a greater polish and professionalism, but that fresh, first-time quality is often missing.

Community theaters can offer their audiences a sense of intimacy. Due to the economics of theater, professional theaters must operate in larger houses than community theaters. The current breaking point seems to be about 600. Without that seating capacity, a professional theater has a difficult time paying its actors and staff the salaries required by theater-related unions. But when seating capacity goes up, a sense of intimacy is hard to obtain. It is that sense of intimacy that facilitates your "leaving your seat" during a performance—getting so caught up with what's happening on the stage that you forget you are in a theater. That's the best theater experience there is.

Perhaps someday theater design will allow larger theaters to retain a sense of intimacy; but until then, usually only the community theaters have it. Operating in houses of small capacity—50 to 200—community theaters can offer every member of the audience close contact with the actors and a marvelous sense of sharing an experience rather than observing from a distance.

In community theater there is often a feeling of community pride—both for the theater people and for the audience. "It's *our* theater," says it all.

And lastly, making theater can be a deeply personal, moving, emotional experience—an act of celebrating life.

Considering these rewards, it's understandable that many participants and audience members develop a loyalty to community theater that they cannot give to professional theaters.

THE BEGINNING

All community theaters start with an ancient idea and desire—to make theater. Although the idea can come from one person, theater by its very nature is a cooperative effort that demands many talents. So the very first step in making theater is the recruiting of those talents.

The first step brings its first problem—agreement on the aims or goals of your community theater. Theater is such a broad term that it means many things to many people. To recruit theater makers who can work harmoniously, you must spell out the aims and goals of the community theater that you envision.

Will your primary goal be to provide a stage for the actors and directors of your community, or will your emphasis be on providing cultural stimulation for your audiences? Do you hope to give equal stress to both goals? Will you seek an audience of children, students, or adults? Will you seek to serve one specific ethnic group or will you serve a general audience? Will you attempt to produce the most recent plays available, or will you revive those plays of the past that have enduring values? Or both? What kinds of plays do you expect to present? Will you produce a variety of drama, comedy, musicals, and children's theater, or will you specialize in one type of play?

Even if you expect to launch your new theater with a single play rather than a season, make up a list of the plays that you can foresee producing in your first two years. Work out a budget for the first two years.

A brief statement of goals, the list of plays, and your budget should give prospective members a basis for deciding whether they can commit themselves to your cause.

Now you are ready to do two things: determine whether there is support in your community and recruit a board of directors.

DETERMINING THE NEED
FOR A NEW THEATER

Talk to people. Announce to the leaders of your community that you wish to launch a new community theater. Discuss your goals. Ask for their advice. Perhaps they can recommend others who should be consulted at the outset.

Mount a publicity campaign. Use the local newspaper to publicize your cause. Use bulletin boards in supermarkets, church bulletins, free radio and TV public service time, and any other media you can find.

Start a mailing list of people who would like to be informed of your first production. Pass out interest survey–registration forms for the mailing list wherever you can. (The card can also ask whether the individual is interested in participating in production work—e.g., "Check one: actor, director, scene design, construction, costumes, publicity, other.")

The number of people who respond to your publicity will let you know if there is ample support in your community.

A BOARD OF DIRECTORS

Developing a significant base of support starts with finding a hard core of dedicated people who are willing to donate their time and energy to the making of theater. Usually this group is called the board of directors, but it may be called an advisory council, trustee council, or governing board.

Of course, you will be interested in finding people with theater skills. But even more important, you must find people with influence in the community, and people who have valuable nontheater skills such as writing (for PR and publicity), accounting (for budget and box office operations), and real estate (for finding a home for the theater, remodeling, and expansion).

Start at the top. Ask the leaders of your community to serve on your board—professional people, politicians, heads of business firms, educators, clergymen, etc. These people need not have any desire to act or direct or work backstage. All they need is a strong desire to have theater in their community. They will attend monthly meetings to discuss the problems of the theater, and they will contribute their intelligence, expertise, and experience to solving those problems. They will be most helpful in determining the theater's policies, raising money, and influencing other people to support the theater as audience. Most important of all, they will represent the community in your community theater.

Many theater organizations start with a clique of actors and directors who zealously guard their organization from the intrusion of outsiders—until they need an audience or financial support. This is a great mistake. The time to involve your community is at the beginning, and all the time thereafter. You must see community theater as a beautiful symbiotic relationship between theater people and the community. The theater people love their art well enough to give their creativity. The community loves theater enough to foot the bills and applaud. One cannot exist without the other. If the marriage is to last, both should be party to the engagement.

ARTICLES OF INCORPORATION

As soon as practical your new community theater should incorporate as a nonprofit, educational organization. There are several good reasons for this.

1. Incorporation will help to insure the continuation of the theater beyond the participation of the founders.

2. You need not pay federal or state taxes on income from tickets sold or on other earned income.

3. You need not file federal or state tax returns, though you may be required to file "information" returns.

4. You may receive gifts (money and property), and those who contribute the gifts may deduct them as a charitable contribution on their income tax reports. Patrons may deduct the cost of their tickets. And the value of a donated prop or set piece is tax deductible, as long as you give the donor a receipt on your theater stationery.

5. You may use "Nonprofit Org." on your mail and take advantage of the bulk mailing rate (annual fee of about thirty dollars) for your flyers.

6. You need not pay property taxes on land owned by the theater.

7. You will not be personally liable for debts of the theater or suits brought against the theater.

The articles of incorporation of the Kentwood Players (Figure 8-1) may serve as an example. But your articles must conform to your state laws governing nonprofit, educational and cultural organizations. Because the laws are slightly different in every state and because the articles are
(Text continues on page 212.)

ARTICLES OF INCORPORATION
OF
KENTWOOD PLAYERS
(A non-stock membership corporation)

KNOW ALL MEN BY THESE PRESENTS:

That we, the undersigned, have this day voluntarily associated ourselves together for the purpose of forming a non-profit, non-stock membership corporation under and by virtue of the general non-profit corporation law of the State of California, and we do hereby certify:

FIRST: That the name of the corporation is

KENTWOOD PLAYERS

SECOND: This corporation is organized and will be operated for exclusively charitable and educational purposes and in furtherance of such purposes and no others, shall:

1.   Promote interest in drama and provide opportunity to all adult residents of the community who may be interested in any phase of little theatre work, to participate in productions of this group.

2.   Cooperate with existing local organizations to promote a community spirit of harmony and good fellowship.

3.   Contract with and be contracted with.

4.   Receive property, by devise or bequest, subject to the laws regulating the transfer of property by Will, and to otherwise acquire and/or own property, real or personal, including shares of stock, bonds or securities of other corporations.

5.   Build, erect, maintain, equip, manage and operate theaters, stages, auditoriums and all usual adjuncts thereto for the members and their guests.

6.   In general have and exercise all of the powers conferred by the laws of the State of California upon corporations formed under the general non-profit corporation laws.

7.   Do each and every thing and exercise all lawful powers for any lawful purpose and such as religious, charitable, educational and for rendering services

Figure 8-1. Articles of Incorporation of the Kentwood Players. (Courtesy of the Kentwood Players.)

which do not contemplate the distribution of gains, profits or dividends of the members hereof, and for which individuals may lawfully associate themselves, all as provided for by Section 9200 of the Corporations Code of the State of California.

THIRD: And it is a corporation which does not contemplate the distribution of gains, profits or dividends to the members thereof. The property is irrevocably dedicated to charitable purposes and upon the winding up and dissolution of this organization, after paying or adequately providing for the debts and obligations of the corporation, the remaining assets shall be distributed to a non-profit fund, foundation or corporation, which is organized and operated exclusively for charitable, educational, religious and/or scientific purposes and which is exempt from Federal income tax. If this corporation holds any assets in trust, such assets shall be disposed of in such manner as may be directed by decree of the Superior Court of the county in which this corporation's principal office is located, upon petition therefor by the Attorney General or by any person concerned in the liquidation.

FOURTH: The County in this State where the principal office of business of this Corporation is to be located is Los Angeles County.

FIFTH: The names and addresses of the persons who are to act in the capacity of directors and who shall be styled directors, and who are to exercise the powers of this corporation, and to control its property and affairs, and who are to serve until the annual meeting of the members hereof, and until the election or qualification of their successors are:

[names and addresses of directors omitted]

The number of directors hereof shall be the number above named, to wit, fifteen.

SIXTH: The authorized number and qualifications of the members of this corporation, the different classes of members, the property voting and other rights and privileges of every class of membership, and the liability of each and all classes to dues or assessments and method of collection thereof, shall be set forth in the By-laws of this corporation.

SEVENTH: Neither the members hereof, nor the directors hereof shall be personally liable for the debts, liabilities or obligations of this corporation, pro-

Figure 8-1. (*continued*)

vided, however, that this clause shall not affect the liability of members for dues and assessments as shall be provided and set forth in the By-laws hereof.

EIGHTH: The existing unincorporated association which is being incorporated under these Articles, is known as Kentwood Players.

IN WITNESS WHEREOF, the above named persons who are to act in the capacity of the first directors, and others desiring to associate with them for the purpose of forming this corporation, have subscribed their names to these Articles this _____ day of _____, 19__.

[signatures of directors omitted]

STATE OF CALIFORNIA   )
)SS
COUNTY OF LOS ANGELES)

On this _____ day of _____, 19__, before me, the undersigned, a Notary Public in and for the County of Los Angeles, State of California, personally appeared (names of directors omitted), known to me to be the persons who executed the within and foregoing instrument, and each acknowledged to me that he executed the same.

WITNESS my hand and official seal.

_____
Notary Public in and for said
County and State

Figure 8-1. (*continued*)

legal documents requiring very careful wording, you will need the services of a knowledgeable lawyer.

Once your articles are filed with your state's Office of the Secretary of State, you will be required to submit copies, plus your bylaws (see Chapter 9), to the District Director of the Internal Revenue Service, the Franchise Tax Board (state income tax service in states where applicable), the State Board of Equalization's Division of Assessment Standards (property tax), and the Office of Administrative Services of the United States Post Office. Check with each office or its equivalent in your state to find out what forms should be submitted and what supporting documents are necessary.

Producing all of this paperwork is inconvenient and time-consuming, but it will immediately start to make and save you money.

From the time of your incorporation on, you must keep abreast of new laws pertaining to nonprofit educational and cultural organizations. It may be necessary to amend your articles periodically to continue your eligibility for the benefits cited above, or to receive new benefits.

RECRUITING CAST AND STAFF

There are two main problems in recruiting cast and staff—not getting enough people and not getting the quality of people that you want.

The tendency is to launch into production once you have a cast, hoping that you can pick up the support staff you need or that the cast members will be able to double in staff positions. Stifle this tendency. Keep repeating to yourself, "Many hands make light work!" Recruit.

Design on paper the production staff that you want, from producer and lighting technicians to curtain puller and box office attendants. Write out job descriptions as if you were about to go to a personnel agency and offer top dollars for each slot. Then set about recruiting with the same methodical, careful approach that huge corporations apply to recruiting their management trainees.

It is wrong to assume that because you are not offering salaries you must settle for less than the quantity and quality of personnel you want. What you cannot offer in salary you must make up for with motivation. If the persons who sweep the stage floor know that they are wanted and needed and that they are contributing to the overall success of the theater, they will stay. You have some important things they want—a sense of belonging and the enjoyment of making theater.

There is too much foot-dragging in recruiting adequate staff—too many negative attitudes: "We just can't get a capable costume designer." Yes you can. You can get the people you want if you will work as hard at recruiting as you expect the recruited to work.

I. Follow up on all names that are submitted as a result of your initial interest survey. The producer or production manager should interview everyone who expressed an interest in backstage work. If more than one person is qualified, ask one to accept an assistant's or committee position. Keep the names of others on file in case vacancies occur. Offer everyone general membership in the theater organization.

2. Ask the board of directors to do word-of-mouth recruiting for positions that are difficult to fill.

3. Also, use all media to advertise those hard-to-fill positions.

4. Go to high schools and colleges. Offer apprenticeship, experience, or summer programs to augment theater classes. Colleges are training many more students in theater than can possibly be absorbed by educational and professional theater (or movies and television). Forced into other occupations, these people welcome an opportunity to apply and develop what they've learned. Community theater can serve them both as training ground and as continuing avocation. But they've got to know that the opportunities are there. Don't go to the educational theater people only when you are strapped for an ingénue. Keep the high school and college theaters in your area constantly aware of the practical opportunities that you have available for their students.

Sometimes you may find teachers reluctant to have their students spend time on nonschool projects. In that case, make it clear that you want their students only during vacations, or upon graduation.

On the other hand, you might find that the school is eager to welcome you into a mutually sustaining relationship. (E.g., The college uses the community theater as a lab for its students. The community theater provides mature and experienced actors to the college when needed.)

5. Senior citizens and retired people should not be overlooked as a source of personnel. More than ever they need a feeling that they can make a meaningful contribution to community life. Transportation may be a problem. Pair senior citizens with younger drivers to insure that they can get to rehearsals, meetings, and performances.

6. Do not overburden those you recruit. Do not expect new members to assume more responsibility than they can handle comfortably. Explain that the theater's policy is to recruit as many people as necessary to make light work of all tasks.

7. Make clear what every task involves. The job descriptions that you wrote (see Chapter 9) should be explored with new members. They should know with whom they will be working and to whom they are responsible.

8. Finally, the people assigned to recruit for your group must be enthusiastic and able to convey a sense of fun. They must keep in their minds a vision of a smooth-running operation where every work call is a pleasant social event. They must like people. And they must communicate all of this when they say, "We'd like you to join us."

FINDING A STAGE

Community theaters exist in incredibly diverse surroundings. For example, imagine the T-shaped hallway of an abandoned railway station. The stage is at the intersection. The arms and foot of the T seat the audience on three sides of the stage. The audience must cross over the stage to get to the seats in the arms. The actors must enter through the audience to get to the stage.

Why the abandoned railway station? We can only assume that it was the most practical place the group could find. (Perhaps they also sought an unusual atmosphere for their theater.)

As you wrestle with practicality, here are some factors to consider:

1. If you have not existed as a functioning theater group for at least a few years, do not consider building your own theater or buying property. Longevity, stability of administration, and acceptance by the community should be well established before you take on the responsibility of property ownership.

2. Where is your audience? Using the addresses from your interest survey–registration forms, place a pin in a street map for every address. Now take a ring with a scaled radius of five to ten miles. Place the ring on the map, encompassing the greatest number of pins. Start looking for a home for your theater in the center of the ring. Proximity to potential audience is a very important factor!

If you are evaluating possible locations in a large metropolitan area, you might want to consult the *Census Tract Book*. (Call your local Commerce Department Field Office to determine where the book is available for study.) This reference will tell you by tracts (small areas of roughly homogeneous socioeconomic population) the educational and income levels of the occupants.

Try both methods and check one against the other.

3. Is the potential site served by public transportation? Is there ample parking? Audience accessibility is another key factor.

4. Is a stage-like facility available? If at all possible, new groups should affiliate with an organization that has a stage. Consider the YMCA, churches, public and private schools, city recreation facilities, and other publicly owned buildings. The disadvantage of using such buildings is a certain loss of freedom. The host organization may want to impose restrictions (e.g., time of use or type of play), but the advantages are great, especially the low operating costs necessary until your group is well established.

5. If you cannot affiliate, or if you are ready to move into your own building, the next step is finding adequate space. Whether you are renting or leasing a private residence, store front, or warehouse (or any other building that was not originally designed as a theater), it is important to set out your minimum space requirements:

Stage space:

Dressing rooms:

Wing and fly space:

Audience space:

Set construction space:

Set and prop storage space:

Costumes (construction and storage):

Box office:

Administrative space:

Rehearsal space:

Lobby space:

It is imperative that your board of directors establish minimums before entering into the always necessary compromises. Assume that you will not find exactly what you want. But up to what point are you willing to compromise? All too often construction, storage, administrative, and rehearsal spaces are sacrificed, to the eventual discomfort of the group.

Must you have the capacity for a proscenium stage, or will you consider working on an open, thrust, or arena stage (see Figure 8–2)? What

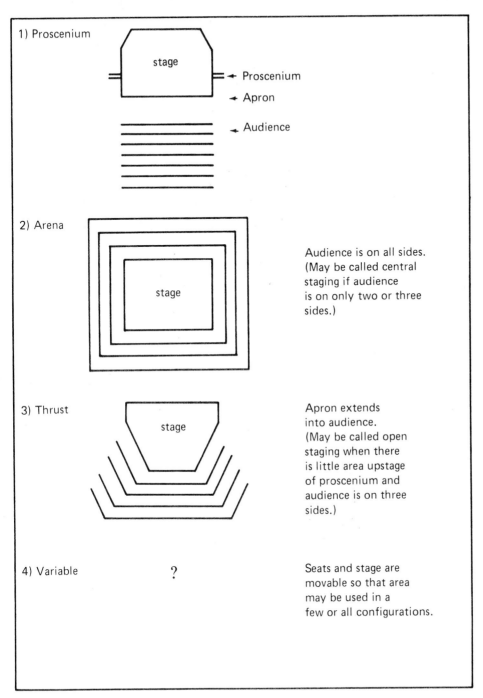

1) Proscenium

stage

← Proscenium

← Apron

← Audience

2) Arena

stage

Audience is on all sides.
(May be called central
staging if audience
is on only two or three
sides.)

3) Thrust

stage

Apron extends
into audience.
(May be called open
staging when there
is little area upstage
of proscenium and
audience is on three
sides.)

4) Variable   ?

Seats and stage are
movable so that area
may be used in a
few or all configurations.

Figure 8-2. Staging Possibilities.

minimums of audience comfort must you have in terms of distance between seats, aisle space, and access to lavatories?

Study local city ordinances covering places for public gathering in
order to meet "safety-to-life" requirements. Sometimes these ordinances
set minimums on aisle, lavatory, and parking space.

Armed with your minimums you are ready to start inspecting buildings
and consulting with realtors. Allow sufficient time. Do not let your anxiety
to start performing in a new home rush you into compromises that you will
later regret.

CHAPTER NINE

Constitution, Bylaws, Standing Rules, Standard Operating Procedures, Handbooks, and Agendas

In the beginning, your theater group was concerned with formulating goals and writing articles of incorporation. As you proceed, you will find it necessary and desirable to record exactly how you want to run your theater.

Written rules will help prevent your wasting time, energy, and money in the needless repetition of past mistakes. They will pass on to new members the collected wisdom of past members. They will remind old members of procedures they may have forgotten.

CONSTITUTION AND BYLAWS

The most formal rules will be written as your constitution and/or bylaws. I use the terms interchangeably, but some community theaters make a distinction: *constitution* refers to the first few articles, which define the name, goals, membership, and leadership; *bylaws* refers to the articles concerning committees and dues (matters of lesser importance). A further distinction exists in the way the rules can be changed—an amendment to an article of the constitution might require a two-thirds vote of the membership, while an amendment to a bylaw might require only a majority vote of the membership or a two-thirds vote of the board of directors.

If all your rules (articles) are equally important and can be amended by the same procedure, then all may be referred to as bylaws.

The bylaws should set out clearly and simply the basic procedures for your theater. Don't chisel them in stone. They are meant to be a guide, not a jail. Include an article that provides for change, or amendment, of the other articles. It is to be hoped that your bylaws will change and grow as they reflect the development of your group.

Periodically a committee should be appointed to review the articles and recommend changes. This committee might be chaired by the vice president, sergeant-at-arms, or parliamentarian. The experience would encourage that individual's familiarity with the bylaws and prepare him or her for other leadership posts with the group.

If the bylaws are to be a working instrument, they must be available to the membership. Copies should be included in a handbook issued to all new members. The members of the board of directors should have copies of the bylaws before them during board meetings. A copy should be kept on the dais during general meetings.

The bylaws that are presented here are those of the Kentwood Players, a Los Angeles area community theater. The Kentwood Players have 200 members and 750 subscribers. They present six plays annually in their 119-seat proscenium theater. Their bylaws, which have evolved over a period of 27 years, are reviewed periodically and amended as necessary.

As will be seen, some repetition is unavoidable.

Only your membership can best determine what bylaws are right for you. Depending on your size, location, purpose, and many other factors, you might need quite different specifics.

If, after studying the Kentwood Players bylaws, you feel that you would like another model, you may write to the American Theatre Association, 1317 F Street, N.W., Washington, D.C. 20004, (202) 737–5606, for their recommended bylaws.

In *Community Theatre Handbook,* by William J. Rappel and John R. Winnie (Institute of Public Affairs, State University of Iowa, 1961), there are three models of bylaws for small, medium, and large community theaters. The book is available in libraries.

KENTWOOD PLAYERS, INC.

BYLAWS

ARTICLE I—NAME

The name of this organization shall be KENTWOOD PLAYERS, INC., hereinafter referred to as Kentwood Players.

ARTICLE II—OBJECTIVES

The objectives of this organization shall be:

Sec. A.   To promote community interest in theater.

Sec. B.   To provide opportunity for members to participate in various phases of community theater work.

ARTICLE III—MEMBERSHIP

Sec. A.   Membership shall be open to adults of eighteen years or over who are willing to subscribe to the objectives and abide by the rules of this organization.

Sec. B. An applicant will become a *Probationary Member* upon payment of his first year's dues to the Membership Chairman.

Sec. C. A *Probationary Member* will become an *Active Member* upon timely payment of his dues for the second consecutive year and providing he has participated in at least one production during his year as *Probationary Member*. The Membership Chairman shall be responsible for determining participation of a Probationary Member.

Sec. D. A member shall not act as a representative of Kentwood Players without the sanction of the Board of Directors.

Sec. E. Probationary Members may not vote at regular or special membership meetings.

Sec. F. A Junior Membership may be awarded, by a two-thirds vote of the total Board of Directors, to any individual under the age of 18 who has contributed his time, efforts and talents in a manner that is deserving of recognition. This membership shall be for one year and will entitle said individual to enjoy all the privileges of membership except voting and holding office.

ARTICLE IV—DUES

Sec. A. Membership dues for probationary members are equivalent to that of a season subscriber, with individual memberships only. A Probationary Member will be eligible to become an Active Member if he has participated in at least one production during the first year. Active Membership dues shall be $10.00 single and $15.00 married couple.

Sec. B. Membership is good for one year from date of joining and dues are not refundable unless, as a cast member, a new member is replaced within the 2-week probationary period.

Sec. C. Each membership card entitles its owner to one performance of each play without charge during the membership year. The membership card is not transferable.

Sec. D.   A member becomes delinquent and loses membership privileges if dues are not paid within thirty days of due date.

Sec. E.   On payment of delinquent dues, within three months of due date, the membership card shall be dated from the due date. After membership has lapsed, upon application, the member may rejoin as a Probationary Member.

ARTICLE V—OFFICERS

Sec. A.   President

1.   Shall be Chairman of the Board of Directors.
2.   Shall preside at all meetings of the organization.
3.   Shall approve and sign all checks drawn by the Treasurer.
4.   Shall appoint all chairmen and committee members as prescribed by the Bylaws and Standing Rules and such others as may be needed.
5.   May serve as a member ex-officio at meetings of all committees except the Nominating Committee.

Sec. B.   Vice President

1.   Shall serve as Plays Committee Chairman.
2.   Shall preside at all meetings in the absence of the President.

Sec. C.   Secretary

1.   Shall keep minutes of all meetings.
2.   Shall conduct all correspondence as directed by the Board of Directors and the President.
3.   Shall maintain a file of all correspondence and records of Kentwood Players.
4.   Shall be responsible for the corporate seal of Kentwood Players.
5.   Shall notify Board members of Board meetings one week in advance of such meetings.
6.   Shall be responsible for notifying the general membership of any change of regular meeting date.
7.   Shall record attendance at Board meetings.

8. Shall notify the Board of the third absence from a Board meeting of a Board member on the occasion of that absence.
9. Shall keep a permanent and separate record of all additions and/or changes to the Bylaws and Standing Rules.

Sec. D.   Treasurer

1. Shall maintain all financial records and funds of Kentwood Players.
2. Shall issue and sign all approved checks in conjunction with the President.
3. Shall give a financial report at all Board and membership meetings.
4. Shall make financial records and audits available to the general membership.
5. Shall prepare all financial records for the annual audit at the end of the fiscal year.
6. Shall accept all monies from and issue receipts to authorized chairmen only.
7. Shall honor only those bills which are duly authorized.
8. May not serve as box office chairman.

ARTICLE VI—BOARD OF DIRECTORS

Sec. A.   The Board of Directors, hereinafter referred to as the Board, shall consist of eleven elected Active Members, in addition to the President, Vice President, Secretary and Treasurer.

Sec. B.   Management of the organization shall be vested in the Board.

Sec. C.   The Board must uphold any motion approved by the general Active Membership.

Sec. D.   In the event a Board member is absent from three regularly scheduled Board meetings, such member may be removed from the Board by a two-thirds majority of the votes cast by the Board without previous notice and the Board shall immediately nominate and elect by plurality vote a replacement.

ARTICLE VII—NOMINATING COMMITTEE

Sec. A.   The Board shall elect a Nominating Committee of five Active Members to nominate candidates for elective offices and the Board. This committee shall be limited to no more than two Board members.

Sec. B.   Consent must be obtained from candidates prior to nomination.

Sec. C.   Members of the Nominating Committee are not barred from nomination for office.

Sec. D.   The members of the Nominating Committee shall be announced at the March regular meeting.

ARTICLE VIII—ELECTIONS

Sec. A.   Nominations shall be made at the April regular meeting by the Nominating Committee and the Active General Membership.
1.   Only active members in good standing may nominate or be nominated.
2.   Consent must be obtained from all nominees prior to nominations.

Sec. B.   Additional nominations may be made and elections shall be held at the annual meeting in May.

Sec. C.   Only Active Members in good standing are eligible to vote.

Sec. D.   All officers and members of the Board shall be elected for a term of one year beginning June 1st, or until their replacements are elected.
1.   The general active membership shall elect the President, Vice President, Secretary and Treasurer.
2.   An officer may not be elected to the same office for more than two consecutive years.
3.   The general active membership shall elect additional members to complement the fifteen-member Board.
4.   The retiring officers may automatically remain on the Board for an additional year.
5.   Nominees not elected to office shall be placed on the ballot for the Board.

Sec. E. The membership chairman shall serve as chairman of the Election Committee. The President shall appoint two members in addition. Proxy votes and absentee ballots shall not be recognized. Election Committee shall be responsible for preparation of ballots, maintaining a list of eligible voters, distribution and counting of ballots. Results of balloting must be given directly to the Chair who will announce the election results.

Sec. F. There shall be two ballots: first for the election of officers and second for the election of Board members.

Sec. G. A majority of the votes cast is required to elect officers. A plurality vote is sufficient to elect Board members.

ARTICLE IX—MEETINGS

Sec. A. The May regular meeting shall be considered the annual meeting.

Sec. B. Regular meetings shall be scheduled monthly on the third Wednesday unless otherwise ordered by the Board.
1. Those Active Members present shall constitute a quorum.
2. All members shall receive 48 hours advance notice of any change in date of meetings.
3. Regular meetings shall be open to the general public unless restricted by the President.

Sec. C. Board Meetings shall be scheduled monthly on the first Wednesday unless otherwise ordered by the Board.
1. Nine Board members shall constitute a quorum.
2. All Board meetings shall be open to the general membership.
3. A special Board meeting may be called by the President, Vice President or any three Board members.

ARTICLE X—CASTING

Sec. A. A cast member must become a paid-up member of Kentwood Players within two weeks after being cast unless excused by the President.

Sec. B. A director cannot cast himself in a leading role.

Sec. C.   All casting shall be open.

ARTICLE XI—REMOVAL AND REPLACEMENT

Procedures for this will be according to Roberts Rules Revised.

ARTICLE XII—ADVANCE NOTICE

Personal or telephone contact 48 hours in advance or a Los Angeles County postmark dated three days, not including Sunday, in advance, shall constitute 48 hours advance notice.

ARTICLE XIII—ANNUAL AUDIT

The Board of Directors shall arrange for an annual audit of the organization's financial accounts by a Certified Public Accountant at the end of the fiscal year. The fiscal year of Kentwood Players shall be from June 1st through May 31st.

ARTICLE XIV—PARLIAMENTARY AUTHORITY

All matters of procedure shall be according to Roberts Rules of Order Revised as interpreted and ruled upon by the President.

ARTICLE XV—AMENDMENTS

Amendments to these Bylaws may be made by the Active Membership by a two-thirds majority of the votes cast at a regular meeting, providing that all members have been notified in writing of such proposed amendments at least 48 hours in advance.

ARTICLE XVI—STANDING RULES

The Active Membership may adopt Standing Rules to govern the operation of the organization, provided they are not contrary to the Bylaws, at any regular meeting by a majority of the votes cast. These rules will stand until amended or rescinded by the Active Membership at a regular meeting by a two-thirds majority of the votes cast or, with 48 hours notice, a majority of the votes cast. Any Standing Rules may be suspended for a specific period of time by the Active Membership by a majority vote without notice at a regular meeting.

STANDING RULES AND
STANDARD OPERATING PROCEDURES

Procedures to be used by members, committees, committee chairpersons, and officers should also be written out in less rigid form than bylaws. These procedures may take the form of standing rules or standard operating procedures. Again, the examples presented here are those of the Kentwood Players, which may or may not be applicable to your theater. If you do not already have your procedures written out, the following may serve as a model. If you do, comparison may trigger some possible changes.

KENTWOOD PLAYERS, INC.

STANDING RULES

1. DUTIES OF CHAIRMEN

    A. Publicity
    B. House Manager
    C. Membership
    D. Mailing List
    E. Special Relations
    F. Season Tickets
    G. Workshop
    H. Production Manager
    I. Producer
    J. Bulletin
    K. Box Office and General Information
    L. Hospitality
    M. Programs
    N. Plays Committee
    O. Miscellaneous
        1. Duties of a Director

    2. Casting

    3. Cast Photographer

    4. Hospitality for Membership Meetings

    5. Scheduling Chairman

    6. Awards Chairman

2. ANNUAL MASQUE AWARDS

3. PRESIDENT'S INTRODUCTION AT READINGS

1. DUTIES OF CHAIRMEN

Sec. A. The Publicity Chairman Shall:

1. Write and release all publicity for Kentwood Players to be presented to the general public.
2. Arrange for publicity pictures for newspapers for each production.
3. Invite reviewers to each play.
4. Serve as liaison with answering service for all authorized complimentary tickets.
5. Coordinate all promotional activities.
6. Have complete and sole responsibility for the Bulletin Boards.
7. Be responsible for coming attraction board in theater lobby.

Sec. B. The House Manager Shall:

1. Maintain and repair the theater building and provide janitorial service.
2. Change marquee for each production.
3. Maintain keys and locks to theater.
4. Open and close the theater for general meetings, castings and other official business meetings.
5. Maintain coke machine operation.
6. Obtain supplies, e.g. coffee cups, stirrers, paper towels, soap, toilet paper, etc.

Sec. C. The Membership Chairman Shall:

1. Collect dues from members.
2. Maintain current membership list. This list should be revised at least twice each year and issued to members.
3. Keep President, Mailing Chairman, Bulletin Chairman, Awards Chairman and Box Office Chairman aware of additions and changes to membership list on a monthly basis.
4. Issue membership cards.
5. Issue copy of Bylaws, Standing Rules, Membership Roster and other pertinent data to new members.
6. Have casting applications and membership forms available for each casting.
7. Notify director 10 days subsequent to casting of intention to remove cast member because of nonpayment of dues as prescribed by casting rules.

Sec. D. Mailing List Chairman Shall:

1. Maintain a list of patrons.
2. Provide a guest book in lobby for patrons' names and addresses to be added to list.
3. Mail postcards for each production so that they will be received two weeks prior to opening of a production.
4. Distribute postcards to cast members.
5. Send a double postcard once every two years to bring list up-to-date.

Sec. E. Special Relations Chairman Shall:

1. Maintain a list of all potential sell-out organizations.
2. Contact organizations for theater parties throughout the year.
3. Order and distribute tickets.
4. Post schedule of sell-outs for each production.
5. Collect all sell-out monies.

Sec. F. Season Ticket Chairman Shall:

1. Notify season ticket holders of renewal date.
2. Order, mail and collect for season tickets.

3. Conduct at least 2 mailing list campaigns for sale of tickets.
4. Maintain card file of ticket holders.

Sec. G. Workshop Chairman Shall:

1. Be responsible for a workshop for each General Meeting.

Sec. H. The Production Manager Shall:

1. Make each producer aware of his responsibilities.
2. Establish budget for each show together with Director and Producer.
3. Protect and conserve all permanent properties, e.g. sound and inter-com system, lighting, etc.
4. Supervise scene dock, flat shed, light booth and equipment.
5. Be responsible for conformance with fire and safety ordinances.
6. Present to the Board a complete budget by producer no later than the board meeting prior to the Work Sunday for said show. Any additional money needed will have to be approved by the Board. No money will be advanced until Board approves budget.
7. Be responsible for making necessary arrangements for providing food at the first Work Sunday of each production (cost excluded from production budget).
8. Be responsible for lending and returning of costumes, properties, etc., after first obtaining approval of House Manager and President. The Board shall be apprised of any such loan at the board meeting following such loan.

Sec. I. The Producer Shall:

1. Coordinate with the Director for design and construction of set.
2. With approval of Director, obtain workers for the following:
   a. Set Designer
   b. Prop Master
   c. Stage Manager
   d. Lights and Sound
   e. Any others necessary for efficient staging of production
3. Disburse all funds required for production. Keep receipts and records for all disbursements which shall be turned over to the Production Manager by the second week of performance.

4. Be responsible for opening and closing of theater during rehearsals and performance.

5. Be entitled to issue up to ten complimentary tickets for production services and arrange for reservations through the Publicity Chairman.

6. Collect funds from cast for lobby portraits.

Sec. J. The Bulletin Chairman Shall:

1. Prepare and mail a monthly bulletin to the General Membership. Bulletin to be received no later than the Monday prior to Membership meeting unless readings occur on that Monday, in which case the bulletin to be received no later than the Friday prior to meeting.

Sec. K. The Box Office and General Information Chairman Shall:

1. Appoint and be responsible for:
    a. Box office chairman for each production whose duties shall be to:
        1) Man box office.
        2) Arrange for reservations with answering service.
        3) Pick up reservations chart for each performance.
        4) Make up ticket board.
        5) Maintain a record of all Kentwood Players attending each production and give list to Awards Chairman.
        6) Deposit box office receipts and report same to the Treasurer.

2. Furnish general information to members and public.

Sec. L. The Hospitality Chairman (for the Year) Shall:

1. Purchase necessary coffee-making supplies for each production.

2. Provide a hospitality chairman for each production who shall:
    a. Provide a head usher who will stay throughout each performance and be responsible for covering the front of the house.
    b. Provide 2 or preferably 3 ushers for each performance who shall also prepare and serve coffee at intermission and clean up afterward.

Sec. M. The Program Chairman Shall:

1. Make up and have printed a program for each play.
2. Be responsible for advertising in program and collect monies for these ads.
3. Be responsible for reviewing printer's proofs with director and producer prior to printing.

Sec. N. Plays Committee Chairman Shall:

1. Preside over the Plays Committee in their preparation and selection of a season calendar, directors, plays and time slots.

    a. Composition of Plays Committee:

    The Plays Committee shall be composed of a Chairman and two additional members. The Vice President (see Bylaws, Article V, Section B) automatically serves as Plays Committee Chairman. The two committee members shall not be members of the Board, but shall be members of Kentwood Players in good standing. The two Plays Committee members shall be elected by the Board at the first Board Meeting in June. If a vacancy occurs on the Plays Committee, the Board shall elect a replacement. If the Plays Committee Chairman is required to assume the duties of President permanently the Board shall elect a replacement for Plays Committee Chairman at their discretion. A Director serving on the Plays Committee may not direct a play that has been selected during his term of office.

    b. Duties—Choosing Plays

    1) The Plays Committee shall choose a season of six plays, starting with the March/April slot, and directors, together with a complete calendar of playing dates. In addition, they shall choose any Tournament Play, Special or other public performance staged under the auspices of Kentwood Players.
    2) Plays Committee Chairman shall secure releases, pay royalties, purchase scripts and in general serve as K.P. liaison with play publishers, directors and Board.
    3) Chairman shall submit each play, director and time slot selection to the Board for approval. At least 5 days prior to

said submission, he shall notify each Board member of the Plays Committee selection.

   c.   Duties—Choosing a Director

      1) No later than the second regular Board meeting the Plays Committee shall submit to the Board, for approval, a list of all directors eligible for the season. Said directors shall be members of Kentwood Players in good standing, with demonstrated ability as directors. The Plays Committee may add directors to said list with the prior approval of the Board.

      2) A guest director shall be considered to be any qualified director not a member of Kentwood Players.

Sec. O. Miscellaneous

1. *Director* must submit a rehearsal schedule to the Scheduling Chairman after casting.
2. *Casting.*
   a. All castings are open to the public.
   b. An actor must read in order to be cast.
   c. There shall be a two-week probationary period during which a director may replace any cast member or any cast member may resign without prejudice.
   d. A Director's choice of cast from among those eligible shall be final. Any dispute as to eligibility shall be decided by the Board.
3. *Cast Photographer* shall take pictures of members of the cast, director and producer, and be responsible for displaying them in the lobby with appropriate name tags prior to the opening of a production. He shall be reimbursed directly from the Treasurer for expenses. He shall be appointed by the Publicity Chairman.
4. *Hospitality (for General Membership Meetings).* This is done on a volunteer basis. Hospitality is authorized to spend up to $5.00 at the expense of Kentwood Players for refreshments.
5. *Scheduling Chairman* is responsible for maintaining an appointment calendar for theater usage. Shall also resolve all usage conflicts. Is appointed by President for each year.

6. *Awards Chairman* shall:
   a. Print ballots and mail to members who have attended all 6 productions.
   b. Receive and keep all returned ballots unopened until end of awards season.
   c. Tally ballots. Purchase trophies and have names of winners inscribed on same.
   d. Maintain secrecy and retain all ballots until Board of Directors votes to destroy them.
   e. Arrange for previous year's winners to present awards.
   f. Preside over annual Masque Awards distribution.
   g. The President shall appoint an Awards Chairman for the next season. In the event the Awards Chairman becomes eligible for an award, the President shall appoint a replacement.

2. ANNUAL MASQUE AWARDS

Kentwood Players shall present Annual Masque Awards for outstanding achievement as follows:

Sec. A. Categories

1. Best performance by an actor in a leading role.
2. Best performance by an actress in a leading role.
3. Best performance by an actor in a supporting role.
4. Best performance by an actress in a supporting role.
5. Best performance by an actor in a minor role.
6. Best performance by an actress in a minor role.
7. Best director.
8. Best producer.
9. Best play.
10. Special Board Award (optional).

Sec. B. Eligibility

1. Plays. To be eligible for awards, a play must have closed before April 30th.

2. Members. Only paid-up members (at time of closing night performance) shall be eligible to receive an award.
3. Category definition. Plays Committee shall coordinate with the director to establish categories. These categories shall be presented by the Plays Committee to Board for approval at a Board meeting before casting of play.

Sec. C.   Masque Awards Balloting Rules

1. Awards Chairman shall check with the box office to determine members who have seen each production and mail ballots to eligible members.
2. There will be a single ballot at the end of the year.
3. Ballots shall be opened and counted by Awards Chairman and two other members who are appointed by the President and approved by the Board of Directors at the April Board meeting.
4. Ties shall receive duplicate awards.
5. You must see all 6 shows to vote.
6. You must be a member of Kentwood Players for all 6 shows being voted upon.
7. The ballots will be listed in the order of the shows and the order of the categories.
8. The final ballot, before it is sent out to the members, must be approved by the Board.
9. The ballots will be signed personally by the Ballots Committee Chairman before they are mailed to the individuals eligible to vote.
10. Special Board Award must be approved by 12 of 15 Board Members.

3. PRESIDENT'S INTRODUCTION AT READINGS

The President, or his designee, will make the following announcements at all readings for play castings for the purpose of stating Kentwood Players' requirements for all cast members:

1. Welcome to open readings.
   Monthly meeting—third Wednesday of each month at the theater.
   Nonprofit community theater.

2. If cast, an actor must:
   a. Join within two weeks. Dues of Probationary Member.
   b. Furnish basic makeup.
   c. Furnish contemporary clothes.
   d. Use Kentwood photographer photo for lobby display—cost $6.50.
   e. Participate in all Work Sundays for set construction.

3. Period costumes will be furnished by Kentwood Players.

4. There is a two-week probation period after the first rehearsal during which time an actor may withdraw from the cast or be terminated by the Director without prejudice.

5. Probationary Members are entitled to attend one full season's plays from date of membership. Membership is not transferable.

6. Probationary Members are eligible to vote for and receive the annual "Masque Award" trophies.

7. Complimentary tickets are not given to cast members for their relatives, friends or agents.

8. Unless specifically announced, scheduled shows which fall on holidays *WILL* be performed.

9. Wednesday Sell Out performances are allowable provided the cast, crew and director are agreeable.

10. No publicity to be released except by Publicity Chairman. NO PRIVATE RELEASES.

11. The signature on a casting application form constitutes acceptance of these requirements.

12. ANY QUESTIONS.

13. Introduce the Director.

14. Remind the Director to announce: Show dates and rehearsal schedule.

STANDARD OPERATING PROCEDURES

Get Acquainted

Kentwood Players built its reputation on being essentially friendly, well organized and businesslike, with polished productions. So many new members enthusiastically volunteer for this or that and then wait at home for the phone to ring. Usually it just doesn't happen. Members become known, recognized and accepted by BEING at the theater when things need doing (or even when they don't). It is incumbent upon the new member to come to the theater. The joy and pleasure one receives from Kentwood Players is in direct proportion to how much one gives to Kentwood Players.

The theater is in continual use and as such offers members (especially new ones) the opportunity of dropping by to observe, learn, become known, relax and enjoy themselves. Members should remember that it is their theater—to be used as a "home" away from home.

Some of the most valuable Kentwood Players members are nonactors who enjoy the "technical" side of a production. "Do-it-yourself" fixers will find ample opportunity to use their skills in set design, carpentry, painting, decorating, script, costume design, makeup, hair styling, sound and lighting effects, stage crew, hospitality, etc. . . . the non-acting spouse of an actor or actress need not feel left out. And there are always those parties to enjoy.

Board of Directors

Responsibility for managing the organization and insuring its orderly progress rests with the Board, which is elected each year. With few exceptions, such as changes to the Bylaws, Board action need not be ratified by the membership. However, any Board action may be subject to review by the membership and may be rescinded by a simple majority vote. Board meetings are on the first Wednesday of each month and are open to the membership with prior notice to the President and meeting host. The Board consists of a President, Vice President, Secretary, Treasurer, and eleven members who chair the following functions:

Box Office and Liaison:	Handles reservations and box office for Friday and Saturday night public performances. Also acts as liaison to the public and membership for any information concerning K.P. in general.
Bulletin:	Handles preparation, printing and mailing of the monthly membership newsletter which includes all local news of upcoming activities, such as members performing at other theaters. Anything deemed

newsworthy by a member may be given to this chairman for publication. Bulletins should be received immediately prior to monthly membership meetings.

House Manager: Handles all functions pertaining to building, facilities, including janitor service, coffee cup and janitorial supplies, coke machine, marquee posting, building keys and maintenance.

Mailing: Handles preparation, printing and mailing of postcards to announce each upcoming play and casting. Maintains guest sign-in book in the lobby for mailing list. Also maintains "addressograph" system of members and mailing list names.

Membership: Handles new membership applications, dues, cards and issues an up-to-date membership roster twice each year. Acts as "greeter" at each of the monthly membership meetings.

Plays: Handles preparation of the season calendar of play dates and presentation to the Board for approval of each play, director and time slot for the season. The Vice President is automatically Plays Committee Chairman. There are two other non-Board members of the Plays Committee.

Production Manager: Guides and assists individual producers for each show. Advises on all production activities of budget, set design, construction and other technical operations.

Programs: Handles preparation and printing of programs for each play. Coordinates program ads, special credits and cast and crew profiles. (*NOTE:* In the biographical data for each actor, no past professional acting credits are allowed to avoid any professional actor's union involvement.)

Publicity: Handles all publicity releases for radio, TV, newspapers, etc. Coordinates and arranges for reviewers. Makes publicity releases for castings,

	show openings and other newsworthy items. No member is authorized to make individual publicity releases of any kind except as approved by the publicity chairman.
Season Tickets:	Handles all mailing, flyers, etc., pertinent to the sale of season tickets to patrons desiring to see all six plays of the year at a special reduced rate.
Special Relations:	Handles Thursday and Sunday night sell-outs to private clubs, organizations, parties, etc. Half-house (50 seats), whole-house (100 seats), and whole-house with complete privacy (119 seats) are available. Sell-out house prices are discounted. Groups may wish to make money for themselves by selling tickets to their members at a higher price. A full season of 6 shows may also be obtained. Periodically throughout the year, "flyers" are sent out to clubs and organizations announcing the current season of plays.
Workshops:	Handles coordination and scheduling of all workshop productions for each monthly meeting.

Membership Meetings

Membership meetings are always held at the theater on the third Wednesday of each month at 8:30 P.M. Pertinent business, including reports by the various Board members and committee chairmen, is followed by a coffee break and the workshop presentation. Members are encouraged to bring guests, and all guests are introduced to the membership by the membership chairman. Hospitality for the monthly membership meetings (not to be confused with hospitality for the run of a play) consists of providing and serving coffee and cookies. Hospitality volunteers are solicited by the President at each meeting and may be reimbursed, up to $5.00, for out-of-pocket expenses if so desired.

Workshop

A workshop is the presentation, by members, of an act, scene, or cutting from a play done with minimum set and props. Workshops are presented at each monthly membership meeting and are for the prime benefit of the members and their guests.

Workshops are good vehicles for new members who want to learn and/or improve their acting or directing craft. Workshops also provide an excellent opportunity to be seen onstage as a reference for casting of major productions. Anyone interested in either acting or directing should contact the Workshop Chairman.

Kentwood Players Non-profit, Nonprofessional Status

Kentwood Players, Inc., is recognized by the State of California and the Internal Revenue Service as a non-profit organization. As such, Kentwood Players is tax-exempt. All monies received by Kentwood Players from any source are "ploughed" back into the business to pay for utilities, mortgage, royalties, production costs, expansion and maintenance, etc. No member receives any salary, payment or fee for any service or activity. All participation is voluntary.

Individual members may declare their K.P. membership as a tax deduction.

Also, any item donated by members to the theater, as confirmed by a written receipt from the Secretary on K.P. letterhead, may also be itemized as a deduction. Kentwood Players is also a nonprofessional community theater. Nonprofessional means that Kentwood Players' policy precludes casting actors who are members of a professional acting union such as Screen Actors Guild (SAG) or Actors Equity. Since K.P. pays no actors, while professional acting unions require that their members be paid, the obvious conflict of interest precludes any accommodation or compromise.

Open Casting Policy

K.P. has an "open casting" policy, which means that anyone may read for a part with the stipulation that, if cast, the person becomes a K.P. member within two weeks. Public notices which announce casting are released through the publicity chairman. Casting for a new show usually occurs on the Monday and Tuesday following the opening of the current show at 8:00 P.M. All are welcome to read or observe. All casting decisions rest upon the director. After casting, there is a two-week probationary period during which an actor may resign or be replaced without prejudice.

Rehearsal

Rehearsals are usually "open," which means that a member may come to the theater and observe. This privilege, however, carries the responsibility of observing in silence. If a conversation is desired, move to the lobby and close the auditorium doors. Occasionally the director may desire to have "closed" rehearsals, which means only those people directly involved in a show are allowed admittance into the auditorium. "Closed" rehearsal notices are usually posted on the front door and all members are obligated to respect the sign.

Work Sundays

The Sunday following the Saturday close of a show is called the "Work Sunday" at which time the new play's cast and crew are responsible for striking the old set and building the new one. ALL cast and crew members share equally the responsibility for set construction, painting, decorating, dressing, etc., until the set is completed, even if more than one Work Sunday is required.

New members should volunteer their time on "Work Sundays" as a means of getting acquainted. This is the one area where help is needed the most. DON'T wait to be called—just come to the theater in work clothes and be ready to help.

Kentwood Players provides a free lunch for all those who participate in the first "Work Sunday." If subsequent Work Sundays are necessary, bring your own lunch.

Cast Portraits—Lobby Display

A condition of being cast in a play includes having a large color photo portrait taken by the Kentwood Players' official photographer. This includes actors, directors and producers. The cost is $6.50 per person, payable in advance. Several proofs are taken and final selection rests with the individual. At the close of the show, pictures are retained by the individual and may be used again in subsequent shows.

Presentations to Directors

It is customary to present to the director at the close of each play, usually at the cast party, a plaque or memento from the cast and crew who each contribute one or two dollars for its purchase. Presentation of this award is decided by the cast and crew.

Cast Parties

It is customary, traditional and just a very good idea to have a cast party on the closing Saturday night of each show. They are held in a private home or at the theater. All party decisions are made by the cast and crew, such as food, location, etc. "Closed" cast parties are for cast and crew only (spouses included). "Open" cast parties mean anyone can come if he notifies the food committee in advance. All parties are B.Y.O.B. Mix and food usually runs $1.00 to $2.00 per person.

During the run of a show, individual cast and crew members usually have parties at their homes or bring cake and cookies to the theater. This makes for a most enjoyable association. Anybody not in the cast or crew who helps—such as set construction, hospitality, etc.—is welcome to attend the closing night cast party. Informality is "the order of the day . . . or night." Board members are automatically included.

Hospitality

Hospitality is one of the easiest jobs to do and yet the best way for new members to get to know the group and vice versa. It consists of handing out programs and ushering patrons to their reserved seats. It also includes making coffee, serving it during the first intermission, and clean up.

The Hospitality Chairman for the year (appointed by the President) appoints a chairman for each play. At the monthly membership meeting prior to a show opening, the Hospitality Chairman for that play prepares and routes a sign-up sheet which lists all performance dates and curtain times. Members are invited to sign up for at least one night of hospitality. At least 3 people are required for each performance.

Hospitality staff should be well groomed to meet the public and arrive at least 3/4 of an hour before curtain time. Their duties include:

1. Visual inspection of auditorium, lobby and bathrooms for neatness, etc.

2. Prepare coffee.

3. Keep auditorium doors closed until 20 minutes prior to curtain time.

4. Check with stage manager prior to opening auditorium for seating of patrons.

5. Hand out programs (one each) and seat patrons in appropriate seats (tearing tickets in half is unnecessary) and return tickets to patrons.

6. Begin pouring coffee 3–5 minutes prior to intermission. Serve in cups (coffee, sugar and cream is provided by Hospitality Chairman of each play).

7. After the intermission, "police up" empty cups, coke bottles and clean coffee pot in upstairs sink.

8. If a last-minute conflict precludes your being able to fulfill your obligation, please obtain your own replacement from the membership roster.

Complimentary Tickets

Kentwood Players' policy provides complimentary tickets to the press for reviewers. The Publicity Chairman is solely authorized to handle press reviews. Also, the producer of each show is authorized up to ten comps for services rendered—such as the loan of special or hard-to-find props by non-members. Use of comp tickets by the cast and crew of a show for friends, relatives, agents, etc., is *not* authorized . . . so please don't ask.

Season Tickets

Anyone wishing to affiliate with Kentwood Players for the sole purpose of attending a full season of plays should become a season ticket holder. As such, there are no obligations to become involved in theater work activities. However, anyone desiring to be active in the theater should join as a member. (See Bylaws for specific requirements.)

Dinner Dance and Masque Awards

At the end of each play season (June through May), a dinner dance is held. At this time the Masque Awards (K.P.'s answer to the movie Oscars) are presented in the various categories. Each member is eligible to vote if he has seen all the plays in the season. Attendance is verified by each member "signing in" at the box office when obtaining his ticket. At the end of the play season, each eligible member receives one ballot which lists all contestants in each category (best lead actor and actress, supporting actor and actress, minor actor and actress, director, producer and play). The dinner dance is the social highlight of the year and all are encouraged to attend.

Ticket Reservations

Phone 645–5156, the number of a 24-hour (medical) answering service, for ticket reservations. Reservations for members and patrons alike may be sold, unless already paid for, if not picked up at 8:15 P.M. the night of the performance, at the box office. The reservation list is usually picked up at the answering service at 5:00

P.M. on the performance date. For last-minute reservations or cancellations, call the answering service or the box office chairman who controls the box office.

Please help by always cancelling reservations as early as possible to help expedite seating of patrons on the "stand-by" list. The best time to make a reservation is in the afternoon or late evening.

Car Parking

Members should park in the garage area underneath the green room, adjacent to the theater, on both sides of the driveway, or on the street. Due to fire regulations, do NOT block the driveway at any time. The last person to leave the theater should always lock the front driveway gate. The key is located in the lobby on top of the main electrical "J" box panel.

Membership

K.P. membership is open to all who are interested in community theater. Members are entitled to see all plays free for one year from date of joining and to participate in all other K.P. activities. Membership cards are NOT transferable to another for use. First-year members are probationary and as such may not hold office, vote at elections, make motions or vote at the monthly business meetings. Upon renewal, second-year members are fully vested to the above privileges. (See K.P. Bylaws for complete description of probationary and active members.)

HANDBOOKS

In some cases you may want to write out even more specific instructions for the positions in your theater's chain of command. This is particularly so if the position is one held by many members for short periods of time. Then a handbook with checklists and references becomes very desirable.

The Kentwood Players' "Producer's Handbook" is used as an example here. Note that in the Kentwood chain of command, the production manager is a member of the Board of Directors and serves for one year. He obtains a producer for each play that is mounted. In other theaters the producer's duties explained in this handbook might be carried out by the production manager, stage manager, both, or others.

KENTWOOD PLAYERS

PRODUCER'S HANDBOOK

I

The Producer is one of the most indispensable persons involved in the show. The success or failure of a show is, in no small part, due to the efforts of this individual.

The Producer is responsible for many aspects of the production. Responsibility for certain items, such as design of sets, costumes, lighting, etc., is established by the director and ratified by the producer to insure a proper balance between artistic intent and practical accomplishment. Unresolved differences will be arbitrated by the Production Manager or they will be referred to the Board of Directors for resolution.

Many of the Producer's tasks can be delegated to others. There are certain tasks, however, which *should not* be delegated by the Producer, as follows:

1. Preparation of the production budget

2. Maintenance of an auditable record of all income and expenses—including receipts for purchases

3. Preparation of the Production Budget Closing Audit Report within one week of the show closing

Although the Producer may delegate authority to others for accomplishing tasks, final responsibility always rests with the Producer. The Producer may withdraw delegated authority if tasks are not properly accomplished. If the Producer encounters any problems not covered by this handbook, he should consult the Production Manager, the member of the Board of Directors who is responsible for

---

Courtesy of the Kentwood Players.

the smooth operation of all shows. The Production Manager is a liaison with the Producer to resolve any problems, offer ideas, and maintain the integrity of the stage and related areas for each succeeding show.

Planning by the Producer—including obtaining a supporting crew—leaves him free to attend to his primary functions of supervision, coordination, and financial administration.

II   GENERAL INFORMATION

When obtaining a supporting crew, sometimes a non-member becomes involved in a show. This is acceptable, although each should be encouraged to join. (One reason for not joining may be an age limit problem.) However, non-members should not be given any theater keys or combinations; nor be given any title or job that gives access to the building or responsibility for theater equipment, properties, etc. Also, be aware of the following important items:

1. City Fire Regulations require that smoking be permitted ONLY in the lobby and on the outside balcony of the rehearsal hall. Violation is a misdemeanor and anyone issued a citation for smoking in the auditorium, stage area, breezeway, dressing rooms, or rehearsal hall may be subject to fines of up to $500.00. It is the responsibility of the Producer and Director to set the example and enforce the safety and smoking regulation. The person in charge may be fined as well as the code violator himself.

2. The Producer is responsible for the following:

    a. When closing the building complex, lock all outside doors and check the security red light warning system.

    b. When closing the building through the lobby, shut off all switches in both electrical panels—except those taped to remain on. Shut off both air conditioning-heating switches.

    c. When closing building through the rehearsal hall, shut off all wall switches for lights and heaters, and shut off the separate remote location switch for the evaporative cooling system.

    d. Make sure all coffee pots, irons, etc., are turned off and unplugged.

3. All uses of the building complex by a major production, including casting,

read-throughs, rehearsals, etc., must be coordinated with the scheduling chairman to avoid any conflicts of facility usage. Priority for usage is as follows:

1) Monthly membership meeting

2) Major production on the boards

3) Major production in rehearsal

4) Specials

5) Workshops and other uses.

Conflicts will be resolved by the scheduling chairman.

4. The following activities are expressly forbidden without the specific consent of the Production Manager:

TO CHANGE, CUT, KNOCK OUT, REMOVE, OR IN ANY WAY ALTER OR MODIFY THE BASIC BUILDING STRUCTURE, including the stage floor, proscenium, apron, ramp, doors and walls. This includes also alterations to loud speakers, proscenium curtains and valance, teasers, stage microphone pickup, doorbell, piping for mounting stage lights, fire extinguishers, work lights, curtain rods, pulley and rope, intercom system, breezeway stair railing, etc. Also, no special wiring may be added nor existing wiring removed, relocated or modified for any special effects. This applies to any and all wiring, whether on stage, in the light booth, or in any other location within the building complex.

5. Readings and monthly meeting workshops may wish to utilize your set, props or lights. Insure the security of your set by monitoring its usage by others.

6. No existing flat, door, or other standard set construction piece is to be cut, altered, or modified. If a special size flat is required, please build it especially for your show, or modify an existing non-standard, specially built flat.

The Producer should announce to the entire cast and crew that they share responsibility for supporting the above critical items.

III CHECKLISTS

Attached are a series of checklists which are keyed to major production events such as "Prior to Casting," "Work Sunday," etc. These checklists provide, in sequence, a guide to insure that nothing is overlooked.

Also attached is a partial list of stores for the purchase of production supplies.

Prior to Casting

1. Read the play; know it well.

2. Meet with the Director. Review personnel requirements for pre-production and production staff, and rehearsal schedule.

3. Contact K.P. Newsletter for cast and description.

4. Determine Director's basic set design requirements and obtain set designer and complete set design. (Obtain stage layout print from Production Manager.)

5. Review existing lumber supply and prepare lumber "List of Material" requirements from completed set design and get bids.

6. Select a "Properties" person and review prop list from script.

7. Select "Costume" person to prepare sketches and review with Director. Review existing costume supply and prepare material cost list.

8. Review special sound and light requirements with Director.

9. Prepare production budget; review with Director and Production Manager and present to the Board for approval.*

10. Approved budget payable schedule to Producer is as follows:

      50%   Upon Board Approval
      40%   Work Sunday
      10%   Tech Sunday
     ────
     100%

11. Obtain combination to building from House Manager.

12. Obtain keys to building from House Manager. Be responsible for opening and closing theater for all show-related usage.

---

*Request for additional funds must be presented in writing to the Board for approval.

13. Offer assistance to Director for selection of script person if required.

14. Obtain Casting Blanks from membership chairman.

15. Offer assistance to Director for selection of music director, choreographer and rehearsal pianist.

16. Consult with Director on size of musical group, determine cost (including piano rental) and hire musicians.

17. Ask for (tech) volunteers at monthly membership meetings.

During Casting

1. Help Director as requested.

2. Provide pencils for casting applications.

3. Check with the current show's Producer to use stage lights for readings (if necessary).

4. Provide Director's table.

5. Return both unused and completed casting applications to membership chairman.

6. Collect extra scripts for crew.

7. Obtain rehearsal schedule from Director and post.

8. Insure that the current stage set, props, etc., are left intact after each night's readings.

9. Ask for tech volunteers.

At First Cast Read-Thru

1. Prepare and issue cast list with phone numbers.

2. Review rehearsal schedule revisions with Director as required.

Prior to Work Sunday

1. Advise cast and crew of K.P. rules and policies, including Work Sundays. Reread President's Message (attached).

2. Prepare for Work Sunday lunch. Money comes from Production Manager, not from show production budget. (Save receipts, from McDonalds to pot-luck; it's your choice.)

3. Order lumber, nails, etc., and arrange for delivery.

4. Obtain set construction plan from designer.

5. Call K.P. members to supplement cast and crew for set construction work.

6. Contact permanent Prop Supervisor to store closing show props and obtain props for new show.

7. Coordinate with Director and K.P. photographer for cast pictures and collect from cast ($6.50 each).

8. Coordinate with program chairman for cast bio's and crew list. Help proof-read program.

9. Contact permanent Wardrobe Supervisor to store all closing show costumes.

10. Arrange for tools required for Work Sunday.

11. Prefab any special set structure.

12. Coordinate costume construction.

13. Coordinate with publicity chairman and Director re publicity pictures.

14. Coordinate with Director all tech work and tech rehearsal.

15. Coordinate with membership chairman for membership dues.

Work Sunday

1. Install plastic protective covers on proscenium curtains prior to tearing down old set—FIRST PRIORITY OF DAY.

2. Fold up all theater seats—SECOND PRIORITY OF DAY.

3. Supervise all Work Sunday activities as well as all other subsequent set construction activities until set is complete for opening.

4. Clean dressing rooms.

5. Strike and store all closing show props, costumes and furniture.

6. Strike all on-stage lights.

7. Store all unclaimed closing show props, furniture, etc., that are not K.P. property in lobby.

8. Strike and clean all flats, etc., and store by size. *Remove all protruding nails.*

9. Erect new set.

10. Keep nails out of driveway and keep driveway clear.

11. Ask house manager to change marquee.

12. Clean light booth.

13. Use work lights, not stage lights, for set construction work.

14. Set up special dressing room requirements, if necessary.

Prior to Tech Sunday

1. Obtain stage manager.

2. Obtain light and sound operator(s).

3. Obtain additional prop people as needed.

4. Have Director approve costumes.

5. Obtain light designer—coordinate with Director—and set lights.

6. Prepare light and sound cue sheets.

7. Instruct new tech people.

8. Obtain postcard show announcements for cast and crew.

9. Obtain scripts for tech personnel.

10. Complete set construction; paint, dress and furnish set.

11. Complete assembly of all props. (The Producer may give out up to 10 complimentary tickets in return for special services rendered to the show for such things as loan of unusual props, etc. Expensive or valuable items loaned to the show may require insurance coverage, the cost of which should be included in the production budget.)

12. Insure stage manager and all tech personnel are on hand for tech Sunday and all subsequent tech and final run-throughs.

Tech Sunday

1. Coordinate with Director on all non-acting aspects of show.

2. Insure stage manager and tech people understand their jobs.

3. Resolve any tech problems.

4. Support stage manager who is generally responsible for all tech activities during tech rehearsals.

5. "Stay loose" and keep smiling to help get through the day.

Prior to Opening Night

1. Clear all scrap lumber, etc., from auditorium and lobby for janitor service.

2. Arrange for opening night party and post-party location sign in the lobby and dressing room.

3. Coordinate with Director for posting of cast pictures in lobby. (K.P. photographer prepares nametags.)

4. Clean all outside areas, including garage. "Police" nails in driveway; the flat tire you save may be your own.

5. Fireproof set as needed—see production manager.

6. Coordinate presentation of flowers at curtain call.

7. Police all Coke bottles.

8. Clean rehearsal hall for next show.

9. Post "call" time and sign-in sheet.

10. Obtain sell-out information from Special Relations Chairman and post in dressing rooms.

During Show Run

1. Insure theater is unlocked and locked at each performance.

2. Insure integrity of show by reviewing all lights, props, etc., for breakage and other damage prior to each performance. (Joint action for stage manager and producer.)

3. Initiate action for closing night cast party.

4. Advise cast and crew that the theater manager is solely responsible for giving permission to start each show and act. (Under no circumstances should house lights be out until patrons have cleared the aisles and are in their seats. This is a safety consideration which must not be ignored. It is better to stop, or at least to prolong the house lights dimming than to have patrons groping in the dark, trying to find their seats. Help prevent unnecessary accidents.)

5. Delegate responsibility for obtaining traditional Director's Award which is presented at cast party.

6. Help stage manager keep all persons not directly involved in show out of the breezeway, stage, and dressing room areas during the performance.

After Show Closing

1. Complete Production Cost Closing Audit Report and coordinate it with Production Manager.

2. Return all borrowed items.

3. See that cast picks up lobby pictures and all personal items.

4. Return all theater keys to house manager.

5. COLLAPSE.

Supply Sources

Item	Location	Hours	Comments
Lumber, Nails, Misc. Hdwr.	Southland Lumber Co. on Aviation 1 Blk. So. of Manchester	Daily; to 12 Noon Sat. Closed Sun.	Discount to K.P. (10%). Will accept cash or charge (if charge list production name on invoice). Will Deliver. Quotes & Orders by phone.
Paint (Luminall) Brushes Dutchman	Chaikin's Paint S.E. Corner La Brea & Manchester Inglewood	Daily thru Saturday. Closed Sun.	Discount to K.P. (Ask for Mr. Chaikin) Cash Only.

Paint	Standard Brands Everywhere	Daily Incl. Sun.	Cash Only
Misc. Hardware	Builders Emporium Ladera Shopping Center	Daily Incl. Sun.	Cash Only
Misc. Hardware	Van Tines Hdwr. Manchester, 1/2 Blk. E. of Hindry	Daily. Sun. 11–4	10% Discount to K.P. Cash Only
Telephone Equipment	Call General Tel, Santa Monica Call Pacific Tel, Inglewood		Give Program Credit for free use of equipment
Costumes	Contact Wardrobe Supervisor—See Membership Roster		
Props	Contact Properties Supervisor—See Membership Roster		
Piano	Angeles Piano Co. Culver City Mr. Schwab, Owner		

DIRECT ALL QUESTIONS TO PRODUCTION MANAGER
DON'T FORGET YOUR RECEIPTS

AGENDAS

Meetings, both general and those of the Board of Directors, should be carefully programmed so as not to waste the time of those present. Planning an agenda and sticking to it can pay off for your theater by making meetings more enjoyable for members.

It is recommended that the presiding officer have a mimeographed copy of the agenda with notes made prior to each meeting. The presiding officer should plan stretch and coffee breaks for lengthy meetings and should set time limits for all committee reports, insisting that they be observed. Any discussion that threatens to bog down the meeting should be referred to committee so that a resolution may be presented to the membership for approval at a subsequent meeting.

A written agenda cannot replace skill on the part of the presiding officer in running the meeting, but it can help.

Following is a sample agenda from the Kentwood Players.

AGENDA

DATE _____

1. Meeting to Order—Check Quorum (Bd. Mtg.) Absentees; Note Time.

2. Minutes—Previous (Accepted, Corrected) + (Reg. Mtg.) Board Action.

3. Treasurer's Report.

4. Membership Chairman
   A. Welcome Guests.
   B. Report.

5. Plays Committee Chairman.

6. Production Manager.

7. House Manager.

8. General & Box Office Chairman.

9. Season Tickets.

10. Special Relations (Sell-outs).

11. Mailing List.

12. Publicity.

13. Programs.

14. Workshop & Scheduling.

15. Bulletin.

16. Temporary & Sub-Committees.
    A. Dinner Dance
    B. Hospitality
    C. Finance
    D. Awards
    E. Social
    F. Other

17. Appointments—(Reg. Mtg.) Hosp. next mtg.

18. Old Business.

19. New Business

20. Announcements.

CONCLUSION

Great paperwork does not necessarily insure great theater. But taking the time to get your policies and procedures into serviceable written form will promote a smoother operation at your theater.

CHAPTER TEN

Grants: Government, Foundation, Corporate

Since passage of the National Foundation on the Arts and Humanities Act of 1965, monies have been made available through state agencies to community theaters. The basis for granting funds varies from state to state. Rules are set up by the individual state agencies following general guidelines from the federal government.

If you are interested in obtaining such funds, the first step is to contact your state agency. The agencies go by a variety of names: State Arts Board, State Commission for the Arts and Humanities, State Council on the Arts, etc. Sometimes when an agency is reorganized, the name and address are changed.

Following is a list of the state agencies, offered with the clear warning that the information is perishable. Your first task in contacting your state agency is to confirm the name and address by calling, writing, or checking with a current telephone directory.

Alabama State Council
on the Arts and Humanities
114 North Hull Street
Montgomery, Alabama 36130
(205) 832-6758

Alaska State Council on the Arts
619 Warehouse Avenue
Anchorage, Alaska 99501
(907) 279-1558

Arizona Commission
    on the Arts and Humanities
6330 North Seventh Street
Phoenix, Arizona 85014
(602) 271-5882

Office of Arkansas State
    Arts and Humanities
330 West Markham
Little Rock, Arkansas 72201
(501) 371-2539

California Arts Council
115 "I" Street
Sacramento, California 95814
(916) 445-1530

Colorado Council
    on the Arts and Humanities
770 Pennsylvania Street
Denver, Colorado 80203
(303) 839-2617

Connecticut Commission
    on the Arts
340 Capitol Avenue
Hartford, Connecticut 06106
(203) 566-4770

Delaware State Arts Council
Twelfth and Market
Wilmington, Delaware 19801
(302) 571-3540

District of Columbia Commission
    on the Arts and Humanities
1012 14th Street, Suite 1203
Washington, D.C. 20005
(202) 724-5613

Fine Arts Council of Florida
The Capitol, Department of State

Tallahassee, Florida 32304
(904) 487-2980

Art and Humanities Council
    of Georgia
225 Peachtree Street, N.E.
Atlanta, Georgia 30303
(404) 656-3990

The State Foundation
    on Culture and the Arts
250 South King Street, #310
Honolulu, Hawaii 96813
(808) 548-4145

Idaho Commission
    on the Arts and Humanities
Statehouse
Boise, Idaho 83720
(208) 384-2119

Illinois Arts Commission
111 North Wabash Avenue
Chicago, Illinois 60602
(312) 435-6750

Indiana Arts Commission
155 East Market
Indianapolis, Indiana 46204
(317) 633-5649

Iowa State Arts Council
State Capitol Building
Des Moines, Iowa 50319
(515) 281-4451

Kansas Cultural
    Arts Commission
509A Kansas Avenue
Topeka, Kansas 66603
(913) 296-3335

Kentucky Arts Commission
100 West Main Street
Frankfort, Kentucky 40601
(502) 564-3757

Louisiana State Arts Council
P.O. Box 44247
Baton Rouge, Louisiana 70130
(504) 342-6467

Maine State Commission
   on the Arts and Humanities
242 State Street
Augusta, Maine 04330
(207) 289-2321

Maryland Arts Council
15 West Mulberry Street
Baltimore, Maryland 21201
(301) 685-6740

Commonwealth of
   Massachusetts Council
   on the Arts and Humanities
One Ashburton Place
Boston, Massachusetts 02108
(617) 727-3668

Michigan Council for the Arts
1200 Sixth Avenue
Detroit, Michigan 48226
(313) 256-3731

Minnesota State Arts Council
314 Clifton Avenue
Minneapolis, Minnesota 55403
(612) 874-1335

Mississippi Arts Commission
Box 1330
Jackson, Mississippi 39205
(601) 354-3538

Missouri State Council
   on the Arts
Raeder Place
727 North First Street
St. Louis, Missouri 63102
(314) 241-7900

Montana Arts Council
235 East Pine

Missoula, Montana 59801
(406) 543-8286

Nebraska Arts Council
8448 West Center Road
Omaha, Nebraska 68124
(402) 554-2122

Nevada State Council on the Arts
4600 Kiepcke Lane
Reno, Nevada 89502
(702) 784-6231

New Hampshire Commission
   on the Arts
40 North Main Street
Concord, New Hampshire 03301
(603) 271-2789

New Jersey State Council
   on the Arts
109 West State Street
Trenton, New Jersey 08608
(609) 292-6130

New Mexico Arts Commission
113 Lincoln Avenue
Santa Fe, New Mexico 87503
(505) 827-2061

New York State Council
   on the Arts
80 Centre Street
New York, New York 10013
(212) 488-5337

North Carolina Arts Council
Department of
   Cultural Resources
Raleigh, North Carolina 27611
(919) 733-7897

North Dakota Council
   on the Arts and Humanities
309 D Minard Hall
North Dakota State University

Fargo, North Dakota 58105
(701) 237-7674

Ohio Arts Council
50 West Broad Street
Columbus, Ohio 04325
(614) 466-2613

Oklahoma Arts and Humanities
    Council
2101 N. Lincoln Boulevard
Oklahoma City, Oklahoma 73105
(405) 521-2931

Oregon Arts Commission
835 Summer N.E.
Salem, Oregon 97301
(503) 378-3625

Pennsylvania Council on the Arts
2001 North Front Street
Shore Drive Office Center,
    Building #3
Harrisburg, Pennsylvania 17102
(717) 787-6883

Rhode Island State Council
    on the Arts
334 Westminster
Providence, RI 02903
(401) 277-3880

South Carolina Arts Commission
829 Richland Street
Columbia, South Carolina 29201
(803) 758-3442

South Dakota Arts Council
108 West 11th
Sioux Falls, South Dakota 57102
(605) 334-7651

Tennessee Arts Commission
222 Capitol Hill Building
Nashville, Tennessee 37219
(615) 741-1701

Texas Commission
    on the Arts and Humanities
1801 Labaca
Austin, Texas 78711
(512) 475-6593

Utah State Division of Fine Arts
617 East South Temple Street
Salt Lake City, Utah 84102
(801) 533-5895

Vermont Council on the Arts, Inc.
136 State Street
Montpelier, Vermont 05602
(802) 828-3291

Commission of the Arts
    and Humanities
400 E. Grace, First Floor
Richmond, Virginia 23219
(804) 786-4492

Washington State Arts
    Commission
1151 Black Lake Boulevard
Olympia, Washington 98504
(206) 753-3860

West Virginia Arts and
    Humanities Council
Capitol Center
1900 Washington Street, East
Charleston, West Virginia 25305
(304) 348-0240

Wisconsin Arts Board
123 West Washington
Madison, Wisconsin 53702
(608) 266-0190

Wyoming Council on the Arts
200 West 25th Street
Cheyenne, Wyoming 82002
(307) 777-7742

The following general guidelines on funding apply to most states and are provided here to give you an overview. Soon after your initial contact, your state agency will probably send you specifics for your state.

1. Only projects directly related to work within the state are considered.

2. Theaters must be nonprofit and tax-exempt, or in the process of applying for that status. They must be certified for accepting charitable contributions under Section 170(c) of the Internal Revenue Code.

3. Only projects designed to improve the standards of production of the theater will be considered, as opposed to those perpetuating the same quality that your group has been doing.

4. Special consideration may be given to projects that are of value to children, disadvantaged, and senior citizens.

5. Special consideration may be given to areas (e.g., rural, ghetto) where theater is less available.

6. The numbers of participants and audience are taken into consideration.

7. Other sources of income will be considered.

8. Competence and qualifications of the theater's personnel working on the project will be evaluated. (This is where your track record counts—with your old programs and reviews to document it.)

9. Funds may not be used for new construction, renovation, reconstruction, permanent supplies, permanent equipment, projects already in progress or completed, or elimination of deficits. Funds are not to be used for prizes, scholarships, or entertainment.

In the past, state agencies have funded the following types of projects:

1. Professional staff development—Money is paid to the theater to bring in qualified personnel who can improve the theater's productions or administration.

2. New audience development—A project is developed to bring in a

new audience to your theater, from another neighborhood or another ethnic group. Or a festival is held where many theaters contribute and new audience is solicited.

3. Technical assistance and training—Consultants, workshops, and short-term training projects are available in management, grantsmanship, bookkeeping, audience development, and writer/artist development.

4. Touring assistance—Money is provided to increase the availability of theater to more remote areas of the state.

Projects are not limited to these general purposes. Community theaters are encouraged to submit other projects that will improve the quality of their productions and their impact on the community.

Several of the states offer mini-grants (up to $500) all year round and major grants ($500 to $20,000) on an annual or semiannual basis. Generally, applications for the mini-grants will be approved or rejected quickly, whereas application for a major grant may require three to six months to be evaluated and determined. Deadlines for application vary from state to state, along with the layout and content of the application forms.

Most state grants are awarded on a matching basis. Since the grants are intended to stimulate rather than replace private and community support, a one-to-one or better match is required. In the budget for the proposed project, the community theater is expected to show that its earned income and "in-kind" contributions will equal or exceed the amount of the requested grant.

"In-kind" contributions are donated goods and services that are necessary to the success of the project: transportation, publicity, volunteer work, office space, rehearsal space, equipment rental, printing, etc. They are valued at their fair market value.

State agencies also offer a wide variety of goods and services. Some states offer a monthly or quarterly newsletter with news of grants and art activities throughout the state. Some offer an annual report of all the funds they have granted in the past fiscal year. (See Figure 10–1.)

A few states offer grant writing workshops, and many that don't, participate in grant writing workshops held by other organizations within the state. Many states will confer with groups seeking grants to give them advice and guidance on their applications. Overall management seminars are offered by some states. They cover such topics as accounting, house management, fund raising, and audience development.

THEATRE

The Theatre Program assists theatres in endeavors to promote theatre productions, to tour performances, and to strengthen the theatre in universities, colleges, and communities.

During FY 1973-74, grants totaling $40,936.45 were made to the following organizations:

Alabama Shakespeare Festival $1,800.00

The *Alabama Shakespeare Festival* in Anniston provides the only Shakespeare Festival in the Southeast. In its third year, the Festival recruited professional actors to assemble a repertory company to present 31 performances of quality family entertainment during the six-week summer period. Mrs. George C. Wallace was honored guest for opening

Cherokee Playhouse, Inc. $1,200.00

The Cherokee Playhouse, Inc. presented *"The Boyfriend"* at the Cherokee County High School auditorium. Authentic costumes were designed and made for use by the cast of the 1920 musical comedy.

Attendance total: 500.

Citadel Players $500.00

In their second season, the Citadel Players *presented* "The Mousetrap," "Streetcar Named Desire," and "Oh, Dad, Poor Dad, Mama's Hung You in the Closet and I'm Feeling So Sad." The Citadel Players are the only community theatre group in the Selma/Dallas County area.

Attendance total: 1,200.

Figure 10-1. Annual Report of the Alabama State Council on the Arts and Humanities. This report gives the amounts granted to community theaters and tells what they did with the money.   (Courtesy of Alabama State Council on the Arts and Humanities.)

Many state agencies offer pamphlets on the following subjects: arts programs within the state, funding guidelines, community theater handbooks, and reading lists of books and periodicals helpful to organizations seeking grants.

Many state agencies also refer community theaters to other organizations supporting community theater within the state and to interstate regional organizations.

Some states require as many as twenty copies of an application or a fee for duplicating your application, plus many supporting documents. Therefore, I would recommend that before submitting your application for a grant, you write a brief letter of intent to the appropriate agency, explaining your project and asking whether such a project would be considered. This procedure might save you a lot of work and bring you the kind of help that could result in a grant. (See Figure 10.2.)

THE NATIONAL ENDOWMENT FOR THE ARTS

The National Endowment for the Arts does not generally fund community theater projects directly from the federal level. However, funds

THE REDWOODS COMMUNITY THEATER

12308 Brackland Ave.
Hidden Valley, California 91352

March 26, 1976

Mr. William Peters
Executive Director
The Stravis Foundation, Inc.
539 Wilshire Blvd.
Los Angeles, California 90017

Dear Mr. Peters:

The Redwoods Community Theater would like the help of
the Stravis Foundation in a project designed to use our
theater as the focal point for the planned integration
of the community of Hidden Valley.

Recent demographic studies by the mayor's planning
commission show that Hidden Valley will experience a
major shift in population over the next few years with
a heavy influx of Mexican-Americans into what has been
a predominantly white, Anglo-Saxon Protestant area.

We propose to stage a series of plays in co-production
with Teatro del Pueblo, a community theater group from
Wilman Heights. Our first joint effort would be an
evening of one-acts, with each group performing half of
the program.

To maximize the impact of this production on our community,
we would like to increase our publicity budget and improve
the quality of our sets and lighting. We also expect some
added transportation costs for the visiting company. We
anticipate that the initial project will cost $900 (or 50%)
more than our normal operating budget for a single production.
(See attachment #1 for detailed budget, as well as the
budget of our last season.)

The project would play for 15 weekend performances from
November 11, through November 17, 1977.

The Redwoods Community Theater has been in operation for
14 years. We have presented over 80 plays and have won
recognition as one of the state's leading community theaters.
(See attachment #2 for our history and attachment #3 for
a resume of our resident director.)

Figure 10-2. A Letter of Inquiry from a Fictional Community Theater. This letter was
tailored to meet the goals and past grant patterns of the Stravis Foundation.

We are a tax-exempt organization as determined by the Tax Franchise Board and the Internal Revenue Service, eligible to receive grants.

If this project falls within the range of interest of the Stravis Foundation, we would be grateful for the opportunity to submit a more detailed proposal, or to meet with you at your convenience to discuss the project more fully.

Very truly yours,

Marshal Wentworth

Marshal Wentworth
President,
Redwood Community Theater

MW:pc

Figure 10-2. (*continued*)

are made available occasionally for theater projects under the following circumstances: (1) the project is innovative and imaginative; (2) the project is applicable to a wide range of situations—i.e., a project that works in one area will also work in other areas on other occasions; and (3) the application for funds clearly states the theater's needs and a method of satisfying those needs.

Most federal funds are granted to professional theaters. However, community theaters may be interested in the National Endowment programs for professional theaters, short season professional companies (summer theaters and ongoing festivals), new plays, new playwrights, new forms, theater for youth, and theater service organizations.

Information on all national programs and the pamphlet *Guide to Programs* may be obtained by writing to The National Endowment for the Arts; Columbia Plaza; 2401 E Street, N.W.; Washington, D.C. 20506; (202) 634-6369.

THE CANADA COUNCIL

Created by an Act of Parliament in 1957, the Canada Council promotes the arts, humanities, and social sciences in Canada through a program of fellowships and grants. Community theaters are eligible to apply for assistance and should contact the Executive Officer of the Arts Division, The Canada Council, 151 Sparks Street, Ottawa, Ontario K1P5V8, Canada. The phone number is (613) 237-3400.

The Council's artists-in-residence program sponsors a limited number of artists. They work within a definable community to the benefit of both artist and community.

FOUNDATIONS

There are thousands of foundations in the United States whose reason for being is to give funds to worthwhile causes. And every year, each foundation receives too many futile applications, useless because the applicants fail to consider the foundation's purpose and past activities. This is a major problem for both the foundations and the community theaters requesting funds.

If you wish to pursue grants from foundations, the best place to start is a good reference library. Find out which foundations give grants, how much, and for what purposes.

The Foundation Directory, a biannual directory published by the Foundation Center and distributed by Columbia University Press (136 S. Broadway, Irvington, New York 10533), is available at most major libraries. This volume lists foundations by state and tells the purpose and activity of each. (See Figure 10–3.)

The 1972–73 Survey of Grant-Making Foundations with Assets over $500,000 or Grants over $25,000, compiled and published by the Public Service Materials Center (104 E. 40th Street, New York City 10016), is designed to be used with the *Foundation Directory.* This pamphlet answers basic questions about the larger foundations: (1) Are there best times of year to submit proposals? (2) Are appointments granted as a result of letters of intent? (3) Is there a specific individual to whom requests should be directed? (4) Does the foundation make grants toward operating budgets?

Giving USA 1973 Annual Report, published by American Association of Fund-Raising Counsel, Inc. (500 Fifth Ave., New York City 10036), gives the general trends in philanthropy in the United States. A section on arts and humanities lists some of the largest donations to theater.

Other good sources are *Grants and Aid to Individuals in the Arts* (Washington, D.C.: Washington International Arts Letter, 1970), *Private Foundations Active in the Arts* (Washington, D.C.: Washington International Arts Letter, 1970), and *Foundation Grants Index* 1976 (New York: Foundations Center, 1977), usually available at libraries.

Two periodicals are highly recommended: *The Foundation News* is published bimonthly by the Council on Foundations. Subscriptions are $20 per year (*The Foundation News,* Box 783, Old Chelsea Station, New York 10011). *The Grantsmanship Center News* is published eight times per year by the Grantsmanship Center, 1015 West Olympic Boulevard, Los Angeles, California 90015. Annual subscriptions are $15. Both magazines offer excellent current information on grants and how to get them.

Another excellent source of information is the state register of charitable organizations. Not all states maintain such a register. Call or write the Office of the State Attorney General or the State Department of Justice to ask if a register is maintained and if it is open to inspection by the public.

```
Stravis Foundation, Inc., The
539 Wilshire Blvd.
Los Angeles, California 90017

Incorporated in 1952 in California

Donor(s):  Members of the Stravis and Behar Families.

Purpose and Activities:  Broad purposes; general giving,
with emphasis on racial and social justice and the inter-
relationship of programs in these areas; to foster democracy
and social and institutional responsiveness in the public
and private arenas of America; to this end seeks to identify
and support energetic, strategically rational, theoretically
well-grounded efforts to effect appropriate institutional
development or change; to redress the imbalances and in-
equities of American life; to establish peace on earth;
religion, the arts, and education.  No grants to individuals.

Financial Data (yr. ended 12/31/76):  Assets, $21,985,413
(M); gifts received, $962,048; expenditures, $2,949,436,
including $2,757,120 for 132 grants (high: $234,000; low:
$100).

Officers and Directors:  Mr. William Peters, Executive
Director ; Mrs. Gertrude B. Peters, President; Mrs. Sarah
Behar, Vice-President; Mr. Arthur B. Tengleman, Secretary;
Mr. Howard Klempton, Treasurer; Miss Leah Behar, Miss Dana
Behar, Mr. Benjamin Shunichi.
```

Figure 10-3. Hypothetical Entry in a Foundation Directory. Note that the previous figure, a letter of inquiry from the Redwoods Community Theater (fictional), matches the information given above.

In California, for example, three copies of the register are kept by the Department of Justice, one each in Sacramento, Los Angeles, and San Francisco. These registers are computer printouts containing information distilled from Periodic Report Forms, CT-2's (discussed below).

The registers show which foundations operated in California in the last year, what their purpose was, and how much money they gave away. For 1975, the California state register lists 14,000 organizations, including all of the community theaters in the state that have filed appropriate articles of incorporation and annual reports so as to be eligible to receive grants. Community theaters have been assigned purpose code 129, performing arts, including ballet. Many of the grant-awarding foundations have a purpose code of 141, general charitable purposes.

The reader can quickly scan the grant-giving foundations to find the administrative officer, the address, and the total amount of money awarded in the past year.

Having done your research at a library and checked the state's register (if available), you will have some understanding of the overall foundation picture. Next, you will want specific information on possible foundation sources for your theater. There are four sources of more specific information: the foundation itself, the Department of Justice in some states, the Internal Revenue Service, and the past recipients of grants.

Some foundations issue annual reports. Call or write to ask if you may obtain a copy.

In many states, all charitable trusts must file a periodic report form (Form CT-2 in California) that gives the name of the foundation's officers, assets, investments, expenses, grants awarded, amount of grants, and who got then. These reports are public documents, and copies may be obtained from the state at a nominal fee. In California the fee is thirty cents per page; the basic document is eight pages, but the larger foundations may submit several more pages of attachments.

When the state government does make foundation reports available to the public, they are generally more up to date than the reports of the Internal Revenue Service. Copies of foundation reports to the federal government are public information and may be obtained by writing to the U.S. Internal Revenue Service Center, P.O. Box 245, Conwells Heights, Pennsylvania 19020. Copies of returns are one dollar per page. They take about six weeks to obtain.

Don't overlook recipients of grants as sources for information. When you read a foundation acknowledgment in a program, or find a theater listed among a foundation's past grantees, contact the manager of the theater and ask how the grant was obtained. The foundation might not consider a similar grant to you, but it could fund a different project at your theater.

Initial letters of inquiry should be brief—two pages at the most, preferably one page, with supporting documents that the reader may check if he or she finds the basic idea worth pursuing (see Figure 10–2). Written under the letterhead of your theater, your inquiry should include:

1. Your objective—its importance, timeliness, or urgency.
2. Your plans for accomplishing your objective
3. The funds you require, with a detailed budget
4. Your timetable for the project
5. Your qualifications to carry out the project
6. Your eligibility to receive grants as a tax-exempt corporation

Do not exaggerate the amount of your request in the expectation that it will be cut by the foundation and still meet your needs. Be realistic and assume that the foundation is expert in evaluating budgets. Don't use passionate prose to sway the reader if the basic facts won't; strive for simplicity in your writing and avoid emotional or elegant phrases.

Timing is very important. Before you submit a letter of inquiry, find out when the foundation meets to consider its grants. If this information is not available at the library or in annual reports, call the foundation to ask. Then submit your letter far enough in advance so that you can send in an extended proposal, if required, before the meeting.

If a more detailed proposal is requested, you will want to expand the information in your initial letter and present it from a problem-solving approach:

1. The history, nature, and extent of the problem
2. What you intend to do about it, how, and when
3. A repeat of your budget information, with expansion of details if your initial budget was not complete
4. Résumés of individuals who will be working on the problem
5. Any other specific information that the foundation requests

CORPORATIONS

Of major importance to the future of the arts are strenuous efforts to stimulate corporations to utilize more of the 5 percent tax deduction that is allowed for philanthropic contributions. If there is fuller general use of this allowance, the arts are likely to gain a fair share of the increase. [*The Performing Arts: Problems and Prospects,* a report by the Rockefeller Brothers Fund, Inc., McGraw-Hill, 1965.]

The federal government provides an incentive to corporations to support charitable organizations, including nonprofit art organizations, by allowing them to deduct up to 5 percent of their income. Corporations, however, do not give this much. Although many corporations are becoming more and more aware of their social responsibility, their contributions in the past have been in areas of health, education, and welfare, rather than the arts. The arts, however, are important to corporations. Corporations gain when their employees have ample opportunities to satisfy their needs for cultural stimulation. So a robust cultural atmosphere is very clearly in the best interest of the corporation.

If community theaters want to obtain the support of business, they must make a greater effort to woo this important source.

Evaluate the corporate situation in your area. What corporations have their offices closest to your theater? Which corporations' employees live in the neighborhood of your theater? Which corporations' officers and employees patronize your theater?

Make a list of the ten largest corporations *near* you. Then try to involve them gradually with your theater. Infiltrate! Get to know their executives personally before you attempt to tap them for a contribution.

Here are a few suggestions to promote involvement:

Start with interactions that won't cost the corporations any money. Place the executives on your mailing list for flyers of your theater's productions. If the corporation is large enough to have an employee recreation office or committee, send a flyer to promote an organization night (see Chapter 13)—a night when the corporation buys out the house. Rather than use this as a fund-raising activity, the corporation would simply pass on the reduced ticket prices to their employees. Follow up your flyer with a phone call, and get to know the person in charge of the corporation's employee relations. Invite that person to attend a performance. If the corporation has an internal newsletter, invite the editor to review your play, or at least promote it.

Invite the corporation to have its employees read for parts or participate in backstage work. Ask if you may post your announcements for readings and solicitations for backstage help, as well as normal advertising for your theater, on corporation bulletin boards.

One of the largest selling points when you later apply for corporate financial assistance will be your ability to show that the corporation is participating in your theater as audience, actors, or crew.

If the corporation has an employee-of-the-month program, donate two complimentary tickets to that program.

Some corporations have community service programs in which they pay their executives, or give them time off, to participate in community projects. Ask a corporation for help in administration, legal support, accounting, or publicity. Even if the corporation has no public service program, you might obtain such help simply by asking for it. These business skills can be a valuable asset to your operations, and once having helped you in this manner, a corporation is more likely to help again in other ways. Additionally, getting someone from the corporation to help you insures that the corporation knows your theater from the inside. When they evaluate any possible larger contribution, this will help.

Solicit other forms of nonmonetary support. Will the corporation let you use their auditorium for rehearsal space? Does the corporation have some storage space that you could use for sets, props, or costumes? Could the corporation donate office space for the use of your publicity staff? Could a corporation truck be used for hauling scenery? You might point out that there are possible tax write-offs involved in such activities.

Ask the corporation executive to serve as a member of your advisory board. Use the board to evaluate the far-ranging plans of your theater: a new building, land acquisition, renovations, etc. In such areas, business expertise could be a valuable asset.

When you have exhausted the possibilities of nonmonetary aid, try the minor sells. Ask the corporation to purchase an ad in your program. Try to sell executives on the purchase of patron tickets (discussed in Chapter 13). If you can get a few executives to purchase patron tickets, escalate: invite the corporation to become a patron by matching the amounts donated by individuals through patron tickets. This would mean making a good case to the corporation that your theater is a cultural asset to the community and a recreational asset to the corporation. List the corporation in your program along with your other patrons.

The next step is the big one—applying to the corporation for support of a project. Like the foundations, the corporations must be persuaded of a project's worthiness. Unlike the foundations, they are open to a wider range of projects.

By this time in your relationship with the corporation you should know executives personally. You should be able to request financial support in conversation, rather than by submitting a letter of inquiry. With an executive's favorable response you will get directions on what formal paperwork (letters, budgets, proposals, etc.) should be submitted.

Of course, you must be ready to accept no for an answer and then bring up a different project in another three months. You must be willing to accept a much smaller contribution than requested—gratefully (consider it a small victory)—and then apply for a larger amount in the future. With any contribution, you must deliver your sincere thanks and follow up with a letter to the corporation telling how the funds were applied.

CONCLUSION

At community theaters, fund raising—from state agencies, foundations, and corporations—is all too often done on a crisis basis with a deficit or mortgage payment imminent. It is done in a hurry, under pressure, and with the wrong goals in mind. All too often, therefore, it is unsuccessful.

It is essential that community theaters break this harmful pattern. A grants chairperson (with a supporting committee if necessary) must be appointed to operate year-round, investigating grants from government, foundations, and business. The grants chairperson must work up a program designed to bring in funds for the coming year, rather than the current one, thus allowing enough lead time for a satisfactory approach. The grants chairperson needs the help of all the theater's officers and other committee chairpersons in formulating projects and writing letters of inquiry, applications, and proposals.

A budget for the coming year should be planned without grant aid.

Separate budgets for grant projects should be carefully considered and made ready to implement.

Finally, it is most important to remember that those who give grants are not interested in your degree of need so much as they are interested in the worthiness of the projects you propose! Obtaining grants takes a lot of selling—selling an idea to people. And this takes hard work, research, and effective communication.

CHAPTER ELEVEN

Raising Funds

It takes money to make community theater, and very often the selling of tickets is not enough to raise all that is needed. In Chapter 10 we looked at government agencies, charitable foundations, and corporations as a source of funds. In Chapter 13 we look at the recruiting and preferred treatment of patrons who can help to support the theater beyond simply buying tickets. This chapter is devoted to still other means of raising funds, from direct mail solicitations to selling items in the lobby, to holding auxiliary events.

In some countries there is much greater government and community support for theater than in the United States. In the United States the community theater is on its own to survive economically as best it can. Community theaters must compete with other forms of entertainment. This means keeping tickets in the one-dollar-to-four-dollar range. Income from selling tickets frequently fails to meet the rising costs of royalties, sets, lights, costumes, makeup, and theater rental—not to mention the cost of land and of building a new theater. Therefore, it is often essential that a community theater consider a broad range of methods to raise funds.

IN THE BEGINNING

When a new group is getting on its feet, the initiators are often called upon to "buy stock." This seed money pays for stationery, postage, and other basic items that are used to find additional supporters and raise money. Sometimes enough seed money can be obtained to cover operating expenses through the first few productions.

Before you ask people to take cash out of their pockets, draw up a careful budget so that you can assure yourself and the people you're asking that you won't be back next week, or next month, to ask for just a few dollars more. Solicit these starting funds from as many people as possible so that no single individual must bear too heavy a burden. Make it clear whether these funds are to be repaid out of future theater receipts.

DIRECT MAIL SOLICITATION

The next step can be broad solicitation for operating or building funds. Asking for money by writing a letter is difficult. The hardest part is preventing the reader from throwing the request directly into the garbage. If you can do that with an attractive, eye-catching format, the next problem is convincing the reader to donate.

If you can afford to use photographs, do so. Photos of actors and actresses in costume can catch the eye quickly. If you can't use photographs, any artwork is the next best choice—possibly logos of the plays of your coming season. At the very least, go for an attractive letterhead and distinctive type and layout. Use color, such as dark green type on light green stationery.

Distinctiveness starts with the envelope. It's a good place for your theater's logo. Or you might want to try hand-addressed envelopes with handwritten minimal return address elements. This usually guarantees that the receiver will at least open the envelope.

Next, use quotes in the margins of your letter or in the body from people well known in the community—anyone from political leaders to newspaper critics. ("We must have live theater in our community."—Mayor William Peters)

In your lead sentence get your reader involved by using the words *you* or *your:*

"Your love of theater should . . . ."

"You and your neighbors deserve a theater . . . ."

Explain the importance of your goals briefly and make sure your readers understand how they can derive a sense of satisfaction from helping to achieve those goals, enjoy theater, and contribute to the community.

"Without your support . . . ."

"Please join your neighbors who have pledged . . . ."

The emphasis should be on emotional appeal; don't weigh the letter down with too many facts. This is not the place for a detailed budget of your operations.

Remember that you have something positive to offer contributors—the feeling that they have made something worthwhile possible (see Figure 11-1).

Your letter must convince the recipients that your organization is capable of using the requested funds to achieve its goals. This may be done subtly in many ways. A statement need not be made in the body of the letter. Photographs with captions might be enough to imply that your track record qualifies you to produce good community theater. A list of your awards (e.g., "2nd Place, Statewide Community Theater Festival, 1977") might also convey this message. One of the best ways is with a list of past contributors, implying that foundations and corporations have already found you worthy of financial support. Quotes from contributors can also help. Listing your board of trustees in the margin might also be effective.

The direct letter appeal for funds may offer a season ticket or patron ticket. (E.g., "Patrons and Angels will receive two season tickets. Benefactors receive two life passes.")

If you have incorporated as a nonprofit organization (see Chapter 8), you can announce in your letter that contributions are tax deductible. (You will mail a receipt with your note of thanks.)

The Lone Birch Community Stage
600 Ventura Avenue
Santa Paula, CA 93060

April 30, 1979

Mrs. Ethel Larkins
1824 Crestwood
Santa Paula, CA 93060

Dear Mrs. Larkins

You can make the difference. Live theater can
survive in our community with your help.

With our new and expanded season our costs will increase.
Yet we are holding the line on the price of tickets in
order to make theater available to all of the people in
our community. This coming year expenses will again
exceed our box office income. So we must ask for
donations.

In retrospect, the past year was a successful one. Warm
and generous critical and public response to our second
season produced a remarkable growth in attendance as the
season progressed -- a token of faith we intend to justify
with our efforts this coming year.

We need and value your interest -- and our survival depends
on your generosity. If you care about live theater in our
community, please contribute. Checks should be made out
to The Lone Birch Community Stage. All contributions are tax
deductible.

We can bring great theater to Santa Paula with your help!

                              Sincerely

                              Phyllis Trinidad

                              Mrs. Phyllis Trinidad
                              President
                              The Lone Birch Community Stage

Figure 11-1. Letter Soliciting Funds.

Sign the letters by hand. This personal touch is not too much effort considering the possible rewards.

"How much is everybody giving?" is a question frequently posed to door-to-door solicitors. Answer this question on your enclosed, self-addressed envelope (see Figure 11-2). Scale your suggested amounts to a list of honorary titles:

Please accept my tax deductible contribution.

____ $10 ____ $25 ____ $50 ____$100 ____$250 ____$500 ____Other.

Name _____ Date _____

Address _____

City _____ Zip _____ Phone _____

FIRST CLASS
Permit No.
Los Angeles, CA.

BUSINESS REPLY MAIL
No Postage Necessary if Mailed in the United States

Postage will be paid by

The Bratenahl Civic Theatre
12308 Woodside Avenue
Los Angeles, California 90036

Figure 11-2. Postage-Paid Reply Envelope. Help the donor decide how much to contribute by printing suggested amounts on the envelope.

$10   —   Friend of the Theater

$25   —   Donor

$50   —   Sponsor

$100   —   Patron

$250   —   Angel

$500   —   Benefactor

The postage-paid return envelope is a must. Even people who are not too lazy to write out a check can be too lazy to hunt for an envelope and a stamp. Generally, the post office charges thirty dollars for the first class business reply permit and five cents for each envelope mailed back.

You may send your letters out at the nonprofit organization rate, but then you may not enclose a "business reply" envelope.

For your address list you might use the local telephone directory, selecting names of the people who have the exchange numbers used in your area. (For further discussion of address lists, see Chapter 3.)

Some city and county governments require that all solicitations be licensed. Check with your county's business license commission and the social service department of your city to determine if you are required to place an "information card" in each letter.

THE PROSPECTUS

A big step up from the letter requesting funds is the prospectus—a complete report of your past activities, projected activities, and budget. Whereas the letter is intended to appeal to the heart, the prospectus is intended to appeal to both the heart and the mind. It is especially intended for the businessperson who is used to seeing investment appeals in this format.

The prospectus may be used to solicit funds not only from government agencies, foundations, and corporations, but also from important individuals who are potentially large contributors.

In raising money by sending out direct appeals, whether letter or prospectus, community theaters should take lessons from professional theater and other art-oriented organizations—dance, fine arts, and museums (see Figure 11–3). Study their methods of appeal and then apply similar techniques.

DOOR-TO-DOOR CAMPAIGNS

Knocking on doors to solicit money, to sell tickets, or to pass out flyers announcing the opening of your theater is hard and sometimes unpleasant work. To make the best of it, go in a group in a festive atmosphere, and go at the right time.

During working hours and on weekends people are not likely to be at home, and many people are afraid to open their doors at night. Therefore, aim at the after-dinner hour during weekdays, preferably when it's still light outside.

If you can set up sound equipment (record player and public address system) on a truck, it's desirable to have attention-gaining music playing, a la the Good Humor Man. Having solicitors in costume can also help. Use taste in selecting costumes. A southern belle can open more doors than Lizzie Borden complete with blood-spattered ax.

Carry flyers, self-addressed envelopes, identification, and any permits required. Even if you collect no money or sell no tickets, this is a good chance to make friends in the community—to show the neighbors that the players are out there in the streets, coming to the community rather than waiting for the community to come to the theater. Give both contributors and noncontributors a flyer. Ask for information as well as a donation. "Do you go to the theater often?" "Would you go if the theater were closer?" "Would you go if it were less expensive?" "What play would you most like to see?"

LOBBY SALES

During intermissions you have a captive audience for ten to twenty minutes, and they would like nothing better than to pursue the national pastime—consuming. Give them something to consume and you can make a profit.

Figure 11–3. Two Pages from the 22-Page Prospectus of the Joffrey Ballet. Note its businesslike format and thoroughness.

(Courtesy of the Joffrey Ballet.)

This Prospectus is modeled after those often utilized by businesses for raising capital. Such prospectuses are usually filed with the Securities and Exchange Commission in connection with registration of the securities offered thereby. This Prospectus is likewise fund-raising material but is not required to be filed with any government agencies and is not subject to any disclosure requirements. Nonetheless, this Prospectus purports to provide a comprehensive description of the activities of The Foundation for The Joffrey Ballet, Inc.

TABLE OF CONTENTS

THE FOUNDATION

The Foundation for The Joffrey Ballet, Inc. ("the Foundation") (formerly The Foundation for American Dance, Inc.) is a not-for-profit corporation established under the laws of the State of New York for the sole purpose of sponsoring The Joffrey Ballet and its affiliated apprentice group, The Joffrey II Company. The Foundation is a tax-exempt organization under Section 501(c)(3) of the Internal Revenue Code.

During its current fiscal year, the Foundation expects to have total operating expenses of approximately $3,440,000, about 63 per cent ($2,180,000) of which will be offset by box office receipts, performance fees and other earned income. The remaining 37 per cent ($1,260,000) of the Foundation's expenses must be raised in the form of grants and contributions from government agencies, foundations, corporations and individuals.

Pursuant to applicable provisions of law, The Foundation files annual information reports with the Internal Revenue Service, the New York State Board of Social Welfare and the Attorney General of the State of New York. Such reports are available for inspection at the offices of The Foundation, which are located at 130 West 56th St., New York City.

2

Figure 11-3. (*continued*)

Start with coffee or soft drinks. Some theaters give away the coffee and punch and then sell the pastry and pretzels. Others sell only items that are individually wrapped. (Check local city and county regulations for licenses needed and standards of cleanliness for vendors.) Investigate the possible consumables that could be sold in your lobby, from gum, cigarettes, and candy to expensive imported confectionery.

Use of vending machines may bring less income than over-the-counter sales, but the ease of operation may be worth it. Or you may find both methods advantageous. For example, you might place a bottled drink dispensing machine backstage for use by the cast and crew and a concession table in the lobby for sales to the audience.

A wide variety of nonconsumables can also be sold in the lobby. The main problem is usually security. If you have display space and secure storage space, you can make a profit in your lobby. The very least needed is a folding table, the willingness of the house manager to preside over it, and the locking up of the merchandise when not on display—possibly in the trunk of a car. Gift store merchandise that you might consider includes books, diaries, address books, calendars, jewelry with masks, bumper stickers with a theater slogan, and other small items.

You can also use the lobby to sell non-items, such as bricks. Audience members are asked to buy a brick as a way of contributing to the building fund for the theater. For a five- or ten-dollar tax-deductible contribution, the donor may be given either a miniature gold brick or a real brick. Or the donor's name may be painted on a brick that is displayed in your lobby.

Seats may also be sold in your lobby. In this case, contributors are rewarded for donations by having their names placed on plaques on the theater's seats—showing that the benefactor bought that specific seat for the theater.

Other items are limited only by your imagination. If a community theater had only thought of the pet rock, the United States would probably have the grandest community theater in the world!

ANNUAL EVENTS

The lobby can also be used to host an annual or semiannual auction, garage sale, or rummage sale—during the day and usually on a weekend. Members of the theater may bring in used items to be sold or auctioned. Members of the community may also be asked to contribute used items—appliances and furniture stored in closets and attics never to be used again. The nonprofit, incorporated community theater can give any donor a receipt for the value of the item. The donor can then deduct that amount from taxes.

This type of auction or garage sale has a few interesting variations. One is the blind auction where donors gift-wrap the items. The auctioneer then gets the bids up by extolling the beauty of the wrap and perhaps the mystery of the shape or weight.

You might want to limit lobby sales to small items like books or records and tapes.

In any case, this type of annual or semiannual event deserves its own promotion. In publicity you call attention to both the event and the next offering of your theater. The annual event can even expand to the running of a year-round thrift shop (e.g., The Prop Shop), an annex to the theater.

Here are some other possible annual events:

The Art Auction

Paintings can be displayed in the lobby during performances to whet interest in an art sale or auction. Artists are asked to donate paintings by entering them in a contest. Prior to the sale or auction, a panel of judges appointed by your theater selects winners (e.g., Best of Show, Best Oil, Best Water Color). Prizes are awarded to winners, thus encouraging donations.

If your lobby is not spacious enough to host this event, you can move outdoors in good weather to a parking lot or to a shopping center mall (with permission, of course, that would probably be obtained with the promise of publicity). Three flats from stock can be joined together to form a free-standing periactus to display the art work.

The Box Luncheon and Variations

The basic idea of the box luncheon is that everyone in the group is asked to prepare a box luncheon or picnic basket for two, and to wrap it attractively. Boxes or baskets are collected on stage and auctioned off to the membership. The contents may or may not be attached and read aloud as each is sold. This event can be held as a separate sociable or in conjunction with a regularly scheduled meeting. Members of the community can be invited to take part.

The wine-and-cheese-tasting party is similar, but each member pays an entrance fee to sample all of the wines and cheese that the members have contributed. In the spaghetti dinner variation, a committee must prepare and serve the food.

The Homemade Bake Sale, Etc.

Baked goods, fudge, doughnuts, cookies, or homemade candies prepared by your members can also bring in small profits. Sometimes such sales can be tied in with appropriate holidays. The general idea is that members donate their time and the ingredients to make the items and sell them at a table in a shopping center. If it's to be an annual or semiannual event, a well-prepared sign is a worthwhile investment; it can easily be stored in the theater.

Sales will increase greatly if you can take the goods to the homes of the consumers via truck in the carnival atmosphere of the door-to-door ticket sales described earlier. If you don't have enough homemade goodies, you may have to contact a wholesaler.

The Pancake Breakfast

A sign advertising "All the pancakes you can eat for $2," ingredients, and willing hands to make and serve can usually raise dollars. An advance sale of tickets is very important. Weekend mornings in a parking lot or in front of your theater are suggested.

Luncheons

The luncheon fund raiser can be held on weekdays if you have enough members who do not work during the day and if you can attract enough housewives from the community. A restaurant with a banquet hall is always happy to provide the space if they cater the meal. The main attraction may be a guest speaker, a fashion show supplied by a local department store, or a demonstration of merchandise (Amway, Tupperware, etc.). Profits come from both the margin of luncheon-ticket price over meal cost and the commission on any merchandise sold.

Garden Parties

A pleasant outdoor fund raiser is the garden party where the host or hostess contributes a spacious backyard (envision beautiful ornamental flowerbeds, a poolside area, or a tennis court) and other members contribute refreshments. Entertainment may be contributed or contracted—from a strolling magician or a singer to a band. It's a social event and people buy tickets partly for the privilege of mixing with the VIPs you invite. Sometimes it's desirable to confer an honor upon a VIP (e.g., Mayor Smith named Honorary Director). This encourages the VIP's friends to contribute their time and energy in promoting the event.

The tribute dinner is indoors but similar. Emphasis is placed on the individual being honored, usually a VIP who is not a member of the theater group but has in some way contributed to the growth of the theater.

USING YOUR THEATER TO HOST EVENTS

If you own or rent your theater you may be able to profit from renting it to others when you are not in production or rehearsal. A rock group might fill your theater with teenagers on a Saturday morning. A children's theater group might also perform on weekends. Besides booking and promoting shows, you may be able to find other groups (such as a ballet school or a barbershop quartet competition) that would like to use your stage. When your theater is dark, use your marquee to advertise that your house is available for rental. Also advertise in your programs. You may also find it advisable to send out flyers to potential renters.

If you know enough film buffs, you might want to set up a club to show 16-mm prints. If not enough membership can be sold in advance, money can be refunded without much risk of capital beyond the cost of advance publicity.

Hosting a bingo party or other fund raiser for another organization is also a possibility. Make sure that you check the legality of bingo and other games of chance with your local police department.

COMMUNITY SERVICES

The car wash is a fairly practical way to earn a few dollars. It only takes a few signs proclaiming the "Annual Community Theater Car Wash," rags, buckets of soapy water, and strong arms. The cooperation of a filling station or an empty lot with driveway access from the street in a heavy traffic area is desirable. Members of the theater wave in drivers to have their cars washed at a nominal fee, while other members provide the service. Flyers may be posted and distributed in advance to drum up business. Members can have their own cars washed to start a line that will encourage business.

Going door-to-door to cut lawns and do yard work or wash windows is another valuable community service. Advertise a per person, per hour rate. Operate from a single truck with a P.A. system if possible.

An unusual fund raiser is the Halloween cleanup service sale. Theater members sell a mimeographed cleanup guarantee in the weeks before Halloween that lessens the homeowner's risk of tricks or pranks. The guarantee gives the number of the theater to call in case of problems. The day after Halloween, the theater members respond to calls by going to homes to sweep up garbage from overturned cans or scrape the crayon from car windows. The whole thing should be done in the spirit of fun with godfather overtones and a humorously written "policy."

On Halloween eve the theater can hold its own party in the streets of the neighborhood where it has sold guarantees and keep an eye out for mischief.

THEATER PARTIES

Just as you sell theater parties, your theater can buy out a performance at a neighboring community theater as a fund raiser. An exotic variation is the theater-travel plan where you sponsor a theater party in New York or London. This must be planned with the help of a travel agent. If you can find fifteen to twenty people who can afford this kind of vacation you can turn a handsome profit for your group. There are some interesting fringe benefits, like being able to take along a deserving member at no cost, or reducing the cost for all.

RAFFLES AND DOOR PRIZES

The raffle, where legal, is an excellent way to raise funds, particularly when the item to be raffled (TV, car, or other) is donated by a neighboring merchant, possibly for publicity consideration—a free ad in your program and mention on all tickets and in all newspaper, radio, and TV publicity relevant to the raffle. When held in conjunction with the other fund raisers described, the door prize or raffle can be used to increase interest and participation.

THE TREASURE HUNT AND OTHER PARTIES

The party game of following clues to find a treasure can be turned into a fund raiser by having each individual pay a fee to participate. A committee prepares clues, which become progressively harder. They lead the players from one place to another, where they find further clues that eventually lead them to a treasure. A party is held to congratulate the finder of the treasure. Progressive dinners, scavenger hunts, and other party ideas can similarly be turned into fund-raising sociables for your members. Of course, in preparing for a scavenger hunt you can be thinking of your prop and set piece needs for the coming season as well as raising money.

A THON

The *Thon* is a modern fund raiser in which members of your theater agree to try to walk, run, swim, or bicycle X number of miles. Members sell their participation to donors, each of whom pledges a specific amount per mile traveled by the participant. The total donation depends on how far the participant is actually able to travel. Donors may pledge money to more than one participant. Amount of the pledge may vary from donor to donor, and each participant has a booklet to keep track of his or her donors and pledges. The money may be collected before or after the event. The thon requires a lot of publicity to let the public know, for example, that members of the community theater are walking from hometown to state capital to dramatize the need for greater state support to the arts.

Variations on this type of promotion are the record-breaking thons where members attempt to break records in the *Guinness Book of World Records* by continuously seesawing or dancing or carrying out some other activity. Again, the public is asked to underwrite each participant by paying so many dollars per hour. Publicity work is especially important in the record-breaking thon. It should call attention to the coming season at the theater as well as the record-breaking event (see Chapter 5 on publicity).

IN SUMMARY

1. Theater managers and ways and means chairpersons must be aware of the fund-raising activities of other organizations in the area. Obviously, it is not good public relations for your theater to plan and promote a fund-raising event that is similar to the fund-raising event of a neighboring organization. (For example: you decide to buy a piano for the theater by collecting trading stamps in the community. At the same time the local Boy Scout troop announces that it will be collecting trading stamps to buy a canoe.) There are so many different types of fund raisers that you need not compete with neighboring organizations.

2. Be realistic about your fund-raising goal. Some of the events described in this chapter have greater income potential than others. When you budget your expenses for conducting the event, also estimate the potential profit. Do not discard an event because the potential profit is small or because it will not completely pay for the new lights you need. Sometimes it is preferable to run a few easy fund raisers than to go all out on a single difficult one. Small profits will add up!

3. Limited fund raisers, even if they do not accomplish your overall goal, show that your group is trying. Your various fund-raising activities should be listed on your applications for grants to foundations, corporations, and government. They are more likely to respond favorably

when they can see that your members are definitely working to raise their own funds.

4. A nonmonetary profit can be made on all fund-raising events through good public relations and publicity. Every time the name of your theater is brought to the attention of your public in a favorable light, it will reinforce their awareness of you. Fund raisers can thus pay off later at the box office even if they don't immediately show huge profits.

5. Keep accurate records of all of your fund-raising activities—where you got your supplies, who did the work, how the work was timed, what problems you had, and how you overcame them. It will be much easier to carry out the event the next time with all of the facts before you.

6. And finally, don't forget to say thanks—to the people who contributed, the organizations that cooperated, and the people who did the work.

CHAPTER TWELVE

Planning a Season

Every year thousands of community theater people throughout the United States, and around the world, go through the difficult process of selecting plays for a season.

For a few reasons, it is desirable to select a season rather than pick one play at a time. Selling season tickets can provide working capital at the beginning of the season. With the sale of season tickets you know that you will have a minimum audience in addition to walk-in patrons. Advance planning of a season also promotes advance production planning.

The process of selecting plays for a season varies from one community theater to another. At some theaters one person may be responsible for the final decision—the resident director, the artistic director, the president of the theater group, or another officer.

More frequently, selection is carried out by a play-reading committee. Any member of the group may submit the name of a play to be considered. Members of the committee sift through the plays and then vie to promote the ones they favor. Through a consensus or vote, the season is selected.

Most frequently, however, the selection results from an interaction between the committee and an individual. Examples: Selections, with perhaps a few alternatives, go to the resident director, who then approves the final slate. Or selections go to the board of directors, which accepts the season or returns the selections to the committee, recommending changes.

Some community theaters package each potential play with a director who wants to direct it. This promotes director affinity and ample preparation time.

Regardless of the process, it takes time to read and evaluate plays. It takes still more time to balance plays for a season and to consider the expectations of your audience. The work of the play readers and their deliberations should not be hurried. Plan their meetings and reports on your annual production calendar.

FACTORS IN SELECTING PLAYS

Orientation of the Theater Group

Paramount among selection factors is the orientation of your theater group. For example, the sole purpose of many community theaters is to bring to their audiences plays that have appeared recently in New York and London. Some groups are dedicated to reviving the best American plays. A few groups want to do only the classics. Some are oriented to musical comedy, and some want to do only Shakespeare or only Gilbert and Sullivan.

First and foremost, therefore, play selection must be within the well-defined aims of your group.

Interests of the Audience

Next, you must consider your audience. If you are completely out of touch with their interests, you will lose them. Evaluate their intellectual level. If they can't understand the play, they won't be entertained.

Be aware of the mores of your audience. Certain plays will offend an audience because of the playwright's attitude toward sex. Some language may be beyond the tolerance of your audience. There are also religious, racial, and moral attitudes that must be considered. If in doubt, sound out leaders of your community before you select a play that may alienate your audience. If still in doubt, post signs in your lobby or box office forewarning your audience.

It takes a special audience to appreciate avant-garde playwrights. Presenting such playwrights to a general community theater audience might frighten them away. But you could do an avant-garde play in addition to your season if you sense that you have an audience for it. Or you might present play-reading evenings. Scripts in hand, actors read and emote parts to an invited audience. In this way you can present offbeat or unusual plays to an interested faction while not turning off the general audience. If there is demand, the readings can be transferred to the stage.

Audience education is desirable. But this is not the same as foisting your tastes on your audience. The standard compromise is to present "educational" plays, partially staged or as readings, on nights when the theater would normally be dark, or to present these plays for short, limited runs. Your audience will quickly tell you whether such plays should be added to your regular season. Such partially staged plays or readings will also allow new actors and directors the chance to try their stage legs.

Variety

Variety is another important factor. Presenting the same type of play time and again in the same box sets will finally bore any audience. Some variety is absolutely necessary. How you introduce variety depends on the response you get from your audience. By studying audience polls and the previous season's balance sheet, you must adjust the ratio between comedy, serious drama, farces, melodrama, mysteries, black comedies, and musicals. Poll your audience for both the types of play they would like to see and their reactions to the specific plays that you are considering for coming seasons. A ballot can easily be printed in, or enclosed in, the program. Besides getting their opinions, polling gives audiences a sense of participation.

In addition to selecting plays from various categories, consider other factors that will enhance the feeling of variety.

Alternating categories. If your season is two comedies and two dramas, alternate them rather than presenting two of the same type suc-cessively. *Indoor/outdoor.* Try not to present a complete season of plays set indoors. Your audience might develop claustrophobia. Even if all of your season might be staged indoors in box sets, go for design that opens up your sets, perhaps playing indoor scenes against a cyc without the traditional walls. *Large cast/small cast.* If possible, choose both small-cast and large-cast plays for the season. Alternate large- and small-cast plays rather than playing the same size casts consecutively. Large-cast plays seem to generate more manpower backstage and usually bring in larger audiences (relatives?). This usually makes up for the added expenses of a large-cast show. *Male/female dominance.* Plays in which the female lead is the dominant character are in the distinct minority. But adding such a play to your season will also enhance the sense of variety. It is a para-dox that there are usually more actresses than actors in community theaters, yet strong roles for actresses are scarce. Look for roles that can be switched.

Other ways of enhancing variety are by presenting costume plays, plays with a distinct foreign flavor, and originals. Be very wary of originals, however. Insist on writing talent. Don't allow a let's-help-the-writer-out at-titude to overwhelm your common sense.

Technical, Casting, and Cost Problems

Technical, casting, and cost problems must also be considered by the play-reading committee. If you don't have the technical capability to mount a demanding production, you may have to forgo it.

It is an easy generalization to say that any technical problem can be overcome by simplification. The audience comes into the theater ready to suspend disbelief. If you suggest rather than present, you can get away with almost anything. (I'm usually ready to stand up and cheer for this argument.) BUT . . . when the audience comes to see the musical version of *Gone with the Wind,* they expect to see Atlanta burn. They remember the scene from the movie. If you cannot deliver a satisfactory burning of Atlanta on your stage, you should not undertake the production.

On the other hand, some play-reading committees immediately discard excellent plays because they call for more than one set. This is the opposite extreme—underestimating your technical capability. Play readers should be aware that split stages, sets-within-a-set, playing a short scene on the apron with little or no scenery, and other techniques can be used easily and successfully.

The committee must also consider the ability of its available actors to handle demanding roles. It is easy to see the need for an actor's actor to play in *Hamlet* or *Cyrano de Bergerac*. *Sleuth* requires two (and is being undertaken by a community theater as I write these words). The play-selection committee simply can't choose these plays in hopes that some new actors will walk in during open casting. It is more difficult to foresee this type of problem when the difficult role is less well known. Sometimes you select a play only to find during casting that no one can be found to meet the challenge of a pivital role. It is best to suspend production and mount another play. Do not allow an actor to undertake a role at which he has no chance for success. It will doom your production.

Being aware of your actors' capabilities does not mean pre-casting all demanding roles. It merely means knowing that your regular pool of actors has the minimum capabilities to meet the script's challenges if even better actors are not found.

Although the committee is not expected to do a complete cost analysis for every play it considers, it should be aware of basic royalty, set construction, costume, and prop costs. Play readers should be alert to any unusually high costs in these areas. Are the royalties high for this play because it is very popular and has just been released? Will the play require extensive or unusual sets that cannot be pulled from stock? Are there unusual props that must be rented or purchased (the magic effects in *Damn Yankees,* for example)?

Some works of well-known playwrights are now in the public domain, and groups may do revivals without paying royalties.

A new copyright law went into effect in the United States on January 1, 1978—Public Law 94–553. It was the first major revision to laws concerning playwrights' royalties and protection since 1909.

Copyright protection now extends for "the life of the author plus fifty years after his death." This brings U.S. law into alignment with international practice.

All copyrights in effect at the time the new law was passed have been extended to seventy-five years from the previous fifty-six-year maximum.

Essentially, all plays with copyrights prior to 1921 are now public domain. Plays with dates of copyright from 1921 to 1977 are protected for seventy-five years and will not start coming into public domain until 1996. If in doubt, check with the publisher of the play.

Timeliness

Timeliness counts. Sometimes you can capitalize on current events and augment your drawing power by presenting a relevant play. Election years are good times to revive political plays like *The Best Man* and *Advise and Consent.* Plays about holidays or plays with scenes of holiday celebrations should be selected and scheduled appropriately. (*Auntie Mame* during the Christmas season, *Diary of Anne Frank* during the Passover season, Lincoln plays in February, etc.)

Sometimes the publicity for a newly released or Oscar-winning movie will greatly benefit the production of the play script. The Oscar sweep of *One Flew over the Cuckoo's Nest* prompted many community theater productions. (Even though the movie is not based on the Dale Wasserman play script, the title alone drew crowds.) Study currently popular movies to see which potential Oscar winners are based on play scripts that are available and suitable. Then schedule your production to coincide with the Oscar presentations, and cross your fingers.

Remember that controversial and heavily publicized pictures can generate as much drawing power as Oscar winners.

Dramatic Values

Finally, choose plays that have strong dramatic values—memorable characters, strong conflict, scintillating dialogue, and insight into human relationships.

Audiences still go to the theater for the same reasons they went thousands of years ago. They want to see characters with whom they can identify. These characters must be suffering from the human condition. They must be believable. They must have problems. The audience wants to be involved with how they resolve their problems and reach their goals.

"Sympathetic character struggles against great odds to achieve a worthwhile goal" is a statement that applies to many short stories and novels. It also applies to many dramas, comedies, and musicals. If you cannot readily identify some of the elements from that statement in the script you are evaluating, you should be suspicious. If you can't identify at least one of the following items as being outstanding—characterization, conflict, dialogue, or the playwright's insight into human relationships—then you should not produce the script. Do not allow yourself to be swayed in your judgment by good reviews of the script at other theaters, the playwright's reputation, or any other factors. Learn to trust your evaluation of the written words.

There will always be someone to tell you that good acting, sets, and costumes can make it come to life. The script is just an outline. Don't you believe it! If you don't see the dramatic values in the script, don't do it.

Policies of the Play-Reading Committee

It is desirable that election of committee members be staggered so that there is some continuity from year to year. If members are elected for periods of two years but only half of the committee is replaced each year, there is both change and continuity.

A file should be kept of all plays previously considered—those performed, those rejected, and those pending.

During deliberations of the committee, don't allow a script to get shelved by one committee member. Buy enough copies for all members and insist that evaluations be completed by deadlines.

Members should not be in the position of being able to select vehicles they can star in or direct. Actors have notoriously bad judgment as to which roles they are best suited for. They have been known to go to great lengths to persuade committees to do plays, not because the plays are in the best interest of the theater, but because they see themselves in the leading roles. Directors should have an affinity for the plays they direct. But is it fair to other directors that one serving on the committee should be able to select the play he or she is to direct? Sometimes directors fall in love wth noncommercial plays that are eminently unsuitable for the theater. Here's the paradox: it's desirable that actors and directors serve on the play-reading committee; their points of view can be valuable. A possible solution is to insist that directors may not stage plays the years that they serve on the committee. Lists of plays under consideration might be circulated to potential directors to see which ones they favor. Actors on the committee might be asked to declare whether they see themselves in the leads of the plays they recommend; if so, other members of the committee could take this into consideration.

Committees must be careful to secure rights to a play before personnel are committed to a rehearsal. A play should not even be announced for production until the rights are secured. Just because the play is listed in a catalogue, do not assume that it is available. Sale of the movie rights, touring companies of a revival, and other factors may force the play service to withhold the rights.

Alternative plays should be selected for every season. For example, if you should find yourself unable to cast a difficult role, you should be ready with another play.

TO FIND GOOD PLAYS

Read, read, read, and then read some more. There is absolutely no substitute for your personal, firsthand knowledge of play scripts. You can augment your knowledge of plays in several other ways, but reading is the most useful because your perception of the dramatic values of the play will not be colored by any production values. Don't allow an outstanding acting performance in a movie to bias your judgment of the play on which the movie was based. Check the play script. You might find that there's very little there.

Another example: You go to see a community theater production that is incredibly good—excellent cast, masterful direction, exceptional sets and lighting. It is a marvelous evening. But when you study the script, you realize that it was the great production you enjoyed, not a great script. Some theater groups can capitalize on a weak script. Can yours?

As you read, fill out an evaluation form that will remind you of the play and its appropriateness for production by your theater (see Figure 12–1). A file of evaluations should be kept so that current committee members can quickly review plays previously considered.

When reading a play that is new to you, ask yourself these questions:

1. Was I interested enough in any of the characters at the end of Act I to want to know what happened to them?

2. Was I involved in the story line until the end of the play?

3. Was I amused or entertained by the dialogue throughout?

4. When I finished reading the play, did I feel that I learned something about human nature, about how and why people interact?

5. Does the playwright have something worthwhile to say?

6. Can it be performed, or is it just good reading?

```
                                    Evaluator_____

                                    Date_____



                        E V A L U A T I O N


Name of Play_____

Author_____

Other Plays by Author_____


Number in Cast ____, ____male, ____female, dominant lead _____
                                                         (male or female?)
      Children: ____, ____male, ____female

Number of Sets ____, ____indoor, ____outdoor

Type of Play (circle one:) drama, comedy, melodrama, farce, mystery,
                      musical, other:_____

Use the reverse side to give a brief summary of the plot.


1.  Is there a really memorable character with whom the audience
    can identify? ____yes, ____no

2.  Is there a well defined conflict?  ____yes, ____no

3.  Is there scintillating or very funny dialogue? ____yes, ____no

4.  Is there outstanding insight into human relationships? ____yes, ____no

5.  Can you see this play staged by our actors?  ____yes, ____no

6.  Can you see it staged in our facilities? ____yes, ____no

7.  Are unusually expensive costumes, sets or props needed?  Describe:

    _____

8.  Would our patrons pay to see it?  ____yes, ____no

9.  Has it been done too much locally?  ____yes, ____no

10. Is it available?  ____yes, ____no  Royalties: $_____

Conclusion:      Highly recommend_____
                 Do it_____
                 Save as an alternative for this season_____
                 Save for another season_____
                 Don't do it_____
```

Figure 12-1. Play Evaluation Form.

Be aware of the length of a play. It may be difficult to estimate playing time as you read, but if it reads long, it probably plays long. Conditioned by watching television and movies, modern audiences are not ready to sit for longer than two hours, including at least one intermission. After two hours, if you expect to hold your audience, you had better have a very good reason. Many, many plays, especially in community theater production, would be well served by judicious cuts. The reading-evaluation stage is not too early to start recommending those cuts.

LEADS TO GOOD PLAYS

Go to movies adapted from plays, watch TV presentations of theater, and listen to the records of great plays (often available at libraries). Seeing plays in other forms does not replace reading, but it serves as a fast introduction to a script.

Study nationally syndicated and local reviews of Broadway openings as a guide to what you should read next. If possible, subscribe to one of the trade papers (*Variety, Daily Variety,* or *Hollywood Reporter*). They carry reviews of Broadway openings, as well as reviews of road shows in major cities. *The New York Theatre Critics' Reviews* is published weekly and contains reviews of most Broadway openings by New York City's drama critics as well as its television reviewers. The yearly subscription is $47.50 (published by Critics' Theatre Reviews, Inc.; Four Park Avenue, Suite 21D; New York, New York 10016; phone (212) 532–2570). It is available at major libraries.

Review studies of the popularity of plays. Annually (since 1938), *Dramatics* magazine has published a survey of the full-length plays and one-act plays most often produced by its member high school troupes (see Figure 12–2).

The Best Plays Series, edited by Otis L. Guernsey, Jr. (New York: Dodd, Mead & Company, yearly), includes statistics on Broadway productions. What plays and musicals ran for how many performances on Broadway? Which play ran the longest—*Harvey, Born Yesterday, Abie's Irish Rose,* or *Life with Father*? Which musical has had the most performances on Broadway—*The Fantasticks, Fiddler on the Roof, Oklahoma!,* or *Man of La Mancha*? There must be reasons why these plays and musicals are so popular. What are they?

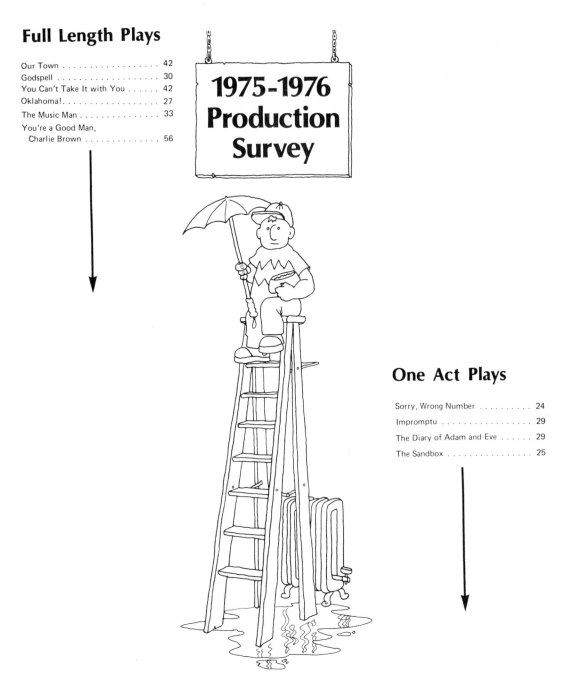

Full Length Plays

Our Town 42
Godspell 30
You Can't Take It with You 42
Oklahoma!. 27
The Music Man 33
You're a Good Man,
    Charlie Brown 56

1975-1976 Production Survey

One Act Plays

Sorry, Wrong Number 24
Impromptu 29
The Diary of Adam and Eve 29
The Sandbox 25

Figure 12–2. Part of a 1975–1976 Production Survey. The sixty-eight full-length plays most often presented by high schools were listed in order of frequency. Seventeen one-acts were listed. See the Sept./Oct. issue of *Dramatics* for the most recent production survey to see what the high schools are doing.

(Courtesy International Thespian Society.)

You may not wish to do revivals simply because of their past popularity. But you should be aware of which plays and musicals have drawn extensive audiences. What are the dramatic values in the scripts of these plays and musicals? Are these values immediately obvious to you when you read the scripts? Can you recognize the same values in other plays that you read?

Lists of prize-winning plays can lead you to some good reading. Check almanacs and theater reference books for the titles of plays that have won awards over the years. The Pulitzer Prize in Drama has been awarded since 1918. The list includes many plays that are worthy of revival. The evolution of the plays reflects changing tastes of audiences— quite a theater history lesson.

The New York Drama Critics Circle Awards go annually (since 1936) to (a) the best American play, (b) the best foreign play, (c) the best musical, or (d) the best, regardless of category.

Since 1947, the League of New York Theatres and Producers has presented the Antoinette Perry (Tony) Awards to the best play and the best musical.

Cumulative lists of the winners of all three awards are published annually in *Theatre World* (Crown Publishers, Inc.; 419 Park Avenue South; New York, New York 10016).

Analyses of plays are presented in a few books. You might find *Drury's Guide to Best Plays,* 2nd ed., by Francis Keese Wynkoop Drury and James M. Salem (Metuchen, N.J.: The Scarecrow Press), helpful.

IDEAS FROM OTHER COMMUNITY THEATERS

Be aware of the plays being presented by other theater groups in your area. What plays have been successful for them? Correspond with a community theater in a neighboring city to find out what plays they are producing. Figure 12–3 lists the plays produced by the Kentwood Players over their twenty-eight-year history. Notice how the balance by season evolved over the years. Figure 12–4 shows one season of four neighboring community theaters that share some cast members as well as audience. Notice the variety offered by each theater.

Write to the play services for their catalogues. Most services provide

1949
The Second Marriage of Santa Claus
50–51
You Can't Take It with You
Laura
For Love or Money
Fresh Fields
51–52
Curse of an Aching Heart
Holiday
Dark Tower
Chicken Every Sunday
52–53
On the Bridge at Midnight
Love from a Stranger
Three's a Family
Arsenic and Old Lace
53–54
Anna Lucasta
Three Men on a Horse
Cry Havoc
Male Animal
54–55
Country Girl
Wizard of Oz (first musical)
Lo and Behold
Night Must Fall
55–56
Time of Your Life
Amphytrion 38
Front Page
56–57
Curious Savage
Hansel and Gretl
(few plays as theater moved)
57–58
Fifth Season
The Sleeping Prince

58–59
Mousetrap
Streetcar Named Desire
Janus
Middle of the Night
Light up the Sky
59–60
Dark of the Moon
Bus Stop
The Big Knife
Blithe Spirit
My Three Angels
Detective Story
60–61
See How They Run
Make a Million
Maybe Tuesday
The Red Shoes
61–62
The Rainmaker
The Desperate Hours
Harvey
The Emperor's New Clothes
Lullaby
All the King's Men
62–63
Papa Is All
Two for the Seesaw
The Drunkard
Dark at the Top of the Stairs
Taming of the Shrew
Snow White
Everybody Loves Opal
Send Me No Flowers
63–64
The Shrike
Ten Little Indians
A Mighty Man Is He

Figure 12–3. Seasons of the Kentwood Players. Note the evolution of the season over the years. By the sixth year, this group started an annual musical. Number of plays per season increased from four to six or seven. A current season consists of two or three comedies, one drama, one mystery, and one musical.   (Courtesy of the Kentwood Players.)

Born Yesterday
Teahouse of the August Moon
The Silver Thread
Time of the Cuckoo
Anne of a Thousand Days
64–65
A Shot in the Dark
The Tender Trap
Picnic
Room Service
Cinderella
Summer and Smoke
The Tenth Man
65–66
Sunday in New York
Auntie Mame
The Glass Menagerie
Kind Lady
Mary, Mary
The Great Sebastians
66–67
Separate Tables
The Irregular Verb to Love
The Happy Time
Gigi
Don Juan in Hell
View from the Bridge
67–68
A Majority of One
Hatful of Rain
A Funny Thing Happened on the Way
  to the Forum
A Thousand Clowns
Carl Sandburg Yes
Who's Afraid of Virginia Woolf
The Rose Tattoo
Come Blow Your Horn
68–69
A Man for all Seasons
The Odd Couple
Night of the Iguana
Barefoot in the Park

Witness for the Prosecution
Generation
69–70
Lion in Winter
The Fantasticks
Don't Drink the Water
Wait Until Dark
Ready When You Are, C.B.
You Know I Can't Hear You When the
  Water's Running
70–71
Of Mice and Men
Guys and Dolls
Cactus Flower
A Case of Libel
Absence of a Cello
The Best Man
71–72
Nobody Loves an Albatross
Man of La Mancha
Angel Street
The Torchbearers
Our Town
The Fourposter
72–73
Look Homeward, Angel
Plaza Suite
Fiddler on the Roof
Lovers and Other Strangers
Rashomon
Arsenic and Old Lace (only revival)
Inherit the Wind
73–74
Forty Carats
Camelot
The Devil's Advocate
Silent Night, Lonely Night
The Dark Soul of Sex
How the Other Half Loves
All My Sons
74–75
Night Watch

Figure 12-3. (continued)

You're a Good Man, Charlie Brown *Finishing Touches*
Black Comedy/Next *Carnival*
Miracle Worker *Cat on a Hot Tin Roof*
Cabaret *Any Wednesday*
Gingerbread Lady *One Flew over the Cuckoo's Nest*
Uproar in the House *77–78*
75–76 *6 RMS RIV VU*
The Price *The Subject Was Roses*
Never Too Late *Oklahoma!*
Sound of Music *Dial M for Murder*
Sunshine Boys *Butterflies Are Free*
Catch Me if You Can *All the Way Home*
Andersonville Trial
Royal Gambit
76–77
Prisoner of Second Avenue

Figure 12–3. (*continued*)

brief synopses of their plays, the number of male and female characters, and some illuminating comments about each play. Some catalogues also contain lists of plays by category (holiday oriented, religion oriented, nationality oriented, etc.).

Torrance Community Theatre   *Chapel Theatre*

  The Lion in Winter   Crawling Arnold (and)
  USA   A Phoenix Too Frequent
  Ten Flights to Clover   It Isn't the Money
  The Good Doctor   Hot Turkey at Midnight
  One Flew over the Cuckoo's   Bad Habits
    Nest   The Silver Whistle

Figure 12–4. One Season (1975–76) at Four Neighboring Community Theaters. These theaters sometimes share audiences, cast, crew, and even staff. They "option" plays on a first come basis. Notice the balance at each theater in terms of small cast, large cast; comedy, drama, melodrama, mystery, original, musical; costume, modern dress; and recent plays, older plays.

My Daughter's Rated X
The Italian Straw Hat
Pure as the Driven Snow

Constant Wife
Right Bed, Wrong Husband

Showcase Theatre Group

The Roar of the Greasepaint,
  the Smell of the Crowd
Royal Gambit
Deadwood Dick
The Effect of Gamma Rays on
  Man-in-the-Moon Marigolds
The Curious Savage
The Championship Season
Godspell
The Sunshine Boys
Camelot

Palos Verdes Players, Inc.

Burlesque
Loot
Move Over Mrs. Markham
And Miss Reardon Drinks
  a Little
Dangerous Corner
Blood, Sweat and Stanley Poole

Figure 12–4. (*continued*)

Anchorage Press, Inc.
4621 St. Charles Avenue
New Orleans, Louisiana 70115

Baker's Plays
100 Chauncey Street
Boston, Massachusetts 02111

I. E. Clark
Box 246
Schulenburg, Texas 78956

Contemporary Drama Service
Box 457
Downers Grove, Illinois 60515

Dramatic Publishing Co.
86 East Randolph Street
Chicago, Illinois 60611

Dramatists Play Service, Inc.
440 Park Avenue South
New York, New York 10016

Eldridge Publishing Company
P.O. Box 209
Franklin, Ohio 45005

Heuer Publishing Co.
Box 248
Cedar Rapids, Iowa 52406

David McKay Company, Inc.
750 Third Ave.
New York, New York 10017

Edna Means Dramatic Service
  Publishers
610 Harmon Street
Tama, Iowa 52339

Music Theatre International
119 West 57th Street
New York, New York 10019

Performance Publishing
978 N. McLean Blvd.
Elgin, Illinois 60120

Pioneer Drama Service
2172 South Colorado Blvd.
Denver, Colorado 80222

Rogers and Hammerstein Library
598 Madison Ave.
New York, New York 10022

Samuel French, Inc.
25 West 45th Street
New York, New York 10036
or
7623 Sunset Blvd.
Hollywood, California 90046

Tams-Witmark
757 Third Avenue
New York, New York 10017

CONCLUSION

Regardless of how you search for plays or the process by which you choose them, the importance of selecting good plays cannot be minimized. In community theater an actor or actress occasionally attains drawing power—ability to draw an audience by publicizing his or her name. But generally, regardless of cast, director, production values, and the overall reputation of the group, the audience is drawn by the play's merit. It is the play that your theater has to sell. Selecting a season of great plays means selecting individual plays that have solid dramatic values and thus can be sold. There is absolutely no substitute for reading play scripts. Your powers of evaluation will mature with experience until you can forecast which scripts will translate into successes for your theater.

CHAPTER THIRTEEN

Recruiting Audience

In community theater there are a few specific techniques for increasing the audience beyond the use of general publicity. These are the encouragement of membership in the theater, the recruiting of subscribers and patrons, the selling of theater parties, and the conscientious pursuit of intergroup relations.

MEMBERSHIP

The first few active members of any theater group are usually obtained through word of mouth and advertising, as discussed in Chapter 8. As your theater grows and you can absorb new members on stage, back stage, and in the audience, you will want to make periodic efforts to recruit new members.

One easy campaign is to encourage each member to recruit two or three new members. The old members may be offered bonus tickets or other incentives to bring their friends and acquaintances into active membership. Or a contest may be held and a prize awarded to the member who can sign up the most new members within a given period.

Annual membership drives are often held between seasons or at the start of the new season. Such drives may be combined with the selling of season tickets. The main instrument of the annual drive is a letter sent to prospective members. Besides telling how an individual may join, it describes the privileges of membership:

1. Free tickets or a discount on tickets
2. Admittance to meetings and workshop offerings not open to the public
3. A voice in the selection of plays for the coming seasons
4. Eligibility to act, direct, crew, or participate in support activities
5. A vote in the election of officers
6. A vote in the awards presented to best actors and director at the end of the season
7. Participation in the social events of the theater

The letter may also list the plays of the coming season. A reply form or application, tear-off or enclosure, should give the prospective member a checklist to indicate his or her specific interest: acting, directing, crew, costumes, scenery construction, audience only, etc. (see Figure 13–1).

SUBSCRIBERS AND PATRONS

The subscriber is anyone who is willing to buy a season ticket. The patron is anyone who is willing to contribute to the support of the theater, usually by buying a season ticket at a price substantially higher than the minimum cost of the tickets. Subscribers and patrons may be recruited through media publicity, but more frequently they are recruited by (1) word of mouth, (2) flyers distributed in the lobby, and (3) letters.

Addresses for letters to prospective subscribers and patrons can be found in telephone books. A guest book in your lobby is an even better way to obtain addresses.

```
YES! I'd like to help support Palos Verdes Players by becoming (check one):
_____ an Active Member($10.)   _____ a Sustaining Member ($20)   _____ a Patron ($50)

    If you are joining us as an Active Member, please check one or more of the
following interest areas:
___ Set Construction    ___ Set Decoration    ___ Set Design    ___ Stage Manager

___ Props    ___ Script/Prompter    ___ Lights    ___ Sound    ___ Costumes

___ Producing    ___ Publicity    ___ Hospitality    ___ Box Office

___ Telephone Committee    ___ Mailing Committee    ___ Directing    ___ Acting

                        ROSTER INFORMATION


_____
Last name,      First name(s)

_____
Street Address                              Apt. No.

_____
City                  Zip             Phone
```

Figure 13-1. Membership Application, Community Theater (Palos Verdes Players).

Usually the most productive method of recruiting subscribers and patrons is through a lobby display. The audience member who has thoroughly enjoyed one of your productions is the person most likely to sign up for future plays and contribute money to your support. The lobby display may simply be a poster or a stack of envelopes on a table. (More on subscription tickets may be found in Chapter 3.)

The key to an effective patron program is special handling. It starts with warm personal greetings at the box office when the patrons present their identifying cards. Box office personnel, normally polite and courteous, should be extra courteous to patrons, and that includes addressing the patron by name.

The house manager can make the whole audience feel at home in a community theater. At some large professional theaters there are uniformed ushers, thick carpets, and huge chandeliers in the lobby, but the members of the audience never feel like welcome guests. The warm personality of an effective community theater house manager can more than compensate for all those trappings. Well dressed and wearing an identification tag, the house manager should greet audience members and circulate during intermissions and after the performance. He or she should be receptive and understanding toward audience comments and should have the ability to make small talk. It takes poise, charm, and a genuine interest in people. A good house manager can make a significant difference in the attitude of the audience toward the theater. The attitude of patrons is particularly important. The house manager should be sure to speak with each patron in the audience.

Publish the names of your patrons in your program. It may take a full page, but it's worth it. It serves as an advertisement for more patrons—to those in the audience who would like to add their names to those of the illustrious. Place a poster in your lobby: "We thank our patrons for their support . . ." and list them there as well.

During intermissions, introduce patrons to the director if he or she is available. After the show, if the patrons wish, introduce them to cast members.

A little camera work can also help. Take pictures of patrons mingling with the other theater guests, the director, or the cast. These pictures can be posted on a patrons' bulletin board, released to local newspapers, and sent to patrons. The cost of this public relations work will pay off in the expansion of your patron program.

If you have any spare space—a patio or hallway or just an alcove in the lobby—it may be dedicated to your patrons by naming it the Patrons' Patio or by placing a bulletin board there with a list of patrons, patron news, and pictures.

Flyers announcing the season, a new play, or extra performances are sometimes mailed to patrons a few days before they are mailed to those on the general mailing list. Or a week is reserved at the beginning of each season when they may phone in reservations before reservations are open to the public.

Sometimes a special reading or performance may be staged for the patrons alone, or they may be specially invited, at no cost, to attend a membership meeting at which there will be some entertainment.

You will undoubtedly find other ways to pamper and distinguish your patrons. If they feel that support of your theater is personally worthwhile, they will return to your patron roster year after year.

THEATER PARTIES

Theater parties are a very important part of the operations of many community theaters. How successful your theater parties are may determine the future success of your theater.

They are called by many names—sell outs, club dates, organization nights, etc. The purpose of the theater party is to fill the house by selling a large block of tickets to an organization, usually at reduced rates, thus allowing the organization to resell the tickets to their members and raise money for the organization.

The theater party offers the theater, in return, a certain amount of financial security. The Kentwood Players found that the money earned from theater parties was often the net profit of the show. Without theater parties many theaters would just break even or lose money.

Perhaps the greater advantage, though, to the theater, is that theater parties develop audiences. Individuals who attend as members of an organization may return on their own for future productions.

Prospects for selling theater parties often become a decisive factor in the selection of plays for the coming season. Although the community theater staff member (sometimes called Special Relations Chairperson) in charge of theater parties may not sit on the play-selection committee, he or she may often advise on what plays will sell to theater parties. It is likely that the light comedy and the musical will be easy to sell, whereas the serious drama will be hard to sell. And certain plays will be extremely difficult to move—the avant-garde or the off-Broadway show that contains vulgar language. The theater party audience is still extremely conservative. It wants to be entertained. It wants to laugh. It does not want a polemic. It does not want to hear dirty words. It does not want to be offended by nudity or explicit sexuality.

Selling theater parties requires a very special person—one who likes to talk about theater and plays, one with a pleasant personality and good telephone voice, one who is cheerful and optimistic, tactful and courteous, one who can accept rejection and bounce right back.

There are two basic approaches—the mailer and the telephone solicitation.

The mailer should include your policy on theater parties, the rules you lay down for buying blocks of tickets, the dates they are available, the cost, and a brief description of the plays you offer.

Mailers should be sent to a great variety of organizations within a fifteen-mile radius of your theater—PTA groups of the elementary, junior high and high schools, Kiwanis, Rotary, Lions, JayCees, Optimists, women's clubs, churches, synagogues, and any other organization you can think of. Check with your local chamber of commerce to get a list of organizations in your area. When at all possible, address your flyers to the person who is responsible for the group's fund raising or social activities.

Address the letters by both name and position. It is worth a phone call to the group to get the right name.

Keep a five-by-eight-inch file card for each organization to whom you send a mailer. List the name of the organization, the address, the name and title of the person contacted, and the phone number (see Figure 13-2). Each time you contact that group, make a note on the card—what plays the group has seen, what kind of plays it wants to see, why it does not favor promoting a theater party, etc. Just before you call again, refresh your memory by reviewing the notes so that you can talk to the group knowledgeably.

You might also put on the card a future date when it would be advisable to contact the group again. Then pull the card from your file and pin it to your calendar so that you don't forget.

The whole file becomes particularly valuable when the position of theater party promoter changes hands.

A simple letter agreement in two copies should be signed by the theater party promoter and the group's representative. The letter should

---

THEATER PARTY POSSIBLE

Organization   DOLLY MADISON WOMAN'S CLUB

Address   c/o MRS. MARCO MURPHY   10667 MADDEN AVE. 90069

Telephone   555-5892   555-6864

Regular Meeting   HOWARD JOHNSON'S   GREEN VALLEY AVE. THURS. NOON

Contact/Title   MRS DORA GLOVER / WAYS MEANS CHAIRMAN

Contact's Home Phone   555-2041 (WEEKEND EVES BEST TIME TO CALL)

Notes LAST PARTY: ENTER LAUGHING 6/20/76   GROUP WAS RAISING FUNDS TO

PROMOTE HOME FOR DELINQUENT GIRLS. INTERESTED IN FUTURE PARTIES-WANTS LIGHT
COMEDIES. DORA RAISES/SHOWS PEDIGREE CHIHUAHUAS, SAYS IF WE EVER NEED DOG IN SHOW, SHE
WILL ARRANGE. 11/13/76-NOT INTERESTED IN DAMES AT SEA; "TOO MANY CONFLICTING ACTIVI-
TIES IN DECEMBER." WANTS TO PLAN SPRING PARTY IN JANUARY. CALL 1/8/77

Figure 13-2. Theater Party File Card.

make clear your policy on return of tickets. (For further information on the handling of group ticket sales, see Chapter 3.)

GROUP RELATIONS

Think of your community theater as a citizen among the other groups in your area.

Let the chamber of commerce know that you exist, how and what you're doing, and what your needs are. Is this your twenty-third consecutive season? If you've been doing it that long, you must be doing something right. Let the chamber of commerce know. They might want to promote your longevity, because it is an asset to have such a recreational institution in their area.

Are you opening a new theater, breaking ground for a new building, burning the mortgage for an old theater, celebrating a birthday (anniversary of founding), or celebrating any other major accomplishment? Share it with your mayor, your councilman, and the city council. Invite local government to share in your accomplishments. Ask for a resolution to commemorate the event. Publicize the resolution and hang it in your lobby.

Now go down the list of all the organizations in your immediate area—schools (public and parochial), service clubs (Kiwanis, Rotary, etc.), and social clubs. Ask if your representative may attend a meeting to brief them on your progress and to find out how your theater and their organization can interact to your mutual benefit. Is the local parochial school having a carnival? Can the theater sponsor a booth? Is the local service club sponsoring a parade? March in their parade.

Be a good citizen and you will find support from other groups at your box office.

CONCLUSION

Your executive committees should carefully review the ideas in this chapter to see which would be most effective for increasing your audiences. Then implement!

CHAPTER FOURTEEN

Organizations to Help Us

Where can we turn for help? Where can we meet others who are working in theater and exchange ideas? How can we form an alliance with another theater for our mutual benefit?

There are many theater organizations—at local, county, state, national, and international levels—with overlapping goals and services. An unaligned community theater should study the field to determine which organization can best serve it, and just as important, which organization it should support.

NATIONAL ORGANIZATIONS

Here are five national organizations: The International Theatre Institute of the United States, The American Community Theatre Association, The United States Institute for Theatre Technology, The American National Theatre and Academy, and Theatre Communications Group.

The International Theatre Institute
of the United States, Inc. (ITI or ITI/US)
245 West 52nd Street
New York, New York 10019, (212) 245-3950

The purpose of ITI is to promote international exchange of knowledge and practice in theater arts.

Through its visitor services ITI assists guests in our country to obtain information about our theaters, introduces them to local theater people, arranges visits to theaters and classes, and in general, helps them to feel welcome. When its members travel abroad, ITI arranges for them to be greeted and similarly served in more than fifty countries.

ITI publishes an annual book, *Theatre.* Its newsletter, *Theatre Notes,* appears ten times per year with reports on national and international theater tours. A list of ITI centers around the world and lists of American theater groups and foreign theater festivals are also published.

ITI maintains an international theater library that is open to the public (Monday through Friday, 10 A.M. to 4 P.M.). The collection, covering 25 years of material on modern theater from 106 countries, includes several thousand books and plays. The focus is on the acquisition of foreign materials that are generally unavailable in the United States: yearbooks, house organs, newsletters, programs, press releases, production schedules, brochures, magazines, monographs, articles, and newspaper clippings. An American section contains files on over 300 U.S. theater groups, Broadway playbills, and scripts.

In addition to ongoing services, ITI takes on special projects periodically. Design 70, for instance, was a two-year touring display of scene design and costumes. Part of the display was sent to Prague to represent the United States in an international design exhibit. The Smithsonian Institution Traveling Exhibition Services then sponsored the exhibit for its tour of the United States.

The American Community Theater
Association (ACTA)
1000 Vermont Ave., N.W.
Washington, D.C. 20004, (202) 628-4634

ACTA is the community theater wing of the American Theatre Association (ATA), described in Chapter 7. The purpose of ACTA is to establish community theater as the great national theater of America.

ACTA works to help solve problems that cannot be handled by individual theaters nor by their state or regional organizations. It promotes high standards in all phases of community theater production. It develops community theater training programs in colleges and universities. It provides a meeting ground, encouraging closer cooperation and communication among individual theaters and state and regional community theater groups. It draws national attention to this country's burgeoning community theater movement. Finally, it enables all community theaters to speak with a strong and unified voice on national arts matters.

ACTA sponsors a community theater festival every two years at regional, state, and national levels. Every fourth year, the winning theater represents the United States at the International Amateur Theatre Association Festival in Monaco.

Floating conferences are held annually for the purpose of exchanging information. Additionally, ACTA provides technical consultants who go to member theater groups to help with local problems.

ACTA publishes a bimonthly newsletter and two pamphlets, *How to Organize a State Community Theatre Festival* and *How to Organize a State Community Theatre Association.* Various bibliographies and lists, such as "ACTA List of Known Community Theatres in the United States," are also offered.

A placement service helps community theaters to find the right people and hopefully helps the right people to find the right theaters. ACTA has also established a repository for community theater records and memorabilia at the University of Wisconsin.

ACTA claims membership of over 2,000 community theater groups.

**The United States Institute
for Theatre Technology (USITT)
1501 Broadway, New York, New York 10036
(212) 757-7138**

USITT studies the technology of theater and disseminates information about theater equipment, production materials, and production techniques. Membership is encouraged from theater planners, owners, clients, architects, engineers, and designers; city officials, builders, administrators, and managers; educators, writers, critics, playwrights, performers, and directors; designers and makers of stage scenery, lighting, machinery, furnishings and equipment; and designers and technicians in all theater disciplines.

USITT arranges meetings, programs, discussions, tours, and demonstrations. It also publishes a quarterly journal, *Theatre Design and Technology,* in addition to a newsletter, newsletter supplements, a membership directory, an annual report, and regional newsletters and reports.

An annual conference is held to further promote an exchange of information between outstanding professionals and the theater people who can use the information.

Beyond this, USITT annually honors individuals, services, innovations, and publications that have made outstanding contributions to the performing arts.

The American National Theatre and Academy (ANTA)
245 West 52nd Street, New York, New York 10019, (212) 757-4133

ANTA West
846 North Cahuenga Boulevard
Los Angeles, California 90038, (213) 462-7026

Chartered by the United States Congress on July 5, 1935, ANTA's purpose is to extend the best in theater to every state in the union. To do this, ANTA works to stimulate public interest in the performing arts. It fosters theatrical activity and supports and produces quality theater locally and nationally. It encourages accredited training in the performing arts in schools and colleges and provides training workshops for professionals.

ANTA West, the chapter serving Southern California, publishes a monthly newsletter containing theater information, casting calls, reviews of plays with emphasis on ANTA members, and other news of ANTA members' participation in theatrical activities. A regularly scheduled FM radio calendar of theater events is broadcast by KUSC, the student radio station of the University of Southern California. Committees of ANTA West stage readings for members, conduct workshops in playwriting and musical theater, and send specialists to speak to interested groups through its lecture and guest artist bureau.

ANTA periodically honors an outstanding contributor to theater with its National Artists Award. Rosalind Russell was the recipient in 1974. The latest recipient was Eva Le Gallienne.

ANTA wants to attract to its membership not only professionals in commercial theater, theater educators and community theater people, but also artists in related disciplines and general theatergoers.

Theatre Communications Group (TCG)
355 Lexington Avenue, New York, New York
10017, (212) 697-5230

Founded in 1961, TCG's goal is to help raise standards and aid in the development of the *nonprofit professional* theater. TCG exists to serve professional theater people, but it is not a membership organization. TCG evaluates a theater, considering factors such as the following: attitude of the staff, length of time in existence, orientation and standards, type of directorship, and length of season. Those theaters that reflect professionalism in most of these areas are eligible to receive publications, informational services, and advisory assistance. Nonprofit status must be substantiated.

TCG provides casting/auditioning services, scheduling auditions in New York City at the request of theaters and maintaining files on over 2,000 actors. Experienced TCG casting directors can provide personal assistance. National student auditions are held annually in the spring. Outstanding graduating students nominated from college drama programs are screened at seventeen regional sites. To include those without formal training, directors of nonprofit professional theaters are also invited to nominate their new talent for auditions.

The TCG referral program attempts to screen stage managers, technical directors, stage technicians, prop builders, costumers, administrators, public relations personnel, directors, designers, and managers. Theaters may examine resumes or request suggestions for filling positions.

TCG's residency/placement service helps universities to locate theater professionals who will augment their staffs in teaching and working with student productions. The purpose is to increase communication between educational theater programs and nonschool theaters.

Travel funds, limited of course, are made available for professionals to observe the work and operation of theaters and to meet with other theater people. Funds must be requested in a letter specifying purpose, destination, and approximate dates of proposed trip.

A highly skilled consultant is available to advise theaters on subscription campaigns and promotional techniques.

Resource files of production schedules, press releases, programs, and other information from nonprofit professional theaters are maintained for research.

TCG also sponsors and hosts conferences and meetings on special topics of concern to theater professionals.

The TCG monthly *Newsletter* is an informational digest of theater activities around the country, including touring, fund raising, new play production, community and educational projects, and reports on TCG programs and services.

Other TCG publications are *Theatre Profiles: An Informational Handbook of Nonprofit Professional Theatres in the United States,* which describes 89 noncommercial professional theater operations; *Theatre Directory,* which lists 138 theaters with their directors, managers, and general performance information; *Information for Playwrights;* and a *Touring Information Service Kit,* which gives technical requirements, fees, and other information for some thirty experimental, ethnic, and other small theaters.

REGIONAL ORGANIZATIONS

In addition to these five national organizations (beyond the educational theater organizations described in Chapter 7), there are many regional organizations. Some are affiliated with the national organizations above and some are independent. These regional organizations share with the national organizations the goal of intertheater communication. In some cases they work from within state, county, or city governments. One example of a regional organization is the ADA.

The Adult Drama Association
of Los Angeles County (ADA)
155 West Washington Boulevard, Los Angeles,
California 90015 (212) 749-6941 x576

ADA holds an annual drama festival in which local community theater groups compete for trophies. It publishes a monthly newsletter, *Divertissement-One,* which tells what's playing at the member theaters, gives casting notes, and presents information of interest to community theaters. Meetings are held periodically to critique activities and to present information to members.

If you or your theater group is interested in joining a local regional theater organization, write to the national organization and ask for the address of their local affiliate. Also call state, county, and city governments to ask if they sponsor, or know of, local theater organizations. Many states have Councils for the Arts or Arts Commissions that can direct you to a theater organization if they do not function as one.

THEATER ASSOCIATIONS

If the organizations above do not interest you, or do not meet your needs, you might want to form your own association. SALT is an example of how a few theaters can band together almost informally, without incurring added expenses, to achieve some common goals.

The Southbay Association of Little Theatres (SALT)
P.O. Box 866, Lomita, California 90717

SALT was begun in 1967 by four little theaters in Southern California that recognized that in unity there is dollar savings. The limited goals they set out to accomplish are met every month:

1. A single bulletin mailed to patrons of all four theaters
2. Exchange of props, set pieces, and costumes
3. Help with casting of actors and the intertheater use of directors and support personnel

Every month representatives of each theater prepare copy on the current production, the next production's needs, group sales, ticket informa-

SOUTHBAY ASSOCIATION OF LITTLE THEATRES

JUNE, 1976 — #111

MOVING? To continue to receive this Newsletter, send your new address with ZIP Code to P. O. Box 866, Lomita, California 90717

TORRANCE COMMUNITY THEATRE
1522 Cravens, Torrance
Reservations: 371-6561

THE GENERATION GAP? WOMEN'S LIB? THE NEW YORK YANKEES? A pig farmer in Washington? FP rating for movies? A haystack in HACKENSACK? A see-through dress? What's happening! Well, it's all happening at TCT where PAUL THORNTON has put together a very funny show that had a great opening night. "MY DAUGHTER'S RATED X" . . . Funny . . . Funny . . . Funny. Featuring RICK IVEY, YVONNE ALLEN, GAIL JOHNSON, ROGER GIRDNER, SHEILA HOLSMAN, JAMES LOVE, TIFFANY and produced by BUDDY SHAFFRON . . . Don't miss it! Just to see PAT PATTERSON'S replica of Gainsborough's BLUE BOY with variations is worth it.

THE ITALIAN STRAW HAT OPENING JUNE 25th HAS BEEN CAST and Director DICK CICIOTTI is busy putting the show together. DC has really come up with a string of hits and this looks like another one.

RICK IVEY . . . THAT EPITOME OF SOUTH BAY THEATRE, is casting June 27th and 28th at 7:30 p.m. for his production of "PURE AS THE DRIVEN SNOW". All types and all ages are needed. Big cast. Some vocalists and also people to do between the acts OLEO. What can be more fun than doing a MELODRAMA . . . A great chance to let it all hang out.

ONE FLEW OVER THE CUCKOO'S NEST and dropped a whole bunch of sold out nights on TCT. Thanks NEAL RECK for a great show . . . . . "S"

SHOWCASE THEATRE GROUP
13752 So. Prairie Ave., Hawthorne
Reservations: 644-5400

Good news! GODSPELL, a musical based upon the Gospel according to St. Mathew, will come to life Thursday, May 27th for a special three week engagement, closing June 12th — a matinee has been scheduled for Sunday, May 30th. GODSPELL is a joyous celebration of life, love and laughter in song and dance — and much more! Remember this is only a three week run, so get your reservations early — Don't miss it! Reservations (for Godspell only) - Nathan Garcia, 374-0871 or 374-6381.

For a reunion of a different nature, be sure to put THE SUNSHINE BOYS on your calendar. This Neil Simon comedy will have a champagne opening June 25th and run to July 24th. Director DAN KUBIK and his cast: JACK BYRON, HARRY HAFTER, BOB BAUMSTEN, RITA DUBLISKI, LOUISE HAANES and GEORGE SYMONDS promise an evening of entertainment you won't forget. (Dan still needs tech. people — set designer, lights, sound, etc.) Reservations: 644-5400.

Readings for CAMELOT will be held Sunday, June 27th at 2:30 p.m. and Monday, June 28th, 7:30 p.m. AL TAYLOR directing. Be prepared to sing songs from CAMELOT. Feature roles and chorus will be auditioned on same days. Al needs musicians — trumpets, violins, sax, piano, etc. If interested, call 326-0302 (token fee paid). Also needed are seamstresses, artist and stage hands.

Break out the habachi! It's time for Showcase's fourth Annual Fourth of July picnic at El Nido Park. More information next Newsletter.

Membership Meeting - Tuesday, June 1st, 8 p.m. Workshop to be presented: OF MICE AND MEN, directed by Jim Betz.

CHAPEL THEATRE
2222 Lomita Blvd., Lomita
Reservations: 373-3636

CONSTANT WIFE will have a champagne opening JUNE 11, and continue through JULY 17. This timeless, sophisticated drawing-room comedy is still as good as the day it came out of Maugham's typewriter; it dissects love, marriage and the modern woman. Cast includes Patricia Lester, Ed Gangel, Billie Galleran, John Chamberlin, Lynda Scarlino, Maree Malone, Marjorie, Myron Sloma and Gene Walker — Jarl Victor directs.

READINGS for RIGHT BED, WRONG HUSBAND, to be directed by Marie Denn, will be held SUNDAY, JUNE 13 and MONDAY EVENING, JUNE 14 at 7:30 p.m. in the Green Room. Four men (1 young bachelor type, 1 old pinch-penny uncle type and 2 other men, any age) and three women (1 young debutante and 2 older women). A door-slamming - hip-slapping comedy!

A BIG THANK YOU to BILLIE GALLERAN and her DELIGHTFUL CAST for a SUCCESSFUL and PROFITABLE RUN of SILVER WHISTLE.

FOR THEATRE PARTIES or SMALL GROUPS — Please call Grace DeRusha at 326-4408 or 545-4328.

Theatre quote for the month from Lillian Hellman's PENTIMENTO "Perhaps the hardest lesson to learn in theatre is not to take anyone too seriously."

PALOS VERDES PLAYERS, INC.
2514 Via Tejon, Palos Verdes Estates
Reservations: 375-7566   Group Rates: 378-3720

DANGEROUS CORNER, NOW THRU JUNE 5th. This suspenseful, mind-teasing puzzle play opened to a near capacity crowd. All enjoyed the play, set and champagne with the cast afterwards. Be sure you are among those attending opening night next time. Our thanks to BRIAN HILLS, GEORGE TREMBLE, FRANK BANE and ALL THE MEMBERS OF THE CAST for giving us this fine interpretation of J. B. Priestley's mystery. Remember Fridays and Saturdays thru June 5th.

BLOOD, SWEAT and STANLEY POOLE, OPENS JUNE 25 DICK JORDAHL, director, has cast some of your favorites including JIM TELLIER, AL KENNGOTT, JERRY GIDEON, BEN SPECTRE, JIM McKAY, KATHY BINA, VAUGHN WILLIAMS and PAM CAPTAIN. At press time, other parts were still being decided. This is an out-and-out comedy, so come and laugh at the problems of the Army. This is one you will want to bring your group to and have a summer theatre party.

NEW SEASON OPENS SEPTEMBER 10th with MUSICAL MELERDRAMA. NO, NO, A MILLION TIMES NO! (or Only a Farmer's Daughter) — a real old-fashioned musical melerdrama will open our 1976-77 season. Casting will be July 11th and 12th at the theatre. Directors for next season are needed; it you are interested, please call John Andrus at 378-9755 so we can consider you and schedule your play dates.

Figure 14-1. SALT Newsletter. Southbay Association of Little Theatres. Ace-Hi Printers.

(Courtesy of the Southbay Association of Little Theatres.)

tion, and even some gossip. They mail it to the printer, whose only editorial function is to cut if there is too much. Every three months one theater takes responsibility for addressing the bulletins to the patrons of all four theaters. The bulletins are mailed at the nonprofit organization rate. If a bulletin is returned by the post office marked, "moved—no forwarding address," the patron's name is removed from the mailing list. Each theater may send out separate mailings to its own patrons if it so wishes.

Exchange of props, set pieces, and costumes is quite informal, starting with the announcement of coming plays and their requirements in the bulletin. The designers and technicians volunteer whatever materials they can. There is no central storage area for props and set pieces, but members know what they have in their garages and remember who lent them things last time they were needed.

If casting bogs down, producers ask producers and directors of the other theaters to recommend actors. Many actors have worked at all four of the SALT theaters. Sometimes technicians and directors are drafted in emergencies.

SALT works. It works because the four community theaters involved understand that there is no competition among theaters—only better theater! And the more theater of better quality, the better future attendance at all four theaters.

Have you got that all straight? Can you tell USITT from ITT from ANTA from ACTA from TCG from ADA from SALT? If you can't, don't feel too bad. I have one friend who says he writes out a check each time any one of them sends him a bill, and he lists most of them under professional expenses at income tax time. But he's never quite sure which one does what for whom. He's happy, though. He gets a lot of ideas, newsletters, and invitations to conventions and meetings.

List your personal needs. List the needs of your theater. Then compare them to the offerings above. Have we found a match?

READER'S COMMENTS FORM

Does this book meet your needs?
If not, please detail reasons:

Did you find it easy to read and understand?

Was it organized for convenient use and application?

Was it well illustrated? If you felt that any additional illustrations might have helped you, please describe.

Was it suitable for your theater?

Type (circle one):   professional   educational   community

showcase   children's   religious

Your name and job title:

Your comments:

I wish to refer to Chapter _____:

Please use reverse side or attach additional sheets as necessary.

Send to: THE STAGE MANAGER
Main P.O. Box 1901
Los Angeles, California 90053

Index